THE SUPREME COURT FOOTNOTE

The Supreme Court Footnote

A Surprising History

Peter Charles Hoffer

NEW YORK UNIVERSITY PRESS
New York

NEW YORK UNIVERSITY PRESS
New York
www.nyupress.org

References to Internet websites (URLs) were accurate at the time of writing. Neither the author nor New York University Press is responsible for URLs that may have expired or changed since the manuscript was prepared.

Library of Congress Cataloging-in-Publication Data
Names: Hoffer, Peter Charles, 1944–   compiler.
Title: The Supreme Court footnote : a surprising history / Peter Charles Hoffer.
Description: New York : New York University Press, 2024. |
Includes bibliographical references and index. | Summary: "A history of the most famous, and infamous, footnotes in leading US Supreme Court cases"—Provided by publisher.
Identifiers: LCCN 2023038945 (print) | LCCN 2023038946 (ebook) |
ISBN 9781479830220 (hardback) | ISBN 9781479830237 (ebook) |
ISBN 9781479830244 (ebook other)
Subjects: LCSH: United States. Supreme Court—Cases—History. |
Constitutional courts—United States. | Judgments—United States.
Classification: LCC KF8741.A53 H64 2024 (print) |
LCC KF8741.A53 (ebook) | DDC 347.73/26—dc23/eng/20231003
LC record available at https://lccn.loc.gov/2023038945
LC ebook record available at https://lccn.loc.gov/2023038946

This book is printed on acid-free paper, and its binding materials are chosen for strength and durability. We strive to use environmentally responsible suppliers and materials to the greatest extent possible in publishing our books.

Manufactured in the United States of America

Also available as an ebook

CONTENTS

INTRODUCTION

"I Will Not Be Bound by a Footnote"

In May, 2022, the legal world was shocked when a draft of the majority opinion in *Dobbs v. Jackson Women's Health* appeared in an issue of *Politico*. The circulation of draft opinions in the Supreme Court is highly confidential, and this one was a bombshell. The majority proposed to do away with the constitutional protection for early term abortion. Overturning *Roe v. Wade* (1973) was long a project for pro-life and conservative forces in and out of government, but the totality of the opinion was a surprise. Chief Justice John Roberts and the author of the draft, Associate Justice Samuel Alito, were furious. The decision itself would go on to rock the election of 2022. But no one in the clamor noticed that the majority opinion and the dissent offered over 140 footnotes, many of them a substantial and telling part of the justices' reasoning.[1]

The present volume is a select introductory history of Supreme Court footnotes, from the first time they appeared in "single spies" to the battalions that marched across *Dobbs*'s pages. They grew in number and importance in significant cases. It offers an exploration of how these forms of citation evolved over time and what they added to our constitutional understanding. The story is full of curious twists and turns, ironies and provocative asides. Typically, although Chief Justice Charles Evans Hughes (1930–41) was reputed to have said "I will not be bound by a footnote," he made a major contribution to the most famous Supreme Court footnote of all (for more on which, see chapter 5).[2]

---

1 Dobbs v. Jackson Women's Health Org. No. 19–1392 597 U.S. ___ (2022); Roe v. Wade, 410 U.S. 113 (1973); Josh Gerstein and Alexander Ward, "Supreme Court Has Voted to Overturn Abortion Rights, Draft Opinion Shows" *Politico*, May 3, 2022, www.politico.com.
2 This aphorism (also used as the chapter's subtitle) was often attributed to Hughes in footnotes but is without reliable authority. This is an example of the paradox of Epimenides of Crete, who is reported to have said, "All Cretans are liars." Can a footnote asserting that courts cannot rely on a footnote be authority for the latter proposition?

Along the way, the book is an exploration of the use of history in judicial writing through the lens of those footnotes. All appellate court opinions are miniature histories. They are the stories of legislative acts that have spawned quarrels and stories of individuals seeking to restore privileges lost or stolen. They are stories of wrongs and rights over time. The footnotes in them are stories within stories, tracing past cases (precedent) and readings of statutes and sometimes the meaning of the Constitution itself. As the justices created constitutional history, they imported their own understandings of it through the footnotes.

Loved, hated, barely tolerated, obsessively deployed, the Supreme Court footnote is now ubiquitous in legal scholarship. It crowds the text off the page in law reviews and routinely adds pages to the bottom of each generation of opinions. Its march into doctrinal battlegrounds seems unstoppable. This is the story of how the lowly footnote ascended to the empyrean heights of our highest law—where it has come under attack from the very guardians of law who rely on it. It is a story of scholars and jurists, lawyers and judges, that began long ago and continues today. For the footnote is a defense of the text, attached to the text by the cords of superscripts, allegedly proving what the author asserts. If the footnotes are persuasive and thorough, the text is safe (or at least rendered safer) from its critics. If the footnote itself is subject to attack, the text becomes vulnerable. The footnote may refer to extralegal materials, for example history or social science, or provide a clue to the judge's thinking generally. Is the footnote then part of the law? Our law rests, in part, on the opinions of our appellate court judges. Do their footnotes become part of precedent? This question is most crucial to the highest appellate court in our land, the US Supreme Court, especially in these days when majority and dissenting opinions engage in a veritable war of footnotes.[3]

* * *

In form, a footnote is a fragment of text that appears at the bottom of a page, separated from the body of the text (an endnote is simply a footnote placed at the end of the text). It is preceded by a number (Arabic

---

3 In the US legal system, appellate or appeals courts decide cases referred to them on legal grounds. The apex in the architecture of US courts, the US Supreme Court's majority opinions and decisions, provide the rules for lower federal courts and state courts.

usually, but sometimes Roman) or a symbol (e.g., an asterisk or a dagger) that corresponds to the same number or symbol in the body of the text. Francis Lieber's classic 1839 study of legal construction, *Legal and Political Hermeneutics,* used both symbols and numbers at the bottom of his pages. The symbols were references. The numbers were extended discussions of topics related to the text. In the text, the number or symbol is either raised (superscript) or in parenthesis and can follow a sentence or a paragraph (block footnote). There can be more than one footnote per page. The footnote contains the source for that piece of text (a citation or reference note) or an explanation or expansion of the text (a discursive footnote) or a relevant piece of information. Footnotes can be quite short or run for entire paragraphs. Footnotes are common in legal opinions, exegesis of scripture, historical writing, social science articles, technical and scientific reports and student research papers, and less often in fiction, journalism, or popular literature.[4]

Princeton historian Anthony Grafton is the very model of a modern scholar of Renaissance history and literature and something of a Renaissance figure himself. His own interests in the cultural history of Europe, the history of books and readers, the history of scholarship and education in the West from Antiquity to the nineteenth century, and the history of science from Antiquity to the Renaissance have birthed ten books. According to his department biography, "Professor Grafton likes to see the past through the eyes of influential and original writers, and has accordingly written intellectual biographies of a 15th-century Italian humanist, architect, and town planner, Leon Battista Alberti; a 16th-century Italian astrologer and medical man, Girolamo Cardano; and a 16th-century French classicist and historian, Joseph Scaliger. He also studies the long-term history of scholarly practices, such as forgery and the citation of sources, and has worked on many other topics in cultural and intellectual history." He is a defender of the book—then and now—and within the book, of the footnote.

From the time he entered graduate school in 1969, Grafton found himself swimming in a sea of the footnotes of his fellow scholars. He learned how much footnotes mattered in historical works. Intrigued, he

---

4 Francis Lieber, *Legal and Political Hermeneutics, or Principles of Interpretation and Construction in Law and Politics,* 3rd ed. (St. Louis: F. H. Thomas, 1880), e.g., 8–9.

searched for the earliest examples of those modern footnotes. He found notes—really marginalia, indexes, and other additions to texts—going back to the church fathers, but in 2012, he declared that the origins of the "modern" scholarly footnote probably belongs to Richard Simon, a Catholic biblical scholar, in his *Critical History of the Old Testament* (1680). Simon's work was a contribution to the contemporary literary and scholarly war of each against all—Catholic vs. Calvinist vs. Lutheran vs. layman—and critics denounced his footnotes as not particularly reliable. He replied to his critics with a *Critical History of the Text of the New Testament* (1687), replacing short fragments of text he offered in the Old Testament tract with entire passage in the notes. Pierre Bayle's *Historical and Critical Dictionary* (1697) enlarged on Simon's innovation. Bayle was a Protestant teacher, editor, and writer at a time in France when Protestantism was under siege. He managed to earn a living and a reputation writing dictionaries of various kinds that questioned authority and irritated (when they did not bore) other writers. His notes were labeled with letters—A, B, C, and so forth—and included both the authorities he used and his own authority for doubting the very sources he cited. The notion of a footnote as a foot soldier in academic contests was now underway.[5]

Bayle cared about his footnotes, and like the fortifications of the French military architect Sebastien Le Presti, the Marquis de Vauban, Bayle surrounded his text with precisely engineered walls, abutments, and trenches to protect his contribution. For "Bayle, like his enemies, silently abridged and consciously or unconsciously misread the texts he instructed his printer to excerpt." He relied on memory and "cited sources he had not read at all, drawing his information from summaries and reviews." Had he Wikipedia at hand, one wonders if he would have used it. Not a very promising beginning, but in the next century, the more familiar footnotes appeared, in histories by David Hume and Edward Gibbon. These were streamlined, in a sense more accurate, designed to supplement rather than merely defend, the text. In the nineteenth century, in the University of Berlin seminars of historians like Leopold von Ranke and later at Johns Hopkins University, a generation

---

5 Anthony Grafton, *The Footnote, A Curious History* (Cambridge, MA: Harvard University Press, 2012), 191–202, 202–4.

of professional historians mastered the footnote. In these laboratories of scholarship, the footnote became a subject of study in itself—precise, learned, and governed by strict rules. Of course, the older tradition of footnote wars among historians continues.[6]

* * *

Just as the early modern footnote was meant to assure the reader of the authority of the author, so the legal footnote developed to lead the reader, student, judge, or practitioner to the source of the author's claims. But the legal footnote has its own story somewhat separate from the developments that Grafton explored. It begins with the problem of legal citation. The common-law tradition to which we subscribe comes to us from medieval England. It is distinct from the Roman-law tradition of codes that dominated continental European law. In England, lawyers and judges, with some exceptions, preferred the use of precedent—earlier decisions—to the use of codes to decide cases. These precedents were kept in students' notes of what the judges said, then in reports called yearbooks (numbered after the reigns of kings), and later in official reproductions of entire opinions. As they multiplied and got more complex, some way of keeping track of the common law was needed, and citation was the answer.[7]

Originally, lawyers and judges relied on memory for earlier cases, but over the course of years, from 1268 to 1535, the period covering the reigns of King Edward I to Henry VIII, the number and variety of cases grew. If the courts were to take proper account of precedent, the exact citation of precedent mattered more and more. But how were the cases and the statutes in these books to be cited in later cases? The answer was messy. "The citation of cases followed much the same development as that of statutes. Initially, citations of court decisions resembled recollec-

---

6 Grafton, *The Footnote*, 211–12. On the citation battles of other scholars in this era, see Barbara Shapiro, *A Culture of Fact: England 1550–1720* (Ithaca, NY: Cornell University Press, 1999), 232. On the history seminar, see Walter Prescott Webb, "The Historical Seminar: Its Outer Shell and Its Inner Spirit," *Mississippi Valley Historical Review* 42 (1955), 3–23. On footnote battles among modern historians, see Peter Charles Hoffer, *Past Imperfect: Facts, Fictions, Fraud—American History from Bancroft to and Parkman to Ambrose, Bellesiles, Ellis, and Goodwin*, 2nd ed. (New York: PublicAffairs, 2007), 141–71.

7 Byron D. Cooper, "Anglo-American Legal Citation: Historical Development and Library Implications," *Indiana University Law Library Journal* 75 (1982), 7.

tions of events more than references to documents in a series. Citations, however, were not used frequently. Medieval judges did not recognize the doctrine of stare decisis. Although they desired judicial consistency, they did not consider previous decisions binding and apparently felt free to disregard them." There were various handwritten abridgments and, of course, manuals, varying in authority and privately (as opposed to officially) prepared. The "rolls" on which the clerks of the high courts of England kept "pleas of the crown" were a potential source of citations, but the rolls could not be carried about from court to court as needed. Parliament kept records of its statutes, but again, these were not handy. The coming of printing to England in the mid-fifteenth century provided the answer. "The printer who had the greatest effect on citation practice was undoubtedly the much maligned, but indefatigable Richard Tottell, who truly had a profound sense of bibliographic control." Tottell was the son of a wealthy and influential public official, and the young man was apprenticed to a printer of lawbooks. What Tottell did in 1553 was gain a patent (a kind of monopoly) to take over the project of printing common-law sources. The original patent was for seven years, but in 1559, Tottell's patent was granted to him for life.[8]

Even the value of Tottell's contribution is debated, however. It is not clear whether his innovations were very innovative, because earlier editions than his circulated before he published his own. Between the years 1493 and 1528, one Richard Pynson (or Pinson) published law books, including compilations of precedent. But the sheer volume of Tottell's publications gave him pride of place. Beginning in 1553, he published some 225 issues of yearbooks. These editions came almost a century and a half before Simon's and Bayle's scholarship.[9]

* * *

The evolution of a citation system for cases in the yearbooks made possible commentaries on the law. Perhaps the greatest of these and certainly a model for later authors was Chief Justice Edward Coke's *Institutes of the Lawes of England* (1628–44), a three-volume collection of laws, cases, and comments expanding the older work of Thomas Littleton, itself a

---

8 Cooper, "Anglo-American Legal Citation," 9.
9 On the history of the early English legal citations, see J. H. Baker, *An Introduction to English Legal History*, 5th ed. (Oxford: Oxford University Press, 2019), 189–94.

handwritten textbook on tenures (property) for Littleton's son. The *Institutes* did not have footnotes, but citations appeared in the margins alongside the relevant text. Coke was not a teacher of law, and it is not clear how his work could have been used in classrooms, so cluttered was it, although Coke himself lamented the "clutter" of authorities.[10]

By contrast to the *Institutes*, a kind of encyclopedia, later commentaries were developed from the lectures of the first law school professors. Not all the early law professors lectured. Some, like William Small and George Wythe at the college of William and Mary, tutored students like Thomas Jefferson, John Marshall, and St. George Tucker. But Jefferson recalled that the *Commentaries on the Laws of England*, by English law professor William Blackstone, a publication growing out of Blackstone's lectures, was essential to student learning. When lectures, delivered orally, became printed volumes, some method was necessary to provide the sources for the lecture's text (something rarely included in the oral presentations). These were the occasion for footnotes.[11]

William Blackstone's *Commentaries on the Laws of England* (1763–70) was a four-volume compendium derived from his lectures as the Vinerian Professor of Law at Oxford University, where he had been an administrator and teacher (along with practicing law as a barrister); Blackstone was later a judge on the Court of Kings Bench and then the Court of Common Pleas. The *Commentaries* were preceded by his *Analysis of the Laws of England* (1756), a sort of annotated syllabus for his students, its chapters divided into short, numbered paragraphs without footnotes. In the *Commentaries*, Blackstone recognized that students were part of his readership. He saw himself as one in a long line of English jurisprudents and urged students to honor that pedigree. Thus, "Besides these reporters, there are also other authors, to whom great veneration and respect is paid by the students of the common law." So the first pages of

---

10 Coke quoted in Cooper, "Anglo-American Legal Citation," 14; Edward Coke, *Institutes of the Lawes of England*, 3 vols. (London: Society of Stationers, 1628–44).

11 W. Edmund Hemphill, "George Wythe, America's First Law Professor," Master's thesis, Emory University, 1932, 15, 19, 22, 28.

Why not endnotes? The answer is that the student will not go to the end of the chapter or the book to find the endnote. They simply ignore it. Only with great effort can we get them to look at the notes on the bottom of the page. Academic presses commonly prefer endnotes to footnotes, however, for reasons that escape most authors, as the decision seems to be based on the customs of trade or popular presses (whose readers are not interested in sources). Law reviews use footnotes for reasons discussed below.

the *Commentaries* introduced footnotes, each preceded by a lower case letter. Later editors of the volumes added their own footnotes, a running commentary on the evolution of English legal thinking.[12]

Blackstone's *Commentaries* were a major influence on American law and American law teaching, well after the Revolution. (Blackstone was an important part of both the opinion for the court and the dissent in *District of Columbia v. Heller* [2008], discussed in chapter 7). It is hard to imagine a late-eighteenth-century student preparing for the bar exam who did not have the *Commentaries* by his side. St. George Tucker, a Bermuda-born Virginia lawyer and judge, who began teaching law at William and Mary in 1790, even prepared a version for would-be Virginian lawyers. But his real purpose was to Americanize Blackstone. The work bewailed the absence of an appropriately republican version of Blackstone, and "these inconveniences had been sensible felt by the Editor [Tucker himself] when he was unexpectedly called to fill the chair of the professor of law in the university of William and Mary, in Virginia." To notes on private law, Tucker added a now classic essay on the origins and application of the new federal Constitution, "a field of inquiry which yet remained to be fully explored." Tucker also kept notebooks of cases he argued before the Virginia courts, then on the bench of the state and federal courts. Something of these reappeared in his edition of Blackstone, but the bulk of them were not published until Charles F. Hobson's three-volume modern edition of Tucker's *Law Reports and Selected Papers* in 2011.[13]

The American versions of Blackstone's opus continued with James Kent's *Commentaries on American Law*, prepared in 1794 for his lectures

---

12 William Blackstone, *An Analysis of the Laws of England* (Oxford: Clarendon Press, 1756); Blackstone, *Commentaries on the Laws of England*, 4 vols. (Oxford: Clarendon Press, 1765–70), 1:72.
13 St. George Tucker, "On the Study of Law," in *View of the Constitution of the United States with Selected Writings of St. George Tucker*, ed. Clyde Wilson (Carmel, IN: Liberty Fund, 1999), 4, 5. This work first appeared as an appendix in St. George Tucker's *Blackstone's Commentaries: With Notes of Reference, to the Constitution and Laws, of the Federal Government of the United States; and of the Commonwealth of Virginia* (Philadelphia: Birch and Small, 1803); *St. George Tucker's Law Reports and Selected Papers, 1782–1825*, ed. Charles F. Hobson, 3 vols. (Chapel Hill: University of North Carolina Press, 2013), 1:xix. Note that Tucker's essay on the Constitution would become one of the classic states rights' works, but scholarly views of his federalism sharply differ; compare Kurt T. Lash, "Tucker's Rule: St. George Tucker and the Limited Construction of Federal Power," *William and Mary Law Review* 47 (2006): 1343–92, with David Thomas Konig "St. George Tucker and the Limits of States' Rights Constitutionalism: Understanding the Federal Compact in the Early Republic," *William and Mary Law Review* 47 (2006): 1279–1342.

at Columbia College in New York and subsequently published in 1826. Kent was largely self-taught, interning with New York State attorney general Egbert Benson for a time and then practicing in Poughkeepsie. In 1790, he joined the New York State assembly, finally becoming a judge in 1793 and the next year a professor at the new college of Columbia (formerly Kings College) in New York City. He became chief justice in 1804 and then in 1814 the state's chancellor or chief judge in equity. His chancery reports were classics, the only state equity source in the United States in its time. After his retirement from the court, he returned to teach law and wrote new lectures, published as the *Commentaries*. Of course, these had to be modified for print. Notes were thus essential to the volume, and the very first page began the notes, lettered rather than numbered, with a reference to a statute in the Journals of the Continental Congress, and the second with a cite to Montesquieu's *Spirit of the Laws*. Each new edition added notes. As the preface to the fourteenth edition in 1896 explained, "An examination of the new notes, which are in double columns at the foot of the pages, and are indicated by the last letters of the alphabet, will best enable an intelligent profession to determine the value of this new material, in which nearly nine thousand cases have been added to the twenty-four thousand cases cited in the last edition, not including the frequent citation of other authorities than the reports and the not infrequent further use made of decisions already cited in that edition."[14]

US Supreme Court Justice Joseph Story, also a professor of law (at Harvard Law School), similarly reduced his lectures to a series of *Commentaries*, all of which were replete with footnotes. Unlike Kent, Story numbered the notes, the modern format. After the Civil War, footnotes became commonplace in treatises on special areas of the law, offering lawyers who did not have access to extensive law libraries to pinpoint relevant cases. For example, Theodore J. G. Sutherland's *Statutes and Statutory Construction* (1891) found that there were so many divergences and complexities that cases of similar type needed to be "collated," and

---

14 Charles R. McManis, "The History of First Century American Legal Education: A Revisionist Perspective," *Washington University Law Quarterly* 59 (1981): 602–3, 605–6; John H. Langbein, "James Kent," in *Yale Dictionary of Legal Biography*, ed. Roger K. Newman (New Haven, CT: Yale University Press, 2009), 314–15; James Kent, *Commentaries on American Law* (New York: O. Halstead, 1826), 1:1, and 12th ed. (Boston: Little, Brown, 1896), vi.

that was best done with footnotes. These are called "string cites." His first footnotes were refences to Kent's and Story's commentaries, naturally.[15]

The reports were compilations of state higher court opinions, and beginning in 1791, of federal courts. After the American Revolution, appellate court judges began to issue written opinions. (The first reports, of Massachusetts cases, by Josiah Quincy, were compiled a decade before the Revolution but were not published until 1865). The first published collection of these appeared in Connecticut, Ephraim Kirby's *Reports or Reports of Cases Adjudged in the Superior Court of the State of Connecticut, from the year 1785, to May, 1788, with Some Determinations in the Supreme Court of Errors* (1791), followed by Pennsylvania and Kentucky. Other states soon followed with their own official reports. The first state reports were commercially published, but there soon followed the appointment of state court "reporters" and official editions. At first, reports were titled by the name of the reporter. The first reporter for Pennsylvania was Alexander James Dallas, and the first of his volumes was labeled 1 and 2 Dallas (the volumes also contained federal cases). In 1801, William Cranch was the second Supreme Court reporter, taking over from Dallas when the court moved from Philadelphia to Washington, DC, and Henry Wheaton was the third. These early reports had footnotes, the first of which are discussed in chapter 1, along with citations in the body of their opinions.[16]

Dallas came to the United States after the Revolution, and his reports, the beginning of the *United States Reports* series, were not entirely accurate nor timely, but they brought him considerable praise at the time. (Although he missed one-third of the Supreme Court cases in his second volume, and his publication of the opinions in *Chisholm* was five years late.) He was not paid for his labors, nor was he in any sense the official reporter of the Supreme Court, but his legal practice was in Philadelphia, and he argued cases before the Supreme Court as well as the state courts. During the 1790s, he was also secretary of the state of

---

15 For example, Joseph Story, *Commentaries on the Constitution of the United States*, 3 vols. (Boston: Hilliard Gray, 1833); J. G. Sutherland, *Statutes and Statutory Construction* (Chicago: Callaghan, 1891), iv, 2, 3, 4.

16 Lawrence M. Friedman, *A History of American Law*, 4th ed. (New York: Oxford University Press, 2019), 308–10; Erwin C. Surrency, "Law Reports in the United States," *American Journal of Legal History* 25 (1981): 48–66. Dallas added a few notes. Cranch's notes were more extensive, including verbatim discussions among the justices. He signaled his notes with letters. Far less frequent were the justices' own notes, signaled by superscript numbers.

Pennsylvania, and after 1800, he was rewarded for his support of the Jeffersonian Republican Party with places in Jefferson's and later James Madison's cabinets.[17]

Cranch was more than a reporter. A judge himself in the District of Columbia, he regularly attended the sessions of the court and included in notes to the cases bits of the justices' comments on the bench. His notes, a selection of which are collected in appendix A, are more annotations than citations. One should note that later editions of these first reports varied in their details and that editors (not the reporters) added, variously, their own notes.[18]

State reporters were lawyers themselves, sometimes judges, and their footnoting was an aid to judges and the practicing bar. The first state reports also had footnotes, again using symbols rather than numbers. Who added them? The evidence suggests that the reporters of the cases were the authors of the notes. The notes were generally references to other cases in the jurisdiction, statutes, and were only occasionally more than a few lines. The first notes in each of the states appear in appendix B.

By the end of the 1860s, "footnote creep" through the state reports had reached the Pacific Ocean. For example, "The first footnote in the *Oregon Reports* appeared in volume 3, in an 1869 reported decision of the Multnomah [Portland] County Court. It is one of two footnotes—denominated 'a' and 'b'—in the court's opinion, and is one of a mere handful in the entire volume."[19]

---

17 George Mifflin Dallas, *Life and Writings of Alexander James Dallas* (Philadelphia: Lippincott, 1971), 16; Raymond Walters Jr., *Alexander James Dallas: Lawyer, Politician, Financier, 1759–1817* (Philadelphia: University of Pennsylvania Press, 1943), 242; Maeva Marcus, ed., *Documentary History of the United States Supreme Court, 1789–1800* (New York: Columbia University Press, 1994) 5:193; Joel Fishman, "Reports of the Supreme Court of the United States" *Law Library Journal* 85 (1995): 648.

18 John O. Newman, "Citators Beware: Stylistic Variations in Different Publishers' Versions of Early Supreme Court Opinions," *Journal of Supreme Court History* 26 (2001): 5. The different versions reflect minor variations in the signal for footnotes. For example, the significant footnote to the report of Hayburn's Case, 2 U.S. (2 Dall.) 409, 410 (1792) (Little, Brown, 1st ed., 1855), quoting the important "opinions" of three circuit courts on each of which different justices of the Supreme Court sat, 10 is signaled by "1" in the 1855 Little, Brown version, by "(a)" in the 1906 Banks version, and by "t" in the version printed by the Aurora Office in Philadelphia in 1798. The Hart and Wechsler treatise reports that this footnote was "added by the reporter." Richard H. Fallon Jr., John F. Manning, Daniel J. Meltzer, and David L. Shapiro, *Hart and Wechsler's the Federal Courts and the Federal System*, 4th ed. (Santa Barbara, CA: Foundation Press, 1996), 100.

19 Jack L. Landau, "Footnote Folly," *Oregon Appellate Almanack* (November, 2006): 203; Cooper, "Legal Citation," 17–18.

* * *

The early nineteenth century was also the opening era of periodical literature in the new nation. Investment in the new rotary press spawned collections of nonfiction essays, poetry, and short stories. A "young America" coterie of writers, including William Cullen Bryant, Henry Wadsworth Longfellow, Oliver Wendell Holmes Sr., Edgar Allan Poe, and Washington Irving, found their audiences. It was thus a welcoming milieu for the *American Law Journal and Miscellaneous Repertory* and its imitators. They did not last long, but the yearly *American Law Register* edited by Asa Fish and Henry Wharton, Philadelphia lawyers, became the prototype of the law review. Its very first article, "Gifts in View of Death," featured thirty-seven footnotes, the majority citations of cases and treatises but one offering a miniature essay on donations.[20]

A magazine for the amusement of lawyers called *The Green Bag* was a short-lived scion of these repertories from the Boston Book Company. From 1889 to 1914, available by subscription, it offered biographies and drawings or photographs of legal figures, short essays on legal subjects, book reviews, synopses of important cases, and anecdotes of the legal profession. It was not associated with any law school, however, and its longtime editor, Horace William Fuller, was a lawyer but not a legal educator. He did belong to the American Bar Association, knew many of the most important lawyers in the country, and *The Green Bag* was always respectful in its humorous offerings. For example, in "Bench Wit in New York City," Fuller found that "there is not one of these nineteen [court of appeals judges] but can be classed as either humorist or wit, and without any sacrifice of dignity."[21]

More recognizable predecessors of modern law journals included the *American Law Review*, founded by Harvard law professor John Chipman Gray in 1866 and published by Little, Brown in Boston. It as a bimonthly collection of legal news and views and remains today in the form of the *United States Law Review*. The first edition of the journal, in

---

20 Michael L. Swygert and Jon W. Bruce, "The Historical Origins, Founding, and Early Development of Student-Edited Law Review," *Hastings Law Journal* 36 (1985): 755; "Gifts in View of Death" *American Law Register* 1 (1852): 6n3. The journal became the *University of Pennsylvania Law Review* in 1908 under the leadership of the law school's dean, William Draper Lewis.
21 "Bench Wit in New York City," *The Green Bag* 9 (1897), 295.

October 1866, featured articles like "The Natural Right of Support from Neighboring Soil" (about suits for damage from collapsing land due to neighboring mining) and did not have any footnotes. The author, one F. V. B., included copious case references in the body of the text. These cases were largely English, but he included some Roman law as well.[22]

The second article, on "Final Process in Courts of the United States as Affected by State Laws," did have something that looked a lot like a footnote. Heralded by an asterisk in the body of the text, the note at the bottom of the page was deemed (by the author) necessary to supply authority for his assertion that the "courts of the United States, as well as every other court" supported the proposition in the text. The asterisk at the bottom of the page was what is now known as a string citation of state cases, listing their citations only. A second asterisk, on the next page, introduced the footnote as a place for an extended discussion of a collateral legal issue, in this case the doctrine of contract. It could not fit in the body of the text, as it was a tangent, but the bottom of the page was a perfect place for it, as well as for display of the author's erudition. Thus, the legal journal footnote arrived, its authority based on the citation to cases alone, or, in the alternative, on the author's command of legal doctrine.[23]

The next, enduring, law review to appear, in 1887, came from Harvard Law School. Two immediate predecessors, from Albany and Columbia Law Schools, had not been successful, lasting only a few issues, although the latter effort may have stimulated Harvard students to try their hand at the project. Their first issues of the *Harvard Law Review* were not an official organ of the Law School but rather the private initiative of the students. Funding came from Law School alumnus Louis Brandeis, among others. The founding editors included such future luminaries as John Henry Wigmore, Julian Mack, Samuel Williston, and Joseph Beale. The *Harvard Law Review* was the first fully student-edited example of the genre. In announcing its arrival, as if it were the first of its kind, the

---

22 F. V. B., "The Natural Right of Support from Neighboring Soil," *American Law Review* 1 (October, 1866): 3–28. Two years later, the House of Lords, in *Rylands v. Fletcher*, 3 H. L. 330 (1868), a suit brought for water damages to a mine caused by a neighboring reservoir bursting, would lead to the doctrine of strict liability for such torts. The case is still taught in American law school courses in property.

23 J. A. C., "Final Process in Courts of the United States as Affected by State Laws," *American Law Review* 1 (October, 1866): 40, 41.

editors explained, "Publication of a law review by any school is justified by the additional contributions to legal literature which it stimulates and the opportunities for better training to students which it affords." Central to those opportunities were the students' editing tasks.[24]

Given that the purpose for the legal footnote was to teach law students how to cite cases and to allow the authors to show their authorities, it was vital that students work on the footnotes to articles published in the reviews. The enterprise of teaching students how to cite cases progressed with the introduction of the first-year law school course in lawyering, and its bible, the *Bluebook*. According to the detective work of Fred Shapiro and Julie Graves Krishnaswami, the first law review footnotes guide was the work of young Yale Law School professor Karl N. Llewellyn. "His 1920 manual had a blue cover (Yale, of course) and became the standard for notes in the law review." Although Harvard Law School dean Erwin Griswold claimed pride of primacy, his parallel, but slightly later, manual of style appeared in 1922. The format was distinct from the evolving format of scholarly footnotes, the former featuring small caps, full caps, italics, and other stylistic devices for citations of different sources. In David Dorsen's biography of Henry Friendly, "According to Judge Henry J. Friendly, 'Attorney General [Herbert] Brownell, whom I had known ever since law school—he was Editor-in-Chief of the *Yale Law Journal* the year I was at the *Harvard Law Review* and he and I and two others [from Columbia and Pennsylvania] were the authors of the first edition of the *Bluebook*.'" Not everyone is a fan of the *Bluebook*. Judge Richard Posner in 1986 insisted that "the legal profession needs a new approach to legal citations and to legal style–the latter a related but more important subject that the Bluebook ignores."[25]

* * *

The rise of the legal footnote has not gone unchallenged, despite the almost universal adoption of *Bluebook* citation in law school courses

24 Editors, *Harvard Law Review* 1 (April 1887), 1; Swygert and Bruce, "Student-Edited Law Reviews," 764–68, 768–71. Wigmore would go on to be the legal academy's foremost authority on the law of evidence, Beale would become the same for diversity of laws, Williston would become a leader in the field of contract law, and Mack would become a federal appeals court judge.

25 Fred R. Shapiro and Julie Graves Krishnaswami, "The Secret History of the Bluebook," *University of Minnesota Law Review* 100 (2016): 1563–98; Richard A. Posner, "Goodbye to the Blue Book," *University of Chicago Law Review* 53 (1986): 1343.

and law journals and the proliferation of footnotes in law reviews. Many appeals court judges still refuse to use footnotes in their opinions. In 1991, legal writer Bryan Garner revealed the extent of the judges' division over footnoting. Then he took sides. He argued that if the material in the note is important to the opinion, it belongs in the opinion. But the opinion that is chopped into pieces then spliced together when citations are embedded in the text is an abomination. "What we're talking about is the noxious habit of interspersing bibliographic references throughout legal analysis (or what commonly passes as legal analysis). It wasn't so bad 150 years ago, when relatively few cases would typically appear over a span of several pages. Today, partly because caselaw has mushroomed, a lot of legal writing has become nearly unreadable." Garner campaigned for the footnote. "In every state where I've spoken to judges, a majority have said that they would prefer footnoted citations. Those who know that they can write better by disburdening their text of bibliographic numbers ought to be able to do so without having some lawyer carp that they're weakening the doctrine of precedent. I predict that within a generation, the citational footnote will be the norm in both judicial opinions and briefs. And it will be one of the greatest helps in improving legal writing."[26]

Some defenders of the footnote went further than Garner. Judge Edward R. Becker was one of these. "As a federal judge for a quarter century," Becker wrote, "I believe in footnotes and am convinced that the judicious use of footnotes allows judges to communicate most effectively with their diverse audiences. I have received much positive feedback about the many footnotes in my opinions." The judge believed that appellate courts' opinions are written for more than other judges and the lawyers and parties in particular cases. According to Becker, "Footnotes enable the opinion to fulfill these disparate, complex functions and thereby respond to multiple audiences while preserving the textual body's coherence and readability." The good footnote also provides context for the judge's reasoning, linking the opinion to a world outside the narrow confines of law. Such footnotes "serve as a repository of scholar-

---

26 See, for example, Bryan Garner, *The Elements of Legal Style* (New York: Oxford University Press, 1991), 91–92; Garner, *A Dictionary of Modern Legal Usage*, 2nd ed. (New York: Oxford University Press, 1995), 364; Garner, *The Winning Brief* (New York: Oxford University Press, 1999), 117, 120–21; and Garner, "The Citational Footnotes," *Appellate Advocate* 13 (2000): 3, 5.

ship." Finally, "Footnotes are also an excellent vehicle for responding to concurring or dissenting opinions," as the reader of this present book will see in chapters 7 and 8.[27]

With something like this in mind, law professor Jack Balkin wrote a meditation on the legal footnote titled "The Footnote." Perhaps it should have been titled "Ode on a Footnote" or "Letter to a Footnote." In any case, he brushed aside the criticism that legal scholars, lawyers, and judges use footnotes as gratuitous displays of legal knowledge. Such criticism found that the lowly note was literally banished from the text, left to be (most often unread) on the bottom of the page, "an inconsequential, inessential, and intellectual bauble that one could, in theory, do without." Balkin dismissed these criticisms. For try as one might in legal writing, he asserted, one cannot do without footnotes. They hold together claims or delay their satisfaction; they can tantalize the reader or relieve the reader; they can even be miniature opinions. Legal writers can raise the lowly footnote to the pedestal of law. Note that both of these essays end in praise of footnote 4 to *United States v. Carolene Products* (1938), the subject of chapter 5 herein.[28]

Footnotes can even be fun to write and read. One former Supreme Court clerk recalled a footnote exchange between Justice Ruth Bader Ginsburg and Antonin Scalia:

> To an expert, for example, even the most straightforward kind of footnote—one that simply cites one or more sources to support a proposition in the text—can turn out to be remarkable for what it cites, or more intriguingly, what it fails to cite. But when the footnotes go beyond mere citation to extend an argument or respond to an argument or to engage in some attenuated speculation about a related point or make a joke, they can become downright entertaining, even fascinating. Footnotes allow the writer to break away from the main text, to use a different tone, to consider tangents—basically to carry on two conversations with the reader at once, or at least one-and-a-half.[29]

---

27 Edward R. Becker, "In Praise of Footnotes," *Washington University Law Quarterly* 74 (1996): 1, 4, 5.

28 J. M. Balkin, "The Footnote," *Northwestern University Law Review* 275 (1988–89): 278, 281, 300.

29 Jay D. Wexler, "Justice Ginsburg's Footnotes," *New England Law Review* 43 (2009): 3–4.

At the same time, the footnote's detractors are many and highly regarded, as both Becker and Balkin were aware. The most recent of these have been judges—Abner J. Mikva, Richard A. Posner, and Justice Stephen Breyer. Mikva's "Goodbye to Footnotes" denounced footnotes "in judicial opinions an abomination." But the judge worried that over the past thirty years (before he wrote his jeremiad), footnote writing "has spread like a fungus and has magnified all of the shortcomings of legal writing." Footnotes in small type were very difficult for older eyes to read, allowed all manner of trivia to infect an opinion, and gave rise to the most unfortunate inducement to carry on assaults on fellow judges. Finally, and most dangerous, "both majority opinions and dissents are replete with examples of black-letter law being made or refined in footnotes."[30]

Judge Posner argued that the references in the notes belong in the text. But Posner had an ulterior motive: targeting Brian Garner's essay. Garner, who thought that opinions were clearer if the citations were moved to footnotes, used two of Posner's opinions as examples. Not fair, the judge decided. The emended versions had changed the meaning of his writing. Breyer's opinion was a little more nuanced. In a 1995 interview with the *New York Times* based on his earlier experience in the Court of Appeals for the First Circuit, Breyer explained that the reason for the judicial opinion in the first place "is to explain as clearly as possible and as simply as possible what the reasons are for reaching this decision. Others can then say those are good reasons or those are bad reasons. If you see the opinion in this way, either a point is sufficiently significant to make, in which case it should be in the text, or it is not, in which case, don't make it." That, of course, is a reason for omitting discursive or tangential notes, not for moving the citations out of the text to the notes. In any case, Justice Breyer never changed his mind. His last major opinion for the court, *June Medical Services v. Russo* (2020), was footnote free.[31]

---

30 Abner J. Mikva, "Goodbye to Footnotes," *University of Colorado Law Review* 56 (1985): 646, 647, 650.

31 Richard A. Posner, "Against Footnotes," *Court Review: The Journal of the American Judges Association* (July 2001): 24, 25; Stephen Breyer quoted in "In Justice Breyer's Opinion, a Footnote Has No Place," *New York Times*, July 28, 1995, Section B, 18. For an example, see June Medical Services v. Russo, 591 U.S. 1101 (2020) (Breyer, J.). Breyer's opinions, often luminous in their learning and compelling in their logic, were less than elegant in style. Broken into pieces by his insertions of

* * *

Neither the defenders nor the attackers of the judicial footnote confronted a difficult but central question: Is the footnote law? In other
words, is it binding as precedent when it is part of a majority decision
of an appellate court? Is it binding on lower courts? Is it precedent in
and of itself? Chief Justice Charles Evans Hughes may have said, "I will
not be bound by a footnote," but footnotes are all over appellate court
opinions. The path to the opinion often leads back to the amicus brief,
in which scholars and lawyers, among others, address the court on particular cases. From these briefs, judges draw arguments and evidence
and put some of it in the notes. When the judge includes such notes in
an opinion, the note acquires a very different status from its status in
the article or the brief. But the question remains the same: Is the note,
by virtue of its inclusion in an opinion, made into law? Is it part of the
precedent created by a majority opinion?[32]

A parallel approach to this conundrum may be suggestive. The preamble to statutes and constitutional texts, for example the preamble to
the federal Constitution, according to Justice Joseph Story's *Commentaries on the Constitution of the United States* (1833), are not self-executing.
This means that one cannot base a legal claim on the preamble's language
unless that language is given effect in the body of the Constitution. For
example, the "blessings of liberty" promised in the preamble did not end
slavery in the country. That required alteration of the Constitution in the
form of the Thirteenth Amendment. The preamble was merely a general
statement of purpose. Who decided that? Well, none other than Story,
in his *Commentaries*. The same was deemed true of the preamble to the
Second Amendment (about which, more in chapter 7). Thus, something
can be part of constitutional or statutory text and not be law—requiring
anyone to do, or not do, anything. Is this true of the footnote? Must its
entire substance be included in the majority opinion for it to be law?[33]

---

citations in the text, they have not achieved the quotability of, say, Justice Antonin Scalia's opinions,
with their footnotes. But in other legal venues, Breyer has proved himself very able and willing with
footnotes. His law review articles and his books are replete with them.

32 Charles Evans Hughes quoted in Douglas E. Abrams, "Those Pesky Footnotes, Part I," *Precedent,
The Quarterly Magazine of the Missouri Bar* (Summer, 2007): 19.

33 Joseph Story, *Commentaries*, 1:145.

There are two kinds of footnotes in Supreme Court opinions, as Bryan Garner explained. Some justices put citations of cases and statutes in footnotes rather than in the text in order to make the text easier, or at least smoother, to read. These materials are already law; that is, they are the precedents and statutes on which the justices are basing their opinions. There is no problem with them as law, except some critics of footnotes want them shifted back into the text of the opinion. The other kind of footnotes add material that is not already law. They may be references that influenced the judge—to history, comparisons with other jurisdictions' doctrines, or citations of social science findings—and they want the reader (and their colleagues) to know about those influences. They are supportive but not definitive. But when they become part of an opinion to which a majority of the court subscribes, do they become part of the law?

The short case studies that constitute the chapters of this book attempt, among other objectives, to answer this question using the historical method. That is, following the trail of the influential footnotes through our constitutional history may help us decide whether we want them to become part of our law. We follow the footnotes in both their legal and their case contexts, that is, what role they played in the particular case. Were they vital to it or ancillary? Then, what role did they play in the later law?

A second question is more diffuse but of particular interest to lay readers who enjoy legal history. All appellate court opinions are miniature histories. The history *in* them are accounts of previous cases, the rehearsal of the arrival of the present case at the court, and an incorporation of the facts of the case from the trial court. But that internal history is enmeshed in a larger, external history, the world of the parties, the litigation, and the courts themselves. This external history surrounds and runs in bumpy parallel to the internal history of the case. The footnotes link the two kinds of histories. They are not perfect links, but in the hands of a skillful judge, the footnotes illuminate the internal history with highlights from the external world. In this, the judges are assisted by friends of the court—briefs by lawyers representing parties who have an interest in the litigation and are permitted, by the discretion of the judge, to present a little of the external history. It is therefore possible, and I believe desirable, to interrogate the footnotes themselves, asking

what they contribute to the opinion and how they help us—the historians—to understand the opinion and the wider constitutional world.
Sometimes condemned as "law office history," the historical materials in
lawyers' briefs for the parties before the court and in friends of the court
(amicus) briefs nevertheless open a window into the heart of constitutional lawmaking.[34]

* * *

Why select the eight cases around which this volume is structured? Why
the opinions therein? What makes them special? All concerned major
issues of the day for the justices. All remain controversial. All contained
new kinds of footnotes. All were fun to revisit. But how do we know
who wrote the footnotes? After all, the first reporters for the court added
their own notes. The reporter became a salaried position in 1817 (Congress paying), and in 1874, the government paid for the reports. The
other editions of the cases, the *United States (Supreme Court) Reports,
Lawyers' Edition* (the *Lawyers' Edition*) and the Westlaw edition, have
headnotes added by the publisher, but the reporters no longer add their
own notes to the cases. In the modern court, the justices have clerks who
are routinely asked to brief the cases, research the notes, or even find
and write the notes. Clerks to the justices played a vital role in *United
States v. Carolene Products* (1938) footnote 4 (see chapter 5) and *Brown
v. Board of Education* (1954) footnote 11 (see chapter 6), but the clerk
authors of those notes insisted that they did not include anything their
justices had not approved. One modern account based on extensive
interviews with former clerks concluded that 30 percent of the opinions
were the work of the clerks. Another insider account documents how
former clerks not only wrote opinions but decided cases. I have made
the assumption that because the justices edit and revise the notes, even
if they do not write them, that the notes are theirs. After all, it is their
names on the opinions, not the clerks.'[35]

---

34 See, however, Rebecca Piller, "History in the Making: Why Courts Are Ill-Equipped to Employ
Originalism," *Review of Litigation* 34 (2015): 191–93 (historians' amicus briefs are bad history).
35 Surrency, "Law Reports in the United States," 48; Artemus Ward and David L. Weiden, *Sorcerers'
Apprentices: 100 Years of Law Clerks at the United States Supreme Court* (New York: New York
University Press, 2006), 23, 46; Todd C. Peppers and Artemus Ward, eds., *In Chambers: Stories of
Supreme Court Law Clerks and their Justices* (Charlottesville: University of Virginia Press, 2012), 183,
235, 316–17, 372. But see an early warning of a legion of liberal clerks taking over the court from an

Finally, let's step back before we examine the following eight case studies and ask, What is the argument of the book? Hopefully, its contribution is pretty obvious—looking at the opinions of the court in a new way, through the back door, as it were, of the footnotes. But what do I conclude from that study? Law reviews tell the reader the author's take on the subject at the very beginning of the piece, in a "headnote." Historians are slyer, dropping clues for the reader to find (think of a good mystery) as they read. But unlike the classic mystery, there is no real culprit at the end of this book (not even the Muppet Grover). Instead, it is the journey through the opinions, and the world of legal ideas beyond, that is the theme.[36]

---

unlikely place: William R. Rehnquist, "Who Writes Decisions of the Supreme Court?" *U.S. News and World Report*, December 13, 1957, 74. There is a rough positive correspondence between the rising number of the justice's clerks (from one to four) and the rising number of footnotes in opinions, but I am not sure what this correlation means.

36 Jon Stone, *The Monster at the End of this Book, Starring Furry, Lovable Old Grover*, 2nd ed. (New York: Golden Books, 2003), 2, in which Grover warns the reader not to turn the page.

[1]

SOVEREIGNTY

Chisholm v. Georgia, 2 U.S. 419 (1793)

The footnotes to Justice James Wilson's opinion in *Chisholm v. Georgia* tell us that for a nation whose new organizing principle was a federal union, no question was more important and more vexing than the nature of federalism. How were the formerly independent states to function in a union with a supreme central government? What were the limitations of the authority of the central government, and what were the powers reserved to the states? In older terminology, these were questions of sovereignty. Could a footnoted survey of ancient and modern states give Wilson, an erudite member of the court, and his readers, reliable answers? Did the footnotes?[1]

The concept of sovereignty was well established when Justice Wilson addressed it in *Chisholm v. Georgia* (1793). It had feudal roots in the contest between princes and their barons, and later between the kings of the new states of western Europe and their nobility. It was part of the conversation between Whigs and Tories in the Revolutionary crisis. For William Blackstone, standing like the colossus astride the common law of England and its American colonies, the sovereign monarch was "a supreme, irresistible, absolute, uncontrolled authority." But within a generation, the notion of popular sovereignty—government ultimately resting on the consent of the governed—triumphed in America. In 1774, Wilson had argued for the sovereignty of the people when he served in the Pennsylvania assembly. "All lawful government are dependent on the consent of those who are subject to it." He sat with the Pennsylvania delegation at the Constitutional Convention when members fashioned a dual federalism—the new national government and the state govern-

---

1 Jonathan Gienapp, *The Second Creation: Fixing the American Constitution in the Founding Era* (Cambridge, MA: Harvard University Press, 2018), 88–91.

ments sharing sovereignty. At the Pennsylvania Ratification Convention, where he led the fight to adopt the new Constitution, he argued that "in our governments, the supreme, absolute, and uncontrollable power remains in the people." For while some might argue that "the supreme power resides in the States, as governments; and mine is, that it *resides* in the PEOPLE, as the fountain of government; that the people have not—that the people mean not—and that the people ought not, to part with it to any government whatsoever. In their hands it remains secure."[2]

* * *

The first footnotes in a US Supreme Court opinion appeared in Wilson's opinion in *Chisholm v. Georgia*. The case was one of first instance, and it was greatly significant as the first real test of legal federalism and the concept of sovereignty. Wilson's views of these issues were predictable, but the court's decision hit the ground with a thud as states'-rights advocates executed a powerful response—changing the Constitution (with the Eleventh Amendment). *Chisholm* was soon a dead letter. Perhaps the majority of the court did not see that response coming. The court had divided 4–1, with Chief Justice John Jay and Associate Justices James Wilson, Francis Blair, and William Cushing agreeing that a South Carolina petitioner could sue the state of Georgia for goods the state owed but had not paid for during the Revolution. Justice James Iredell dissented, finding that Georgia remained a sovereign in the federal union and could not be sued without its consent. Georgia, infamously, did not appear to defend itself, although it had in the circuit court the previous year and despite the fact that its agent in Philadelphia was there to represent the state in *Georgia v. Brailsford*.[3]

---

2 William Blackstone, *Commentaries on the Laws of England*, 1:48; Daniel Hulsebosch, *Constituting Empire: New York and the Transformation of Constitutionalism in the Atlantic World, 1664–1830* (Chapel Hill: University of North Carolina Press, 2005), 33; Eric Nelson, "Prerogative, Popular Sovereignty, and the American Founding," in *Popular Sovereignty in Historical Perspective*, ed. Richard Bourke and Quentin Skinner (Cambridge, UK: Cambridge University Press, 2016), 187–211; James Wilson, *Considerations on the Nature and Extent of the Legislative Authority of the British Parliament* (Philadelphia, 1774), in *Works of James Wilson*, ed. Bird Wilson (Philadelphia: Bronson and Chancey, 1804), 3:206; Wilson, December 4, 1787, *The Debates in the Several State Constitutions*, ed. Jonathan Elliot (Philadelphia: Lippincott, 1876), 2:456; but see Edmund S. Morgan, *Inventing the People: The Rise of Popular Sovereignty in England and America* (New York: Norton, 1988), 236–62 (consent of the governed was a fiction; the elite was sovereign).

3 Chisholm v. Georgia, 2 U.S. 419 (1793); Maeva Marcus, ed., *Documentary History of the United States Supreme Court, 1789–1800* (New York: Columbia University Press, 1994), 5:130, 6:81; H.

The issues in the case were far more important than its facts. On October 31, 1777, the Revolutionary Executive Council of Georgia authorized Thomas Stone and Edward Davies, as commissioners of the state, to purchase goods from Robert Farquhar, a South Carolina merchant. At the time of Farquhar's death in 1784, he had not received payment for his merchandise. The estate filed a claim for the debt with the Georgia legislature in 1789, but a committee of the legislature refused to pay. It suggested that he sue the two commissioners who had taken the funds from the state treasury for themselves. Chisholm sued Georgia in the federal circuit court in 1791 (at that time a trial court), rightly assuming that a Georgia court would find for the state. That was one reason that Article III, Clause 2, Section 4 gave to the federal courts jurisdiction in cases "between a State and citizens of another State." But riding circuit in Georgia, Justice Iredell dismissed the case because Georgia, he opined, could not be sued without its consent. Chisholm appealed to the US Supreme Court, which, he claimed, had jurisdiction when a state was a party to a suit. Attorney general of the United States Edmund Randolph represented Chisholm when the court met to hear the case. Georgia did not appear, and judgment was entered for the petitioner. When it learned of the decision, the state's legislature declared the decision unconstitutional.[4]

* * *

James Wilson was born in Scotland in 1742 and arrived in the colonies two decades later. Here he studied and practiced law. He was a strong supporter of the protests against Great Britain leading to independence and served in the Continental Congress, where he signed the Declaration of Independence. At the Constitutional Convention, he supported Madison and other nationalists. He was one of the four men that new president George Washington appointed to the US Supreme Court in 1789, on which he served until his death in 1798. A leading legal theorist,

---

Jefferson Powell, "Imagining the United States: Reflections from Constitutional Law," *Law Contemporary Problems* 85 (2022): 6. Note that the issue of sovereignty reappeared in the Civil War. See Peter Charles Hoffer, *Seward's Law: Country Lawyering, Relational Rights, and Slavery* (Ithaca, NY: Cornell University Press, 2023), 117.

4 G. Edward White, *The Law in American History*, vol. 1 (New York: Oxford University Press, 2012), 202–4; John V. Orth, *The Judicial Power of the United Stats: The Eleventh Amendment in American History* (New York: Oxford University Press, 1987), 12–20.

in his capacity as the first professor of law at the College of Philadelphia (later to become the University of Pennsylvania), he taught the first course on the new Constitution. He was also deeply in debt for improvident land speculation and would spend much of his tenure on the court dodging his creditors. He died with them breathing down his neck in Edenton, North Carolina, while on circuit (although he did not come to court that day).[5]

Wilson was familiar with footnoting. The first footnote of his *Commentaries on the Constitution of the United States* (1792), the published version of his speeches in the ratification debates in Pennsylvania, called out the opponents of the Constitution by name. The second cited Blackstone (but did not indicate which volume). The third, fourth, and fifth footnotes cited a parliamentary history, parliamentary debates, and again Blackstone, but did not indicate the authors or publication dates, only the pages. While intimates may have known more about the works cited, a casual reader would have been mystified. In short, Wilson was not a particularly careful footnoter, and the notes he did add were more reminders to himself than revelations to his readers. Wilson's *Lectures on Law* (1790–92) featured somewhat less cryptic footnotes, however, proving that he cared more about them in his scholarship than in his politics.[6]

The footnotes to Wilson's opinion in *Chisholm*, appearing with letters at the bottom of the pages, were simple citations in almost coded form. In the handwritten original draft of the opinion that Wilson gave to Dallas, there were no footnotes. Instead, Wilson made notes in the margin of the sources for some of his allusions and quotations. These were the first (and last) time that Wilson added notes. In *Georgia v. Brailsford*, 2 U.S. 402 (1792), for example, Wilson's opinion was four paragraphs long, without notes. His other opinions in Supreme Court cases were similarly short and to the point and devoid of notes. In *Chisholm*, however, he

---

5 Charles Page Smith, *James Wilson, Founding Father, 1742–1798* (Chapel Hill: University of North Carolina Press, 1956), 376–89; Michael Taylor, *James Wilson, Anxious Founder* (Lanham, MD: Lexington Books, 2021), 206–7.

6 James Wilson and Thomas McKean, *Commentaries on the Constitution of the United States* (London: Debrett, 1792), 20, 30, 43; James Wilson, "Lectures on Law," in *Works of James Wilson*, ed. James DeWitt Andrews (Chicago: Callaghan, 1890), 1:xxi: e.g., citation to "R.O. bk. A, p. 22." But some, with reference to the text, were decipherable, for example, "de leg. 1, 2, c. 23" is a reference to Cicero's *De Legibus*, book 1, page 2, chapter 23. On xxii, "Bl Com 410" is Blackstone's *Commentaries on the Laws of England*, 1:410.

added twenty-five notes to a very long opinion. Examining them, one can surmise why he thought footnoting essential. They were primarily from the text of the Constitution but included treatises like Cicero, Bracton, Vattel, and Blackstone, English high court opinions, and literary works like the *Iliad*. Some of the notes had already appeared in his *Lectures on Law*, delivered over the previous two years. He had turned the opinion into a miniature treatise, likely because he saw it as his legacy.[7]

As was the custom at that time, each of the justices read their opinion from notes. Only Wilson's draft opinion had references in the margins. He turned over a clean copy to Alexander James Dallas, the volunteer reporter for the court, sometime after February 13, 1793. The footnotes were not added by Dallas, although editors of later Dallas 1–4 (U.S. 1–4) published in the 1880s did add footnotes to the cases (one finds these editions of the *Reports* in law libraries.) Dallas's version of Wilson's marginalia used letters, and the later editions, following the custom of their times, used numbers. One should add that Wilson's opinion is the first great statement of federal courts' jurisdiction, preceding *Marbury v. Madison* (1803) by a decade. And *Chisholm*, had it stood, would have been the first in the canon of great constitutional tests.[8]

Wilson was a nationalist; he believed in a strong central government. In the Constitutional Convention and during the ratification contest in Pennsylvania, he made the case that without a strong central government, the confederation of states that existed from 1781 would collapse or fly apart. Thus, for him, *Chisholm* was a "case of uncommon magnitude." He also believed that sovereignty, the authority of government, cannot easily be divided. The revolutionaries had concluded that the ultimate sovereign was the people, and the Constitution's prefatory "We the People" seemed to confirm that tenet. Finally, the Supremacy Clause of the federal Constitution (Article VI, Clause 2) seemed to answer the question where sovereignty lies short of the people.[9]

---

7 Marcus, *Documentary History of the Supreme Court*, 5:193–214, reproduces a facsimile of the original draft opinion and annotates the changes that Dallas made for the print version. Apparently, Dallas moved the marginalia to the bottom of the page and labeled the notes a, b, c, and so forth, beginning anew with each page. See Article III, Section 2, of the federal Constitution, under which Chisholm brought the suit against Georgia.

8 Randy E. Barnett, "The People or the State: Chisholm v. Georgia and Popular Sovereignty," *Virginia Law Review* 93 (2007): 1730; Powell, "Imagining," 7.

9 Chisholm v. Georgia, 2 U.S. 419, 453 (1793) (Wilson, J.).

Here, then, was the nub of his argument: "One of the parties to [the case] is a State; certainly respectable, claiming to be sovereign. The question to be determined is, whether this State, so respectable, and whose claim soars so high, is amenable to the jurisdiction of the Supreme Court of the United States?" The tone was almost snide; after all, Georgia was the least populous and arguably the most corrupt of the states in the Union. For although the other party was a mere citizen of South Carolina, behind his claim lay the weight of Article III and the federal courts. "This question, important in itself, will depend on others, more important still; and, may, perhaps, be ultimately resolved into one, no less radical than this 'do the people of the United States form a Nation?'"[10]

Wilson's subject was the nature of sovereignty, both as a matter of general principles and as applied to the Constitution and the federal union. It was more a disquisition that a judicial opinion. In it Wilson ranged far and wide beyond the facts of the case. In fact, he did not bother to give them, nor did he discuss, the procedural history of the suit. Instead, "I am, first, to examine this question by the principles of general jurisprudence." It is true that he had little federal precedent to guide him, did not look at the precedents of his own state of Pennsylvania, and ignored the law that the Articles of Confederation made. Instead, remember that Wilson was a student of the so-called Scottish Enlightenment, whose second wave of theorists included Edinburgh philosopher Thomas Reid. "What I shall say upon this head, I introduce by the observation of an original and profound writer . . . Dr. Reid, in his excellent enquiry into the human mind, on the principles of common sense, speaking of the sceptical and illiberal philosophy." Reid rejected metaphysics, and concluded that the common sense of a subject should guide one's consideration of it. "Every proposition is either true or false; so is every judgment."[11]

What had Reid to say about sovereignty? This was a stretch, given that a Scottish political philosophy was not obviously relevant for the case, but Wilson eagerly made it: "The language of philosophers, with regard to the original faculties of the mind, is so adapted to the prevail-

---

10 2 U.S. at 453 (Wilson, J.); Charles F. Hobson, *The Great Yazoo Lands Sale: The Case of Fletcher v. Peck* (Lawrence: University Press of Kansas, 2016), 34.

11 2 U.S. at 453 (Wilson, J.); Thomas Reid, *Essays on the Intellectual Powers of Man*, ed. James Walker (Boston: Phillips, 1855), 349. First published 1785 by Maclachlan and Stewart (London).

ing system, that it cannot fit any other; like a coat that fits the man for whom it was made, and shews him to advantage, which yet will fit very awkward upon one of a different make, although as handsome and well proportioned." Scottish common sense philosophy, for Wilson an excellent guide to constitutional thinking, warned that "it is hardly possible to make any innovation in our philosophy concerning the mind and its operations, without using new words and phrases, or giving a different meaning to those that are received." So a concept like sovereignty was, in effect, up for grabs among those who wished to claim its mantle. "With equal propriety may this solid remark be applied to the great subject, on the principles of which the decision of this Court is to be founded." How Reid was an authority might be questioned by modern jurists but perhaps not in the inception of this formative era of federal constitutional jurisprudence and certainly not by this framer of that jurisprudence. On his own authority, Wilson warned that "the perverted use of genus and species in logic, and of impressions and ideas in metaphysics, have never done mischief so extensive or so practically pernicious, as has been done by States and sovereigns, in politics and jurisprudence."[12]

Georgia did not make any of these claims; recall that it did not argue its own brief before the court. Its assertion of sovereignty was naked— "Catch us if you can. Make us if you can." By contrast, Wilson supplied the state's brief, then answered it: "In these purposes, and in this application, I shall be justified by example the most splendid, and by authority the most binding." Against a silent Georgia, Wilson raised "the example of the most refined as well as the most free nation known to antiquity; and the authority of one of the best Constitutions known to modern times." His authorities would come from the store of ideas in Western civilization, reaching back to ancient Greece and spanning the rise of the great Western nations.[13]

The crucial principle of revolutionary constitutionalism and the major difference between the British imperial constitution and American constitutions was that here, the only sovereign was the people. That was why there was no mention of sovereignty in the federal Constitution. "States and Governments were made for man." Here Wilson found

---

12 2 U.S. at 454 (Wilson, J.).
13 2 U.S. at 454 (Wilson, J.).

Cicero useful, as "Cicero says so sublimely, 'Nothing, which is exhibited upon our globe, is more acceptable to that divinity, which governs the whole universe, than those communities and assemblages of men, which, lawfully associated, are denominated States.'" For the state was subordinate to the citizenry, but in all else, the objects of government were subordinate to the state. Wilson had used the Cicero quotation in his lectures on law as well.[14]

Wilson thought that states were nothing more than combinations of people. States were not metaphysical entities; they were simply aggregations of men, subject to the same legal and moral obligations. Then, "Is there any part of this description, which intimates, in the remotest manner, that a State, any more than the men who compose it, ought not to do Justice and fulfil engagements? It will not be pretended that there is." Georgia was not doing what it should, and hiding behind the abstraction of sovereignty would not alleviate it of its financial obligations. "If Justice is not done; if engagements are not fulfilled" the state fails just as an individual, sovereign in his political role, fails. "Upon the same principles, upon which he becomes bound by the laws, he becomes amenable to the Courts of Justice, which are formed and authorised by those laws. If one free man, an original sovereign, may do all this; why may not an aggregate of free men, a collection of original sovereigns, do this likewise? If the dignity of each singly is undiminished; the dignity of all jointly must be unimpaired."[15]

Reasoning by analogy and relying on Reid's idea of common sense, Wilson reached for the heart of the matter: "A State, like a merchant, makes a contract. A dishonest State, like a dishonest merchant, wilfully refuses to discharge it: The latter is amenable to a Court of Justice: Upon general principles of right, shall the former when summoned to answer the fair demands of its creditor, be permitted, proteus-like, to assume a new appearance, and to insult him and Justice, by declaring I am a Sovereign State? Surely not." The fact that Georgia did not appear to defend itself in Philadelphia, even though it was there to prosecute in *Brailsford*, may have given wings to Wilson's rhetoric. After all, there were Georgian members of both houses of Congress who could have been asked by the

---

14   2 U.S. 455 (Wilson, J.); Cicero, *De Re Publica*, 1, 2 c. 33, also cited in Wilson, "Lectures on Law," *Works*, 1:271.
15   2 U.S. 456 (Wilson, J.).

state government to speak for it. In any case, Wilson had not held back his aspersions.[16]

Turning next to a more conventional approach to sovereignty, Wilson found little in the Constitution to sustain a strong claim by the state. This was clearly his nationalistic stance. One could argue that the states retained their sovereignty as polities; James Madison, for example, made this argument in his *Federalist*, no. 45, and he continued to make it literally next door (the Supreme Court met in the upstairs courthouse at the other end of the Constitution Hall from where the House of Representatives sat) in opposition to Alexander Hamilton's proposal for a national bank. The three of them had worked together to insure ratification. No longer: "On this subject," Wilson concluded," "the errors and the mazes are endless and inexplicable."[17]

Wilson conceded that according to some writers (here citing Emmerich de Vattel's *Law of Nations*), "every State, which governs itself without any dependence on another power, is a sovereign State." But in the federal system, Georgia had to concede that tariffs, war, diplomacy, coinage, and many other government functions exclusively belonged to the new federal government. Even then, the citizens of Georgia had not surrendered all their rights to the state. "As a citizen, I know the Government of that State to be republican; and my short definition of such a Government is, one constructed on this principle, that the Supreme Power resides in the body of the people."[18]

Now came a bit of clever reasoning. "As a Judge of this Court, I know, and can decide upon the knowledge, that the citizens of **Georgia**, when they acted upon the large scale of the Union, as a part of the 'People of the United States,' did not surrender the Supreme or Sovereign Power

---

16 2 U. S. 456 (Wilson, J.).

17 2 U. S. at 456 (Wilson, J.); Martha A. Field, "The Eleventh Amendment and other Sovereign Immunity Doctrines," part 1, *University of Pennsylvania Law Review* 126 (1978): 515; James Madison, *Federalist*, no. 45: "The powers reserved to the several States will extend to all the objects which, in the ordinary course of affairs, concern the lives, liberties, and properties of the people, and the internal order, improvement, and prosperity of the State. The operations of the federal government will be most extensive and important in times of war and danger; those of the State governments, in times of peace and security." James Madison, Speech on the Bank Bill, February 2, 1791: "It would directly interfere with the rights of the States, *to prohibit* as well as to establish Banks, and the circulation of Bank Notes." *The Papers of James Madison*, ed. Charles F. Hobson and Robert A. Rutland (Charlottesville: University Press of Virginia, 1981), 13:372.

18 2 U. S. at 456 (Wilson, J.).

to that State; but, as to the purposes of the Union, retained it to themselves" (bold in original). The purposes of the union included allowing
suits against the state, one assumes. "As to the purposes of the Union,
therefore, **Georgia** is NOT a sovereign State" (bold in original). That is,
insofar as the present case, the federal courts' jurisdiction of these suits
was one of the enumerated powers explicit in the Constitution.[19]

He could have stopped there. But Wilson was a legal historian, and
in his library, he found many claims of sovereignty in other times and
places. These he laid out in the footnotes. There was feudal Europe ruled
by the princes of France and Germany. Sovereignty rested on the king's
person, "and like many other parts of that system so degrading to man,
still retains its influence over our sentiments and conduct, though the
cause, by which that influence was produced, never extended to the
American States." The feudal sovereignty of the king made its way to
England, "introduced by the conqueror the Norman lord William . . .
and to this era we may, probably, refer the English maxim, that the King
or sovereign is the fountain of Justice." Then he offered a recitation and
refutation of the king's powers from Blackstone to refute the imaginary
Georgia case, for everyone had Blackstone at hand. "This last position
is only a branch of a much more extensive principle, on which a plan of
systematic despotism has been lately formed in England, and prosecuted
with unwearied assiduity and care." Lest anyone still rely on Blackstone,
"Of this plan the author of the *Commentaries* was, if not the introducer,
at least the great supporter." The American principle was entirely different: "Laws derived from the pure source of equality and Justice must be
founded on the CONSENT of those, whose obedience they require. The
sovereign, when traced to his source, must be found in the man." There
were precedents for this latter source of sovereignty—ancient Greece, for
one: "In those days, law, liberty, and refining science, made their benign
progress in strict and graceful union: The rude and degrading league
between the barons and feudal barbarism was not yet formed."[20]

Other precedents demonstrated that suits against sovereigns were allowed. So Columbus's son Diego sued King Ferdinand of Spain for what
Columbus had been promised, and after much travail and in the Coun-

---

19 2 U.S. at 456 (Wilson, J.).
20 2 U.S. at 457 (Wilson, J.).

cil of Indian Affairs, he won his claim. The kings of Sparta similarly bowed to the Ephori, as did the constable of France before his council. Hottoman's *Franco-Gallia* described how the king of Aragon had to accede to the judgment of the justiciar. Even in England, under Saxon laws, according to Sir Edward Coke, and then under the first Normans, the king could be sued. "Bracton, who wrote in the time of Henry III, uses these very remarkable expressions concerning the King 'in Justitia recipienda, minimo de regno suo comparetur' 'in receiving Justice, he should be placed on a level with the meanest person in the Kingdom.'" In this fashioning of a response to the imagined case for Georgia, history was vital; indeed, the entire case—and its refutation—rested on history. It was not especially good history, because it was source-mined and used to make a case, but Wilson took it very seriously.[21]

In example after example drawn from his research, he found that even in England, the sovereign king was not above the laws. "True it is, that now in England the King must be sued in his Courts by petition, but even now, the difference is only in the form, not in the thing." The crown must participate; it must allow the production of evidence against itself, and at least for Frederick the Great, prince of Prussia, "Judges ought to know, that the poorest peasant is a man as well as the King himself: all men ought to obtain Justice; since in the estimation of Justice, all men are equal; whether the Prince complain of a peasant, or a peasant complain of the Prince."[22]

Returning from Prussia, Wilson visited France with "an anecdote, which is recorded concerning Louis XIV, who has been styled the grand Monarch of France." What was the result of his tyranny? It was the oppression of his people, for he had "been accustomed to consider his Kingdom as his patrimony, and his power over his subjects as his rightful and undelegated inheritance." He was the state, he reportedly said. Then Wilson traveled back to Britain, and "the British Government, as described by Sir William Blackstone and his followers. As described by him and them, the British is a despotic Government. It is a Government without a people. In that Government, as so described, the sovereignty is possessed by the Parliament: In the Parliament, therefore, the supreme

---

21 2 U.S. at 458 (Wilson, J.).
22 2 U.S. at 461 (Wilson, J.).

and absolute authority is vested." For Parliament was little more than a collective tyrant, an "incontrollable and despotic power." The people were nowhere.[23]

Carried away by his recitation of foreign precedents, Wilson left the argument (and the case) behind entirely to discourse on states' rights. "In the United States, and in the several States, which compose the Union, we go not so far: but still we go one step farther than we ought to go in this unnatural and inverted order of things. The states, rather than the People, for whose sakes the States exist, are frequently the objects which attract and arrest our principal attention." Were this a political essay, Wilson's points would hit the mark. Here, he was carrying his participation in the framing and ratification into the court. "This, I believe, has produced much of the confusion and perplexity, which have appeared in several proceedings and several publications on state-politics, and on the politics, too, of the United States."[24]

In retrospect, one has to conclude that apart from antiquarian interest, the footnotes had not aided his case. Wilson was aware of the centripetal effect of the notes, and he tugged at it to bring the opinion back to the topic. "With the strictest propriety, therefore, classical and political, our national scene opens with the most magnificent object, which the nation could present. 'The PEOPLE of the United States' are the first personages introduced." We the people were not well served by thirteen states held together by an inadequate confederation. It had no executive and no courts. A federal Constitution alone could form a more perfect union. The preamble laid out the purposes of the new government, but Wilson did not think the preamble was without executory force. It con-

---

23 2 U.S. at 461 (Wilson, J.). Among the other notes in the margins, some of which Dallas did not include, are the following: Hist. of Germanic Body, p. 157. 8, Bynk. c. 3.c.4; [John, Lord] Som[ers], [Exchequer] Sup. c. 3; fed Const. Art. 1. &. 2.; Art. 3. s. 3; Art. 3. s. 3; [Emmerich de] Vatt[el]. [*Law of Nations*] B. 1. c. s. 4., 113; Charles Jean Henault, [*Chronological Abridgement of the History of France*] Ant. p.; Blackstone's *Commentaries*, 241, 242; R. A. 231.Sid. 131; Francis Hotman, *Francogallia*, 71; David Houard, *Traits sur les Costumes Anglo-Normandie*, Book 31; 4; C. A. N. 487; John Comyns, *Digest of the Laws of England* [the same Com. As for Blackstone] 104.; [Henry de] Brac[ton] [*On the Laws and Customs of England*] 107; Blackstone's *Commentaries*, 46–52, 147, 160–161; ibid., 153, ibid. 158; 104; Charles York [G. F.] *Some Considerations on the Law of Forfeiture* [G. F.] 124; Comyns, *Digest of the Laws of England*; Charles Hargreaves, *Collections Juridicia*, 68.; Jacques Pierre de Warville, *Theory des Loix Criminelles*, 343, 46–52. 147. 160–162, 155.; 153; Iliad, I., 2. v. 54. one of the words, of which democracy in compounded.; Fed Const Art I, sec. 10; Bracton, 107, "It would be superfluous to make laws, unless those laws, when made, were to be enforced."
24 2 U.S. at 462 (Wilson, J.).

strained the state of Georgia at the same time that it protected the people of that state. Georgia must obey the federal government. "The Constitution ordained and established by those people; and, still closely to apply the case, in particular by the people of **Georgia**, could vest jurisdiction or judicial power over those States and over the State of **Georgia** in particular" (bold in the original).[25]

One could, Wilson opined, simply state that Georgia was obligated to obey the court, or one could reason one's way to it. He chose the longer route. The Articles of Confederation did not bind the people of the states, only the states. "This defect was remedied by the national Constitution, which, as all allow, has an operation on individual citizens." It was defective reasoning to assume from the latter that the Constitution did not operate on the states. "It cannot, surely, be contended that the Legislative power of the national Government was meant to have no operation on the several States." That was the power of Congress. Did the executive branch share it? Did the courts? "Ever since the time of Bracton, his maxim, I believe, has been deemed a good one 'Supervacuum esset leges condere, nisi esset qui leges tueretur.' It would be superfluous to make laws, unless those laws, when made, were to be enforced." The conclusion was inescapable: "The Constitution ordained and established by those people; and, still closely to apply the case, in particular by the people of **Georgia**, could vest jurisdiction or judicial power over those States and over the State of **Georgia** in particular" (bold in the original).[26]

A last look at the preamble confirmed Wilson's argument. "A third declared object is 'to ensure domestic tranquility.' This tranquility is most likely to be disturbed by controversies between States. These consequences will be most peaceably and effectually decided by the establishment and by the exercise of a superintending judicial authority. By such exercise and establishment, the law of nations; the rule between contending States; will be enforced among the several States, in the same manner as municipal law."[27]

Missing, however, and conspicuously so, were any references to the Constitutional Convention and the Pennsylvania Ratification

---

25 2 U.S. at 463 (Wilson, J.).
26 2 U.S. at 464 (Wilson, J.).
27 2 U.S. at 465 (Wilson, J.).

Convention—that is, to speeches that Wilson himself had made. True, the delegates at Philadelphia had agreed on the first day to keep their deliberations confidential, and Madison's notes on the convention debates would not be published for three more decades, but Wilson surely had notes on his own contributions, and his speeches at the Ratification Convention, like his *Lectures on Law*, were already in print. Why not make the case positively rather than negatively, by citing abuses of the rights of the people? Why go all over the landscape of European and England prerevolutionary legal history when evidence for his views was so much closer to home?

Which brings us to a question: What was Wilson doing with the notes? Why add notes at all? Although in his draft, they may have been just for his eyes, but the notes appeared in Dallas's *Reports*, presumably with Wilson's consent. There they were meant to be read. Was Wilson reminding his reader that he, unlike the other justices, was a legal scholar? This is not the same as showing off, but the citations are learned rather than purely formulaic. Bracton and Cicero were familiar to the generation that wrote and read the revolutionary pamphlets. Blackstone's *Commentaries* went everywhere in the Anglophone legal world. Was this a prelude to Wilson's plan to footnote all his opinions? If so, he did not carry through the plan. Instead, he hurried the opinions in the remaining cases in which the justices offered opinions. In his personal life, his unwise investments in land had made his circuit riding for the federal system a harried attempt to satisfy creditors while hearing cases. Nevertheless, the footnotes were the beginning of tradition in Supreme Court opinion writing.[28]

* * *

Or perhaps we owe the first federal footnotes to Dallas himself. Very likely, he was in court to hear Wilson read the opinion. He knew Wilson. Wilson entrusted the draft notes to Dallas. From Wilson, Dallas obtained a clean copy of the opinion. It was Dallas who turned Wilson's

---

28 John Fabian Witt, *Patriots and Cosmopolitans: Hidden Histories of American Law* (Cambridge, MA: Harvard University Press, 2007), 15–82, suggests that Wilson was a poor prognosticator of political realities, which made his erudition brittle and in the end unsuccessful. Witt suggested to the author that Wilson's footnotes may even have spurred a negative reaction to reliance on foreign and international law at the time. Witt to author, June 11, 2023.

marginalia into footnotes, because it was almost impossible to set type with marginalia.

But let us join Wilson as he prepares the notes. The books are from his library. He has amassed a small collection of books. He regards himself as an intellectual as much as a lawyer, an example of the transatlantic intelligentsia. His background is Scottish, not English, so he grew up under a foreign king—George II of England and Hanover rather than the deposed Scottish Stuarts. He has been thinking about sovereignty for many years, thus about kings who ruled over peoples not their own and about kings, this time George III, who ruled as tyrants over their colonial possessions. He has taken a small part in overthrowing a sovereign to whom he had sworn allegiance and then an even more central part in creating a new sovereignty—the United States of America. He watched its first uncertain years under a confederation of states, each cleaving to its own interests. To repair that fault, he helped frame a new sovereignty, the federal union. But its powers are as uncertain as its future. The sources he cited in his footnotes reflect these experiences. They draw from two bodies of political and legal authority, that of ancient and modern kings and that of a sovereign people. Back and forth he went between them, the notes tracking the comparison. He had little use for Georgia's claim to sovereignty, because during the confederation era, such claims had almost wrecked the revolutionaries' achievement of independence. See, then, in the footnotes his own long journey from a subject of Britain to an citizen of a republican union.

* * *

Setting aside just who was responsible for the footnotes and the limitations on sovereign immunity today along with the unfortunate fate of *Chisholm*, it is conceivable that had Wilson's career on the court matched his influence in the crafting and ratification of the Constitution, the Supreme Court opinions would have followed his precedent of incorporating the constitutional ideas of other countries. After all, he taught the law of nations in his *Lectures on Law*. But this much is clear from his footnotes; at least one of the original justices saw the Constitution as part of international law and believed that the examples of other countries had a direct bearing on our fundamental law. From its inception, American constitutionalism was part of a much wider experiment in self-government under law. That concept has been a red thread running through American constitutionalism, for ours was a sovereignty among sovereigns. Learned, comparative, and deeply researched essays on the nature of law in the footnotes of constitutional opinions remind us that Wilson was right: the Constitution is part of a Western tradition in lawmaking.[29]

Chisholm is not widely taught today; it is not part of the constitutional canon, certainly. That is because state sovereignty was reaffirmed in the Eleventh Amendment: "The Judicial power of the United States shall not be construed to extend to any suit in law or equity, commenced or prosecuted against one of the United States by Citizens of another State, or by Citizens or Subjects of any Foreign State." What seemed to be a victory for a robust and final state immunity from suit has been narrowed and hollowed out by state laws on certain subjects, waivers of immunity in certain cases, and the "abrogation doctrine" whereby the federal government, acting under explicit powers in the Constitution, may allow a breach of state immunity. Agencies of the state, municipalities, and counties, as well as individuals in state offices, may also be sued. In this sense, the logic, if not the specific circumstances, of *Chisholm* still lives. What is more, the alteration of the Constitution by explicit amendments, the result of *Chisholm*, may be a lesson from it that needs to be recalled.[30]

By 1801, when William Cranch took over the reporter's job, footnotes became a regular feature of the Supreme Court reports. He included snatches of lower court decision, oral argument before the high court, and evidentiary material. Most, however, remained, as they were in the first state reports, citations of earlier cases and procedural matters. But looks could be deceiving, as the six footnotes to *Dred Scott v. Sandford* (1857) reveal. For in those six footnotes, as in the second of Chief Justice Roger Taney's dicta, the question of federalism returned: Could Congress keep slavery out of the western territories?[31]

---

29 Stephen G. Breyer, *The Court and the World: American Law and the New Global Realities* (New York: Alfred A. Knopf, 2015), 283; David Golove, "The American Founding and Global Justice," *Virginia Journal of International Law* 57 (2018): 624; Golove and Daniel J. Hulsebosch, "The Law of Nations and the Constitution: An Early Modern Perspective," *Georgetown Law Journal* 106 (2018): 1593–1658; Hulsebosch, *Constituting Empire*, 255.

30 Barnett, "*Chisholm*," 1737; Orth, *The Judicial Power of the United States*, 136–52.

31 For a representative sample of Cranch's additions, see appendix A.

[2]

Slavery

Dred Scott v. Sandford, 60 U.S. 393 (1857)

The vexing problems of sovereignty raised in *Chisholm* continued to echo in the antebellum era (1800–60) of American legal history. While the Eleventh Amendment put to rest the precise issue in *Chisholm*, a far more ominous specter had risen on the horizon. The three sets of footnotes in *Dred Scott v. Sandford* (1857) demonstrate that for the justices of the antebellum Supreme Court, the greatest question of the day was the expansion of slavery. In the years from 1815 to 1860, national politics became sectional politics as the country fractured over the question of the expansion of slavery to the West. With pro- and anti-abolitionist mobs roaming city streets and vigilance committees helping runaway and stowaway slaves find stops on the underground railroad, courts faced that question repeatedly. A majority of the US Supreme Court tried to answer these questions definitively in *Dred Scott v. Sandford* (1857)—with calamitous results. Against the better judgment of some of his colleagues, Chief Justice Roger Taney of Maryland offered a solution that triggered an explosion of popular opinion in free and slave states alike. Taney wrote with a long career as a jurist and Jacksonian politician behind him. As a young man, he expressed his personal antagonism to slavery, and he freed slaves he had inherited. But he believed that the future of slavery was a matter for the state governments to decide. Whether his opinion on the merits was sound, two obiter dicta (parts of the opinion not necessary to render the decision) had detonated the blast. Condemned in the North and celebrated in the South, the decision helped bring on what New York senator William Henry Seward called an "irrepressible conflict."[1]

---

1 Timothy S. Huebner, "Roger Taney and the Slavery Issue," *Journal of American History* 97 (2010): 39–62; *A Memoir of Benjamin Robbins Curtis*, ed. Benjamin R, Curtis (Boston: Little Brown, 1879), 1:207–8; James H. Kettner, *The Development of American Citizenship, 1608–1879* (Chapel Hill:

* * *

Although the high court had earlier tiptoed around the slavery question with narrow opinions in cases like *Prigg v. Pennsylvania* ([1842]: the state could not interfere with federal slave law), *Strader v. Graham* ([1854]: slave status followed the slave to free states), and *Jones v. Van Zandt* ([1847]: runaway slaves remained the possession of the master even in free states), the prior caution was abandoned in *Dred Scott v. Sandford*. Dred Scott was the slave of US Army doctor John Emerson and traveled with him to Army posts in the free state of Illinois and free territory of Minnesota, where he and the doctor were domiciled. At Fort Snelling in the Minnesota Territory, Scott married a slave named Harriett and had children, a marriage to which Emerson consented and that was recorded. In 1843, Emerson returned to a family home in Missouri, a slave state, and Scott went with him. Emerson died, and in 1846, Scott sued for freedom for himself and his family. After two trials and four years had passed, the Missouri trial court ruled in his favor. In 1852, the Missouri Supreme Court reversed that decision. In the midst of the crisis over slavery in the territories, a majority of that court abandoned its own precedents that if a slave was freed in the North, the individual's return to Missouri did not reimpose bondage. Northern personal liberty laws, the response to the Fugitive Slave Act of 1850, angered Missouri slaveholding interests, and the majority opinion of the state's supreme court in *Dred Scott* reflected that anger. The court found Scott, his wife, and their two daughters to be slaves.[2]

But Scott's cause had also gained new friends—Free Soil Party and abolitionist interests that saw his case raising crucial issues. Because Dr. Emerson's estate had a New York executor, John Sanford, Scott's counsel, Roswell Field, brought a suit for freedom in federal circuit court under federal diversity jurisdiction. This litigation could only go forward if Scott were a deemed a citizen of Missouri in the federal circuit court. Sitting in St. Louis, district judge Robert Wells, a native Virginian who

University of North Carolina Press, 1978), 324–32; Mark A. Graber, *Dred Scott and the Problem of Constitutional Evil* (Cambridge, UK: Cambridge University Press, 2006), 19–21; Peter Charles Hoffer, *Seward's Law: Country Lawyering, Relational Rights, and Slavery* (Ithaca, NY: Cornell University Press, 2023), 77–92.

2 Don E. Fehrenbacher, *The Dred Scott Case: Its Significance in American Law and Politics* (New York: Oxford University Press, 1978), 259–60; Prigg v. Pennsylvania, 41 U.S. 539 (1842); Strader v. Graham 51 U. S. 82 (1851); Jones v. Van Zandt, 46 U.S. 215 (1847).

moved to Missouri after it gained statehood, allowed counsel to argue the jurisdictional issues. Wells found that "the law is for the plaintiff [Scott]" and permitted the case to go to trial. The jury found Scott a slave in Missouri and that therefore diversity did not exist. A slave did not have standing to bring a suit on the basis of diversity of citizenship.[3]

With the circuit court decision a dead end for Scott, his new counsel, Montgomery Blair, one of the founders of the Republican Party, filed a writ of error from the circuit court to the US Supreme Court. Sanford's defense was conducted by former and future US senator Reverdy Johnson, a proslavery Democrat from Maryland. The political clout of the opposing counsel signaled the growing importance of the case. Dred Scott's counsel had based the case for his freedom in part on the Northwest Ordinance, and the Constitution had explicitly incorporated the Free Soil territorial ordinances of the Confederation. The court could have declined the invitation by citing the political question doctrine (political questions would be left to elected government bodies) established in *Luther v. Borden* (1849), but the case was now so widely discussed and had become so important to the debate over slavery in both North and South that justices on the Supreme Court felt obliged to take it on. Oral argument in 1856 took four days, and the court's final ruling was delayed another year, after the presidential election of 1856. It was reported that when president-elect James Buchanan approached Taney for a "brief chat" before Buchanan took his oath of office; they may have discussed the case, and Buchanan may have urged Taney to settle the matter once and for all.[4]

There was no doubt that newly elected Democratic president Buchanan wanted Bleeding Kansas (the little civil war between pro-slave and Free Soil emigrants to the territory) and the popular sovereignty (the doctrine that the settlers of a territory could determine whether the state they formed would be slave or free) questions resolved. His predecessor, Frank-

---

3 Dred Scott v. Sandford, U.S. Circuit Court for the Eastern District of Missouri (1854), November 2, November 16, 1853; April 25, 1854. Equity and Law Final Record Books, 1831–1915, 506–14, NARA, Kansas City, Missouri. The abstract of the proceedings was copied into the final record because the case papers were sent to the Supreme Court after the appeal.
4 Luther v. Borden, 48 U.S. 1 (1849). Buchanan wrote to Catron on February 3, 1857, and Catron replied on the tenth. The subject of the correspondence was the *Dred Scott* case. Fehrenbacher, *Dred Scott*, 307. Paul Finkelman, *Dred Scott v. Sandford: A Brief History with Documents* (New York: Bedford, 1997), 46, mentions the conversation.

lin Pierce, had tried—and failed—to settle the controversy by executive decree. Congress had not only stumbled over the issue, it had brought the legislative branch to its knees. Buchanan, himself a lawyer, hoped that the federal courts could do what the other two branches had not—settle the question once and for all. *Dred Scott* was thus a test of separation of powers as well as the relationship of federal and state courts, and the role of courts in the most vexing political issue of the age.[5]

There were three sources of law the court might draw on to accommodate Buchanan's desire. The first was the Comity Clause of the Constitution. If Northern states could be made to give "full faith and credit" to the "public acts, records, and judicial proceedings" of Southern courts as specified in Article IV Section 1 of the federal Constitution and follow the provisions of Section 2 of that article requiring the return of persons "held to service or labor" in Southern states, perhaps the South would be satisfied. If, in turn, the Southern states (as they had before the 1850s) allowed slaves freed in the North to return to the South as free persons, the dispute might be mitigated. Unfortunately, the Comity Clause of the Constitution did not look to the justices like a promising place to find a solution against the background of Northern states' personal freedom laws—not while "fire-eaters" in the South were opening mail from the North to be certain that it did not contain abolitionist literature.

The next source of law within the traditional jurisprudential role of courts was the interpretation of congressional legislation. Under Section 3 of Article IV, Congress had "the power to dispose of and make all needful rules and regulations respecting the territory or other property belonging to the United States." This power was expressed in the Missouri Compromise of 1820 and the Kansas-Nebraska Act of 1854. The former barred slavery in lands acquired in the Louisiana Purchase north of the 36° 30' latitude line. This would have included Kansas. The Kansas-Nebraska Act repealed the Missouri Compromise and gave to the settlers of the territory the privilege of deciding whether it would join the Union as a free or slave state. The court might simply have interpreted these statutes, in effect deferring to Congress, but by 1857, it had

---

5 Buchanan referred to the case in his inaugural address, hinting that the court was the proper branch of the federal government to settle the question once and for all. Jean Baker, *James Buchanan: The American Presidents Series: The 15th President, 1857–1861* (New York: Macmillan, 2004), 83.

become clear that Congress could not compromise the passions slavery and anti-slavery engendered.

Finally, the court might find legal grounds to settle the slavery controversy in its own precedents. But in the past the court had prudently steered away from the sort of sweeping ruling that Buchanan wanted. Still, by basing a ruling solely upon these precedents, including the dictum in *Strader*, the court could have resolved *Dred Scott* without churning slavery law.

While the court might still have saved its store of public confidence, or at least not exposed itself to the virulent politics of the day, by issuing a narrow ruling, perhaps along the lines that the circuit court trial envisioned, division over slavery on the court had come to mirror divisions in the nation. Facing the prospect of a wide-ranging antislavery opinion by Ohio Free Soil and presidential aspirant Justice John McLean, Chief Justice Taney of Maryland, scion of a wealthy slave-owning family in Baltimore and himself a former Democratic politician, expanded his own opinion. As Justice Charles Evans Hughes later wrote, Taney's opinion in the case was a "self-inflicted wound." Its contents were not binding precedent, for only Virginia's Justice Peter V. Daniel fully adhered to it, but by not deferring to the elective branches and seeking to settle the slavery issue once and for all, Taney put the court into the center of the most divisive issue in national politics.[6]

Joined by six of the other justices, Taney ruled that the Missouri Supreme Court and the lower federal court were correct—under Missouri law, Scott had no case and Missouri law disposed of the suit. Nor should the case have come to the federal courts, for Scott was not a citizen. The law behind this decision was clear, and it was enough to resolve the case. But Taney was not done. He added two dicta, readings of history and law that were not necessary to resolve the case (and were not subscribed to by the other justices save Daniel), but would, if followed, have imposed on all African Americans a species of civil servitude. Taney wrote that no person of African descent brought to America to labor could ever be a citizen of the United States. They might be citizens of particular states,

---

6 Charles Evans Hughes, *The Supreme Court of the United States* (New York: Columbia University Press, 1928), 50; Francis P. Weisenburger, *The Life of John McLean: A Politician on the United States Supreme Court* (Columbus: Ohio State University Press, 1937), 207; Carl B. Swisher, *Roger B. Taney* (New York: Macmillan, 1935), 485–511.

but this did not confer national citizenship on them, for "they were not intended to be included, under the word 'citizens' in the Constitution, and can therefore claim none of the rights and privileges which that instrument provides for and secures to citizens on the United States." Adding gratuitous insult to injury, Taney continued, Blacks "had for more than a century before [the drafting of the federal Constitution] been regarded as beings of an lower order, and altogether unfit to associate with the white race, either in social or political relations; and so far lower that they had no rights which the white man was bound to respect."[7]

Taney had not finished. In a second dictum, he opined that the Fifth Amendment to the Constitution, guaranteeing that no man's property (and slaves were personal property under the law) might be taken without due process of law, barred Congress from denying slavery expansion into the territories. Although Article IV, Section 3 of the Constitution had explicitly given to Congress full and untrammeled authority to set laws and regulations for the territories, it could not rule out slavery, because the Fifth Amendment was added to the Constitution after ratification, and it must be read to modify Congress's powers over the territories. In effect, Taney retroactively declared the Missouri Compromise of 1820 unconstitutional. This was retroactive judicial review with a vengeance, for although the Missouri Compromise was undone by the Kansas-Nebraska Act of 1854 and its doctrine of popular sovereignty, Free Soil advocates might fear that Taney and the court were opening the rest of the West to slavery. That the court with a stroke could undo what Congress had labored so long and so hard to accomplish was a chilling challenge to the separation of powers doctrine.[8]

Keep in mind that the case in the Supreme Court was not an appeal from the Missouri rulings. It was an appeal from the federal circuit court sitting in Missouri. The issue in the appeal was not slavery per se, although a decision returning the case to the lower court with instructions to allow Dred Scott to sue in diversity was a proxy that he was free. The issue was whether he could sue in diversity. The provision for diversity in the Judiciary Act is that "the circuit courts shall have original cognizance . . . or the suit is between a citizen of the State where the suit is

---

7 60 U.S. at 407 (Taney, C. J.).
8 Fehrenbacher, *The Dred Scott Case*, 388; Hughes, *The Supreme Court of the United States*, 50.

brought, and a citizen of another State." Dred Scott did not have citizenship in Missouri, but had he gained US citizenship? More important, but
lurking next to the citizenship question, was the power of Congress to
legislate for the territories, a power that raised federalism questions, for
slave states had an interest in expanding their "peculiar institution" to
the West. If Congress could bar slavery in the territories, might it assay
an assault on slavery where it already existed?

The concepts of state and national citizenship were already mentioned
in the original US Constitution adopted in 1789, but the details were un-
clear. The passages were not directed to the general issue of citizenship.
For example, "No Person shall be a Representative who shall not have
attained to the Age of twenty five Years, and been seven Years a Citizen
of the United States, and who shall not, when elected, be an Inhabitant
of that State in which he shall be chosen" (Article I, Section 2, Clause 2);
"No Person shall be a Senator who shall not have attained to the Age of
thirty Years, and been nine Years a Citizen of the United States, and who
shall not, when elected, be an Inhabitant of that State for which he shall be
chosen" (Article I, Section 3, Clause 3); "No Person except a natural born
Citizen, or a Citizen of the United States, at the time of the Adoption of
this Constitution, shall be eligible to the Office of President; neither shall
any person be eligible to that Office who shall not have attained to the Age
of thirty five Years, and been fourteen Years a Resident within the United
States" (Article II, Section 1, Clause 5); "The Citizens of each State shall be
entitled to all Privileges and Immunities of Citizens in the several States"
(Article IV, Section 2, Clause 1). Article IV, Section 3, Clause 2 did create
an opening for Congress to expand the concept of citizenship, but the
opening was oblique rather than frontal: "The Congress shall have Power
to dispose of and make all needful Rules and Regulations respecting the
Territory or other Property belonging to the United States; and nothing
in this Constitution shall be so construed as to Prejudice any Claims of
the United States, or of any particular State." Combined with Article VI,
Section 1, "All Debts contracted and Engagements entered into, before the
Adoption of this Constitution, shall be as valid against the United States
under this Constitution, as under the Confederation," the powers of Congress were by implication extended to the barring of slavery, as this had
been done in the Northwest Territory during the confederation period.
Under the former provision, Congress had settled the disputed 1819 state-

hood application of Missouri by allowing slavery in the state but barring it in the Louisiana Territory north of the 36° 30′ latitude line.[9]

Were Black persons citizens of the United States? There was much in prior law to dispute Taney's first dictum. Both New York's chancellor James Kent, in 1827, and William Rawle, a Pennsylvania Quaker and US attorney, in 1829, defined national citizenship in broad terms: "Every person born within the United States, its territories or districts, whether the parents are citizens or aliens, is a natural born citizen in the sense of the Constitution, and entitled to all the rights and privileges appertaining to that capacity" (Rawle); "Natives, are all persons born within the jurisdiction of the United States" (Kent). But both works described slavery as property, and property does not have citizenship. Justice Joseph Story had both these works in his library, and it showed in his opinion in *Inglis v. Trustees of Sailors' Snug Harbor* (1830).[10]

In *Inglis*, a trust for the creation of a home for "aged, decrepit, and worn out sailors" was challenged. In the course of his opinion upholding the trust, Justice Joseph Story explained, "Two things usually concur to create citizenship; first, birth locally within the dominions of the sovereign; and secondly, birth within the protection and obedience, or in other words, within the ligeance of the sovereign. That is, the party must be born within a place where the sovereign is at the time in full possession and exercise of his power, and the party must also at his birth derive protection from, and consequently owe obedience or allegiance to the sovereign, as such, de facto." By this, whether Black or white, a person born in the United States was a citizen of the United States. But Story was dissenting, and his opinion had no weight as law unless it was adopted at some point by the majority of the court.[11]

In the meantime, state and federal governments faced cases of disputed Black citizenship. These came in the form of due process claims by counsel for alleged runaway slaves. Chief Justice Lemuel Shaw of Massachusetts and Governor William Henry Seward of New York had answers. Residents of their states were presumed to be citizens and thus could avail

---

9 Earl Maltz, *Dred Scott and the Politics of Slavery* (Lawrence: University Press of Kansas, 2007), 2–3, 5, 72–72.

10 James Kent, *Commentaries on American Law*, 33, 43; William Rawle, *A View of the Constitution of the United States of America*, 2nd ed. (Philadelphia: Carey and Lea, 1829), 80.

11 Inglis v. Trustees of Sailor's Snug Harbor, 28 U.S. 99, 155 (1830). *Ligeance*, now archaic, is the mutual bond of sovereign and citizen, an exchange of obedience for protection.

themselves of procedural guarantees against slave catchers. In *Commonwealth v. Aves* (1836), Shaw faced the question of slavery directly. The slave in question, a six-year-old girl named Med, was brought to Boston from New Orleans by her owner's wife, Mary Slater, and there given to the care of one Thomas Aves, with the purpose of keeping her until Mrs. Slater could return with Med to New Orleans. They had been in Boston for four months when a suit against Aves was brought by the Massachusetts Anti-Slavery Society. Benjamin Robins Curtis, who as a US Supreme Court justice would later dissent in *Dred Scott*, here represented Samuel Slater. Curtis argued that the Massachusetts court had to follow the law of Louisiana with respect to a slave owner merely visiting the commonwealth and that such a decision worked no harm on Massachusetts or its law. What was more, slavery was not immoral in itself. Ellis Loring, representing the state, disagreed. He argued that comity, the full faith and credit clause of the federal Constitution, did not impose an absolute rule on Massachusetts in doubtful cases. Slavery contravened the laws, the sentiments, and the precedents of Massachusetts, and, as a matter of choice of law, Massachusetts, the state in which the case was to be heard, had the authority to prefer its own laws to that of a foreign jurisdiction. On top of which, slavery was repugnant to the people and the laws of Massachusetts.

Lemuel Shaw agreed with Loring.

> The precise question presented by the claim of the respondent is, whether a citizen of any one of the United States, where negro slavery is established by law, coming into this State, for any temporary purpose of business or pleasure, staying sometime, but not acquiring a domicile [i.e., permanent residence], here, who brings a slave with him as a personal attendant, may restrain such slave of his liberty during his continuance here, and convey him out of this State on his return, against his consent.

Med was a little girl, and that is why the state of Massachusetts represented her. "It is not contended that a master can exercise here any other of the rights of a slave owner, than such as may be necessary to retain the custody of the slave during his residence, and to remove him on his return." In other words, no one could be made a slave in the state.[12]

---

12 Commonwealth v. Aves, 35 Mass. 193, 207 (1836) (Shaw, C. J.).

Shaw knew that the case was a novel one and one of great moment. Federal law did not apply, as Med was not a runaway subject to return under the Rendition Clause of the Constitution and the 1793 Fugitive Slave Act. This was a state case decided under state law. "Until this discussion, I had supposed that there had been adjudged cases on this subject in this Commonwealth; and it is believed to have been a prevalent opinion among lawyers, that if a slave is brought voluntarily and unnecessarily within the limits of this State, he becomes free." The reason for this was "not so much because his coming within our territorial limits, breathing our air, or treading on our soil, works any alteration in his *status*, or condition, as settled by the law of his domicile, as because by the operation of our laws, there is no authority on the part of the master, either to restrain the slave of his liberty, whilst here, or forcibly to take him into custody in order to his removal." He looked back to the course of slavery in Massachusetts and then to the provisions for slavery in the federal Constitution. But that is not where he stopped or where he found grounds to free Med. This was because slavery had "crept in" to the colony, despite its laws (as he read them), and slavery was customary throughout the colonies. But Massachusetts, he emphasized, had ended slavery during the war "upon the ground that it is contrary to natural right and the plaint principles of justice. "The whole tenor of our policy, of our legislation and jurisprudence, from that time to the present, has been consistent with this construction, and with no other."[13]

In 1839, three free Black merchant seamen on the crew of the New York ship *Robert Carter* concealed Isaac, a Virginia slave carpenter brought aboard the ship to make repairs, and smuggled him to the port of New York. Slave catchers retrieved the runaway, and Lieutenant Governor Henry Hopkins of Virginia requested the extradition of the three free sailors for trial in his state, "an offense peculiarly and deeply affecting the general interest of the good people of this Commonwealth, recognized as felony and severely punished by our laws." Governor William Henry Seward, after studying the request for some time, declined. "There is no law of this state which recognizes slavery." Because the act of the three sailors was committed in New York harbor, it would not

---

13 35 Mass at 208, 210 (Shaw, C. J.).

have "contravened any statute." Seward then added his own view that "in my opinion the offense is not within the meaning of the constitution of the United States."[14]

But federal courts enforced the 1793 Fugitive Slave Act, which assumed that a Black person was not a citizen but a slave when that person was claimed to be a runaway from slavery. In *Prigg v. Pennsylvania* (1842), Justice Joseph Story's detestation of slavery was genuine, but domestic slavery remained the law in half the nation. As he had written in his *Commentaries on the Conflict of Laws*, among all nations, "the state of slavery will not be recognized in any country whose institutions and policy prohibit slavery." Slavery was "strictly territorial." But the United States presented a different case, for although the individual states were sovereign and slavery was a matter of domestic law in those states, the federal government had, at the behest of the slave states, taken a hand in questions of runaway slaves. It might seem to Story that the Rendition Clause and the Fugitive Slave Act of 1793 made no sense on their face. After all, was the labor of the unborn "owed" to anyone? Still, no free state could deny to citizens of the slave states their right to property, and the Rendition Clause of the Constitution, as explained in the 1793 Fugitive Slave Act, barred states from interfering. At the same time, states like Pennsylvania believed that they had the duty and the right to protect due process for their free Black citizens. The question then became how Pennsylvania might do this in the face of federal law. The answer was the state's anti-kidnaping act, which provided that slave catchers must bring suspected runaways before a state magistrate, where the captured party could provide evidence that he or she was in fact not a runaway.[15]

The first part of the Rendition Clause concerned the rendition of felons, a common provision of both domestic and international law. The second was much newer; it read, "No person held to service or

---

14 William H. Seward, *An Autobiography*, ed. Frederick Seward, (New York: Derby and Miller, 1891), 1:420; William Henry Seward to Lieutenant Governor Hopkins, September 30, 1839, in George E. Baker, ed., *Works of William H. Seward*, (New York: Redfield, 1884) 2:452.

15 Prigg v. Pennsylvania, 41 U.S. 539 (1842); Joseph Story, *Commentaries on the Conflict of Laws* (Boston: Hilliard and Gray, 1834), 138; United States v. the Da Jeune Eugenie (Cir Ct. MA 1822) (Story, J.), quoted in Joseph Story, *Life and Letters of Joseph Story*, ed. William W. Story (Boston: Little and Brown, 1851), 1:350. The story of the state act and the case is told in H. Robert Baker, *Prigg v. Pennsylvania, Slavery, the Supreme Court, and the Ambivalent Constitution* (Lawrence: University Press of Kansas, 2012).

labor in one State, under the laws thereof, escaping into another, shall, in consequence of any law or regulation therein, be discharged from such service or labor, but shall be delivered up on claim of the party to whom such service or labor may be due." Its origins lay in the history of the Constitutional Convention. Story: "Historically, it is well known that the object of this clause was to secure to the citizens of the slave-holding States the complete right and title of ownership in their slaves, as property, in every State in the Union into which they might escape from the State where they were held in servitude." Whether the clause was necessary to keep the slave South in the Union was a question that Story elided. He simply asserted that "the full recognition of this right and title was indispensable to the security of this species of property in all the slave-holding States, and indeed was so vital to the preservation of their domestic interests and institutions that it cannot be doubted that it constituted a fundamental article without the adoption of which the Union could not have been formed." Note how he seemed to shove abolitionism, gaining strength at that time in domestic politics and already the rule in the rest of the Anglophone world, to one side. "Its true design was to guard against the doctrines and principles prevalent in the non-slaveholding States, by preventing them from intermeddling with, or obstructing, or abolishing the rights of the owners of slaves."[16]

Justice Samuel Nelson, in his concurring opinion in *Dred Scott*, cited correspondence between "Lord Stowell and Judge Story, in 1 vol. Life of Story, p. 552, 558, to this effect: Story wrote 'I have read with great attention your judgment in the slave [Grace] case, &c. Upon the fullest consideration which I have been able to give the subject, I entirely concur in your views. If I had been called upon to pronounce a judgment in a like case, I should have certainly arrived at the same result.'" Story replied, "In my native State (Massachusetts), the state of slavery is not recognized as legal, and yet, if a slave should come hither and afterwards return to his own home, we should certainly think that the local law attached upon him, and that his servile character would be redintegrated [restored]."[17]

---

16 41 U.S. at 611 (Story, J.).
17 60 U.S. at 467 (Nelson, J.).

Slaves, apparently, were not citizens when state law did not accord them this privilege. But were free Black persons citizens of states? Could they then be citizens of the United States? So the narrowest point of law in *Dred Scott* was that he could not bring a suit in the circuit court in Missouri on diversity grounds (citizenship in separate states) against Sandford, a citizen of New York, because Missouri did not consider slaves like Dred Scott to be citizens. End of story. But not for Taney and the justices who subscribed to his opinion. Belabored, repetitious, infelicitously framed, that opinion was mammoth (seventy-six printed pages) and occasioned concurring or dissenting opinions from every one of the other justices.

Taney's first dictum, on citizenship, came late in his opinion:

> A free negro of the African race, whose ancestors were brought to this country and sold as slaves, is not a 'citizen' within the meaning of the Constitution of the United States. When the Constitution was adopted, they were not regarded in any of the States as members of the community which constituted the State, and were not numbered among its 'people or citizens.' Consequently, the special rights and immunities guaranteed to citizens do not apply to them. And not being 'citizens' within the meaning of the Constitution, they are not entitled to sue in that character in a court of the United States, and the Circuit Court has not jurisdiction in such a suit.[18]

While historians focus criticism on this dictum, it did not stray all that far from popular opinion, even in free states. There, Black persons were second-class citizens at best. It was a second dictum that most concerned contemporary free people. The source of the outrage was not the denial of the possibility of Black citizenship, for the footnotes tell a different story. Return to Taney's opinion, lay it alongside Justice Campbell's and Daniel's, and see that the real thrust of the opinions was the guarantee that slaveowners could carry their property into free soil:

> The difficulty which meets us at the threshold of this part of the inquiry is whether Congress was authorized to pass this law [the Missouri Compromise] under any of the powers granted to it by the Constitution [in Article VI, Section 1]; for if the authority is not given by that instrument, it is the

---

18 60 U.S. at 403, 407, 409, 416, 422 (Taney, C.J.).

duty of this court to declare it void and inoperative, and incapable of con-
ferring freedom upon anyone who is held as a slave under the laws of any
one of the States. . . . The power is given in relation only to the territory of
the United States—that is, to a territory then in existence, and then known
or claimed as the territory of the United States. . . . No one, it is believed,
would think a moment of deriving the power of Congress to make needful
rules and regulations in relation to property of this kind from this clause of
the Constitution. Nor can it, upon any fair construction, be applied to any
property but that which the new Government was about the receive from
the confederated States. . . . And if the Constitution recognizes the right of
property of the master in a slave, and makes no distinction between that
description of property and other property owned by a citizen, no tribunal,
acting under the authority of the United States, whether it be legislative,
executive, or judicial, has a right to draw such a distinction or deny to it
the benefit of the provisions and guarantees which have been provided for
the protection of private property against the encroachments of the Government. . . . Upon these considerations, it is the opinion of the court that
the act of Congress which prohibited a citizen from holding and owning
property of this kind in the territory of the United States north of the line
therein mentioned is not warranted by the Constitution, and is therefore
void, and that neither Dred Scott himself nor any of his family were made
free by being carried into this territory, even if they had been carried there
by the owner with the intention of becoming a permanent resident.[19]

Taney had denied the constitutionality of the Missouri Compromise,
even though by 1857 it was a dead letter (superseded by the Kansas-
Nebraska Act of 1854). Because he did not require Congress or the court
to do anything about this (again, because the Compromise line was no
longer applicable), his dictum stood as law. It was a brilliant piece of
constitutional lawyering, similar to Marshall's opinion in *Marbury v.
Madison* (1803). Like *Marbury*, in which the court did not delivery any
remedy, it was based on the limitation of what Congress could do under
the Constitution. It could not take from the slaveholder his property
without due compensation. On its face, it was a legal argument, not a
political one. But Abraham Lincoln, in Illinois, a state carved from the

---

19 60 U.S. at 432, 436, 437, 451 (Taney, C.J.).

Northwest Ordinance, hence free, saw the threat immediately. The logic of Taney's dictum would make slavery national rather than sectional. Lincoln raised that threat repeatedly in his 1858 campaign for the Senate. So did the rest of the Free Soil advocates. The threat of slavery national swelled the ranks of the Republican Party, and in 1860, the one unshakable premise of their presidential platform was no extension of slavery. Although no steps were taken by the court or the proslavery Democrats to bring this doctrine to life, the demand to amend the Constitution to guarantee slavery could go into the territories would explode the 1860 Democratic Presidential Convention in Charleston and lead to the secession of South Carolina eight months later.[20]

The six footnotes show that members of the court recognized that the voiding of the Missouri Compromise was far more portentous to constitutional law than Taney's strictures on citizenship. States could still confer citizenship on people of color. But the potential for making slavery national instead of confining to where it already existed brought differences of opinion on the court to a boil. Relations among the later Taney-court justices were never entirely cordial. Relations between the chief justice and Justice Benjamin Robbins Curtis of Massachusetts, the divide between Democrats and the one Whig, Curtis, exploded. Justice Campbell, well liked by everyone despite his being a slaveowner and states' rights advocate, tried to smooth the roiled waters. But his concurrence in *Dred Scott* argued that slaveholders had the right to take their property with them wherever they went in the United States. That was the last straw for Curtis, and after *Dred Scott*, he resigned.[21]

Clues to what the justices were thinking about the application of the dicta appeared in the portions of their opinions that were footnoted. The important take away is that the justices were not as concerned with the citizenship issue as with the congressional power to legislate for the territories. Modern scholarship has focused on the former, for obvious reasons. Our interest on racism in the law is a major theme of recent legal history, and Taney's racism was obvious. But it was a bias largely

---

20 Eric Foner, *The Fiery Trial: Abraham Lincoln and American Slavery* (New York: Oxford University Press, 2010), 94; Stephen Berry, *A House Dividing, The Lincoln Douglas Debates of 1858* (New York: Oxford University Press, 2016), 9, 29; Fehrenbacher, *Dred Scott*, 363.
21 Timothy S. Huebner, *The Taney Court: Justice, Rulings, and Legacy* (Santa Barbara, CA: ABC-Clio, 2003), 19–20.

shared by his brethren. By contrast, the checks and balances question, of the power of the court to revisit acts of Congress, and the authority of the federal government over territory that would become states, hence the federalism question, was far more important to the justices. There were six footnotes in three of the justices' opinions in *Dred Scott*, two by Justice Daniel, two by Justice Campbell, and two by Curtis. (Taney's opinion, while full of references to earlier history, had no notes.)[22]

Daniel not only signed on to Taney's opinion; he was even more convinced than Taney that slavery should be national rather than sectional. Daniel was appointed to the court by President Martin Van Buren at the end of his administration, one of the Democratic members who dominated the court. He served until his death in 1860. An avatar of the Virginia slaveholding aristocracy, he sought higher office in Virginia, and along with service as lieutenant governor, he occupied a place in the governor's council for twenty years. He led the court in dissents, writing fifty solo dissents, although he wrote majority opinions seventy times. Learned, a family man, he owned a few household slaves. He had little influence on the court, and his opinions are not greatly valued today. He believed that the nation was a confederacy of sovereign states and had little use for the commercial, financial, and technological developments that Taney himself favored. His view of the case was plainly a defense of slavery rather than a question of federal jurisdiction:

> Now the following are truths which a knowledge of the history of the world, and particularly of that of our own country, compels us to know—that the African negro race never have been acknowledged as belonging to the family of nations; that, as amongst them, there never has been known or recognized by the inhabitants of other countries anything partaking of the character of nationality, or civil or political polity; that this race has been by all the nations of Europe regarded as subjects of capture or purchase, as subjects of commerce or traffic; and that the introduction of that race into every section of this country was

---

22 A speculation of my own. If Taney had deployed an armada of footnotes to support his dicta, would they have escaped some of the criticism contemporaries and moderns shower on them? Modern scholarship focuses on the citizenship questions: For example, Martha S. Jones, *Birthright Citizens: A History of Race and Rights in Antebellum America* (New York: Cambridge University Press, 2018), 128–45, on which Taney was surely mistaken. But the second dictum, on the Missouri Compromise, was more arguable and could have been better defended with footnotes.

not as members of civil or political society, but as slaves, as *property* in the strictest sense of the term.[23]

In Justice Daniel's concurring opinion, one finds "Footnote 1 *Vide* Gibbons's *Decline and Fall of the Roman Empire*. London edition of 1825, vol. 3d, chap. 44, p. 183." The first footnote derived from Gibbon's account of the Roman Empire, during which "the first Caesars had scrupulously guarded the distinction of *ingenuous* and *servile* birth, which was decided by the condition of the mother [just as in Virginia] The slaves who were liberated by a generous master immediately entered into the middle class of *libertini*, or freedmen, but they could never be enfranchised from the duties of obedience and gratitude, whatever were the fruits of their industry." The comparison with the United States Daniel found obvious and telling. But the placement of the footnote in the text came in the prelude to his discussion of the denial of the master's rights by barring slavery from the territories. That act created disorder in the slave states and denied the rights of property to the master class. One cannot find a stronger defense of the expansion of slavery, even in the works of US senators John C. Calhoun and Henry Hammond of South Carolina.[24]

The second footnote, footnote 2, "Letter from James Madison to Robert Walsh, November 27th, 1819, on the subject of the Missouri Compromise," quoted from ex-president James Madison, went to the same point as the first footnote. As the crisis over the admission of Missouri loomed, Madison seemed to deny to Congress the power to take from Missouri any of the rights that the original states enjoyed. What mattered to Daniel was the expansion of slavery:

James Madison, in the year 1819, speaking with reference to the prohibitory power claimed by Congress, then threatening the very existence of the Union, remarks of the language of the second clause of the third section of article fourth of the Constitution "that it cannot be well extended beyond a power over the territory *as property*, and the power to make

---

23 60 U.S. at 475 (Daniel, J.); E. Lee Shepard, "Peter Vivian Daniel," Newman, *Biographical Dictionary*, 148–49; Hoffer, Hoffer, and Hull, *Supreme Court*, 2nd ed., 84–85; generally, John P. Frank, *Justice Daniel Dissents: A Biography of Peter V. Daniel, 1784–1860* (Cambridge, MA: Harvard University Press, 1964).
24 60 U. S. at 479 (Daniel, J.).

provisions really needful or necessary for the government of settlers, until ripe for admission into the Union. . . . As to the power of admitting new States into the Federal compact, the questions offering themselves are whether Congress can attach conditions, or the new States concur in conditions, which after admission would *abridge* or *enlarge* the constitutional rights of legislation common to other States; whether Congress can, by a compact with a new State, take power either to or from itself, or place the new member above or below the equal rank and rights possessed by the others; whether all such stipulations expressed or implied would not be nullities, and be so pronounced when brought to a practical test. It falls within the scope of your inquiry to state the fact that there was a proposition in the convention to discriminate between the old and the new States by an article in the Constitution. The proposition, happily, was rejected. The effect of such a discrimination is sufficiently evident.[25]

For Daniel, this gist of this long quotation was that Congress could not place new states fabricated from national territory on different ground from existing states—and that included denying citizens of existing states the right to take their slave property with them when they went west. In effect, Daniel was arguing from the authority of a framer that slavery was indeed national.

Justice Campbell added two notes. In *Dred Scott*, he did not discourse on the issue of citizenship, but he went to great lengths to argue against the Missouri Compromise and the premise that Congress could bar slavery from the territories. He would later try to mediate a compromise on secession, but when the die was cast, he resigned his seat on the court and returned to Alabama and then to New Orleans. There he was tapped to serve as the assistant Confederate secretary of war. Briefly imprisoned after the war, his former colleague Curtis represented him in his attempt to return to legal practice. In his later years, Campbell waged a vigorous campaign against congressional Reconstruction. He died in 1889.[26]

His footnotes showed his opposition to laws enlarging federal control in the newly acquired Louisiana Territory. In the first footnote, quoting members of Congress:

---

25 60 U.S. at 491–492 (Daniel, J.).
26 See, generally, Robert Saunders, *John Archibald Campbell: Southern Moderate, 1811–1889* (Tuscaloosa: University of Alabama Press, 1997).

Mr. [Joseph Bradley] Varnum [of Massachusetts] said: "The bill provided such a Government as had never been known in the United States." Mr. [William] Eustis [of Massachusetts]: "The Government laid down in this bill is certainly a new thing in the United States." Mr. [John] Lucas [of Pennsylvania]: "It has been remarked that this bill establishes elementary principles never previously introduced in the Government of any Territory of the United States. Granting the truth of this observation," &c. Mr. [Nathaniel] Macon [of North Carolina]: "My first objection to the principle contained in this section is that it establishes a species of government unknown to the United States." Mr. [John] Boyle [Kentucky]: "Were the President an angel instead of a man, I would not clothe him with this power." Mr. G. W. [George W.] Campbell {Tennessee]: "On examining the section, it will appear that it really establishes a complete despotism." Mr. [James] Sloan [New Jersey]: "Can anything be more repugnant to the principles of just government? Can anything be more despotic?"—Annals of Congress, 1803–1804.

The footnote implied that such a despotism of the federal government over the new territory would surely have brought disunion, or worse.[27]

Campbell's second footnote quoted ex-president Thomas Jefferson's concern over the consequences of federal intrusion in Missouri: "The Missouri question is the most portentous one that ever threatened our Union. In the gloomiest moments of the revolutionary war, I never had any apprehension equal to that I feel from this source." Jefferson was not arguing for the extension of slavery, however, and the quotation was misleading. Jefferson saw the danger that Story and Lincoln would see if the slavery issue became the focus of national politics. This was Campbell source mining at best and quoting out of context at worst, but the point is that Campbell was not concerned with citizenship, but with the expansion of slavery. One notes, again, that he and Daniel were southerners, slave owners, and defenders of the institution of slavery.[28]

In dissent, Justice Curtis offered two notes. Curtis was the only member of the court appointed by a Whig president (Millard Fillmore) and the only member up to that time to hold a law degree (Harvard Law School, after Harvard College). He was, in this sense, the most formally educated

---

27 60 U.S. at 508 (Campbell, J.).
28 60 U.S. at 518 (Campbell, J.).

of the justices although Joseph Story was as learned. His career in Massachusetts did not reveal him as an abolitionist, and his dissent in *Dred Scott* was not predictable (unlike his colleague McLean, an avowed abolitionist). Custis's dissent was a closely reasoned essay on pleading. The section on citizenship was compact: "Slaves were not, in legal parlance persons, but property. The moment the incapacity, the disqualification of slavery, was removed, they became persons." Dred Scott had become a person when the status of slavery was lifted from him in Illinois and the Michigan Territory. It could not be imposed again. One cannot go from personhood back to property. Taney's history was wrong at worst and biased throughout: "The fact that free persons of color were citizens of some of the several States, and the consequence that this fourth article of the Confederation would have the effect to confer on such persons the privileges and immunities of general citizenship, were not only known to those who framed and adopted those articles, but the evidence is decisive."[29]

The conclusion was similarly terse: "I can find nothing in the Constitution which, *proprio vigore*, deprives of their citizenship any class of persons who were citizens of the United States at the time of its adoption, or who should be native-born citizens of any State after its adoption, nor any power enabling Congress to disfranchise persons born on the soil of any State, and entitled to citizenship of such State by its Constitution and laws." Citizens of the United states were citizens of individual states. "One may confine the right of suffrage to white male citizens; another may extend it to colored persons and females; one may allow all persons above a prescribed age to convey property and transact business; another may exclude married women." Along with the provision of the Constitution that guaranteed the privilege and immunities of one state's citizens to citizens in other states, the question of Dred Scott's citizenship, hence his capacity to bring a federal suit in diversity, was settled. "The language of the Constitution is "The citizens of each State shall be entitled to all privileges and immunities of citizens in the several States." If each State may make such persons its citizens, they became, as such, entitled to the benefits of this article if there be a native-born citizenship of the United States distinct from a native-born citizenship of the several States."[30]

---

29 60 U.S. at 573 (Curtis, J.).
30 60 U.S. at 573, 575, 576, 583, 584 (Curtis, J.).

Curtis's dissent devoted relatively little space to the question of the constitutionality of the Missouri Compromise. The law that mattered was the law of the states and territories in which Dred Scott sojourned. He refused to give significance to Taney's remarks, dismissing them with his silence. That silence was deliberate. He wished the prospect of national slavery to go away. That had been the hope of the conservatives in the Whig Party, his party, from its inception. A moderate Whig who believed in compromise over slavery, he never ran for public office and often crossed the aisle to work with the Democratic Party. As the Whig Party broke apart in the 1850s, many of its members shifting to Free Soil and then to the Republican Party, Curtis remained as unpolitical as a public figure could be. But his grim-visaged silence was as telling as Daniel's and Campbell's avidity.[31]

His footnotes concerned trivial issues, by implication reducing Taney's thunder to mere noise. Footnote 3/1: "This statement that some territory did actually pass by this cession is taken from the opinion of the court, delivered by Mr. Justice Wayne, in the case of *Howard v. Ingersoll*, reported in 13 How. 405. It is an obscure matter, and, on some examination of it, I have been led to doubt whether any territory actually passed by this cession. But as the fact is not important to the argument, I have not thought it necessary further to investigate it." Footnote 3/2: "It was published in a newspaper at Philadelphia, in May, and a copy of it was sent by R. H. Lee to Gen. Washington on the 15th of July. *See* p. 261, Cor. of Am.Rev. [*American Review*], vol. 4, and *Writings of Washington*, vol. 9, p. 174." These were of an entirely different character from Daniel's and Campbell's.[32]

Had the majority followed Curtis's example, even if not to his conclusion, the case would not have created the furor that it did. When the case was first argued, in the previous term, an opinion by Justice Nelson had circulated, and its narrow holding would almost certainly have averted the firestorm that followed the Taney opinion. But the footnotes in Daniel's and Campbell's opinions demonstrate what mattered greatly to them, and likely to Taney. Unwittingly, they created the controversy to protect the South's "peculiar institution," for slavery advocates believed

31 Richard H. Leach, "Benjamin Robbins Curtis: Judicial Misfit," *New England Quarterly* 25 (1952): 508; Michael F. Holt, *The Rise and Fall of the American Whig Party* (New York: Oxford University Press, 19999), 332–33.
32 60 U.S. at 593 (Curtis, J.).

it must grow or die. And those who sowed the wind would reap the whirlwind. In 1857, Curtis left the court to resume his private practice. He had long felt the financial burdens of serving on the court (he had twelve children, three wives, two of whom died, and a country home in the Berkshires as well as domiciles in Boston and the District). Daniel died before secession became a reality, his Virginia aristocracy soon to be shattered by war. Campbell left Washington to serve the Confederacy and ended his life in New Orleans, almost in exile from the Reconstruction. Only Taney remained on the during the Civil War, a relic of the Jacksonian Democracy's flirtation with national slavery. His reputation has never recovered from *Dred Scott*.

But the six apparently innocuous footnotes tell us what *Dred Scott* meant to the justices and thence to the nation. While the gratuitous denial of citizenship to free Black persons angered white and Black antislavery people in the North, the finding that the Missouri Compromise had been unconstitutional meant to both Free Soilers and proslavery men, Republicans and Democrats, that the court might yet find that slavery was a national rather than a sectional institution and that slave property might be taken by their owners wherever they traveled. This, in turn, meant that the irreconcilable conflict between freedom and slavery, in William Henry Seward's words, could not be resolved by the courts. A political conflict had become a constitutional crisis.[33]

---

33 Michael F. Conlin, *The Constitutional Origins of the American Civil War* (New York: Cambridge University Press, 2019), 220. Looking ahead, the citizenship of US-born Black people living in the United States was resolved by the Civil Rights Act of 1866, Section 1:

That all persons born in the United States and not subject to any foreign power, excluding Indians not taxed, are hereby declared to be citizens of the United States; and such citizens, of every race and color, without regard to any previous condition of slavery or involuntary servitude, except as a punishment for crime whereof the party shall have been duly convicted, shall have the same right, in every State and Territory in the United States, to make and enforce contracts, to sue, be parties, and give evidence, to inherit, purchase, lease, sell, hold, and convey real and personal property, and to full and equal benefit of all laws and proceedings for the security of person and property, as is enjoyed by white citizens, and shall be subject to like punishment, pains, and penalties, and to none other, any law, statute, ordinance, regulation, or custom, to the contrary notwithstanding.

And by the Fourteenth Amendment, Section 1, Clause 1: "All persons born or naturalized in the United States, and subject to the jurisdiction thereof, are citizens of the United States and of the State wherein they reside."

COMPARATIVE LAW

Viterbo v. Friedlander, 120 U.S. 707 (1887)

After the Civil War, no one could ignore the emergence of the United States as an international player. Already a major influence in the Western Hemisphere, the diplomacy of the war years made the nation a center of Western European attention. Finally, the acquisition of Alaska and the presence of the United States in Hawai'i and Japan drew the nation into Pacific Rim affairs. Treaties with other nations were an important subject of the federal Constitution, but what obligation did the United States owe to the private law of other nations? To what extent were these extraterritorial laws incorporated in our own? Justice Horace Gray's footnotes in *Viterbo v. Friedlander* demonstrated how foreign law and domestic law had become intertwined as American rose to a world power.[1]

* * *

The Civil War all but destroyed the sugarcane industry in the bayou country of southeastern Louisiana. But so stable was the demand for the crop that the end of slavery and the defeat of the Confederacy did not prevent the recovery of the sugarcane industry. "Production, which averaged 177,000 tons per year from 1857 through 1861, amounted to only 5,400 tons in 1864, and did not recover to its pre–Civil War average until 1888." But the demand for the product skyrocketed in the years after the war, making investment in it an attractive prospect. Contract labor, largely from the sugar growing areas of the Caribbean, provided a supplement to domestic wage laborers (many of them children) in the sugar fields. While capital in the South after the war was limited (much

---

1 Generally, see Eugene Volokh, "Foreign Law in American Courts," *Oklahoma Law Review*, 66 (2014), 219–43. On wartime diplomacy, see Peter Charles Hoffer, *Seward's Law: Countrylawyering, Relational Rights, and Slavery*, (Ithaca, NY: Cornell University Press, 2022), 93–124.

of it coming from northern investors), the depression of 1873 flattened what had been an uneven growth. With the original owners staggering under the burden of repairing levees, bridges, buildings, and fields, the opportunity was wide open for foreign investment, and in it, the French connection was particularly strong.[2]

Traveling in the bayou, one could not miss the impress of sugarcane culture on the land:

> The landscape of sugarcane plantations in post-war Louisiana was cruelly impressive: Towering over the cane fields, the sugarhouse chimneys denote the location of a sugar factory-an agricultural factory in the field. A cluster of barns and sheds surrounds the sugarhouse forming a centrally located outbuilding complex. Nearby is the quarters, a village grouping of nearly identical laborers' dwellings which is either centered upon a single road in a linear pattern or grouped in a block pattern based on a grid of streets. In a location separate and exclusive from the other buildings in the settlement complex, the mansion, a prominent structure, is set amid moss-draped oaks. On larger plantation enterprises, a company store and sometimes a church are located on or near the plantation holdings. Extensive fields covering hundreds, even thousands, of acres unbroken by fences stretch long and narrow from levee crests at the stream banks to backswamps downslope from the streams. Long, straight ditches divide the fields and also give them a characteristic linear appearance.[3]

The breaking of a levee was foreseeable but very unfortunate, for unlike rice, sugarcane could not grow under water. (In Atlantic Coast low country rice culture, by contrast, water was moved about through a system of dikes and ditches.) These dangers did not deter foreign investment in Louisiana sugar plantations, however. But the total destruction

---

2 Roy A. Ballinger, "A History of Sugar Marketing through 1974," 8, 9; US Department of Agriculture, www.ers.usda.gov; Stanley Engerman, "Contract Labor, Sugar, and Technology in the Nineteenth Century," *Journal of Economic History* 43 (1983): 635–59; Khalil Gibran Muhammad and Tiya Miles, "The Barbaric History of Sugar in America," *New York Times Magazine*, August 14, 2019, www.nytimes.com. John Alfred Heitmann, "The Modernization of the Louisiana Sugar Industry," University of Dayton History Faculty Publications, paper 121 (1987), 1–19.

3 J. B. Rehder, "Sugar Plantations in Louisiana," Talltimbers, 1979, 114, https://talltimbers.org/wp-content/uploads/2014/03/Rehder1979_op.pdf.

of a sugar plantation by flooding was the grounds for a lawsuit in *Viterbo v. Friendlander* (1887).[4]

The lessee (renter) was a Frenchman, one Viterbo, and the lessor was a Louisiana owner of the Friedlander plantation:

> A sugar plantation, leased for five years, with the buildings, mules and implements necessary for the cultivation of sugarcane, and with the growing crop of cane (which the lessee agrees to cut and plant as seed cane, and, by way of reimbursing the lessor for, to leave a certain amount of growing cane on the plantation at the end of the lease), is overflowed for three months, all the cane destroyed, the canals and ditches necessary for drainage filled up, the bridges swept away, and a deposit from three to six inches deep left over the whole ground, making it necessary, in order to cultivate it as a sugar plantation the following year, to spend large sums of money to dig out canals and ditches, repair bridges, and buy seed cane.[5]

Almost as far away from these unfortunate events as one could travel in the United States at the time, US Supreme Court Justice Horace Gray worked in his Washington, DC, home at 1601 I Street NW. Built in 1874, it was three solid stories of bricks. Boston bred in wealth and prestige, with a family going back to the city's beginnings, Gray attended Harvard College and its Law School. He was, with other members of the city's elite, an abolitionist, and his tract, *A Legal Review of the Case of Dred Scott*, argued that a Black person could indeed be a citizen of the United States, contrary to what Chief Justice Roger Taney had written in his *Dred Scott v. Sandford* (1857) opinion. The sixty-two-page tract even questioned whether Taney's opinion represented the opinion of a majority of his brethren. "We feel bound to say that the opinion of the Chief Justice is by no means the ablest or soundest of the opinions in this case. It bears marks of great labor, and of an anxiety to meet, and,

---

4 Viterbo v. Friedlander, 120 U.S. 707 (1887). Rice cultivation along the Georgia and South Carolina coast rivaled the cane sugar crop before the war but did not recover after it. Rivals in Asia emerged to lower demand and the destruction of the low country but the war lowered production. Charles Joyner, *Down by the Riverside: A South Carolina Slave Community* (Urbana: University of Illinois Press, 1984), 41–89; Peter A. Coclanis, *Shadow of a Dream: Economic Life and Death in the Low Country, 1670–1920* (New York: Oxford University Press, 1989), 111–58.

5 120 U.S. at 708.

as far as possible, to reply, to, all objections which might be raised to its conclusions. But in its tone and manner of reasoning, as well as in the positions which it assumes, it is unworthy of the reputation of that great magistrate."[6]

Although his family wealth was based on shipping and commerce, Gray chose to pursue a career at the bar, became the reporter of the state high court opinions in 1854, and was named to the state Superior Court of Judicature in 1864, becoming its youngest member. Nine years later, he became its chief judge, and in 1882 was named to the US Supreme Court by President Chester Arthur. On the court, he favored giving latitude to state legislative action, under the doctrine of the state's police powers. His most famous opinion was *Wong Kim Ark* (1898) (to which we will turn at the close of this chapter) that found the Fourteenth Amendment guaranteed citizenship for all who were born in the United States, including the children of Chinese immigrants.[7]

Gray was noted for the length of his opinions, along with their copious scholarship. He was particularly enamored of studious digressions into early English legal history. He loved the history of law, and in extrajudicial writings of many hundreds of pages (replete with footnotes) demonstrated his mastery of historical sources. These were the stuff of ancient law but did not include contextual materials in the social and cultural history of the past. Thus, his knowledge of case and statute was deep but not broad. Nevertheless, his library at his death contained over two thousand books and other sources on legal history and comparative law.[8]

In his writing for the court, he had help in the form of newly graduated Harvard Law students, whom he hired as clerks; they were recommended to him by his half-brother, Harvard Law School professor John Chipman Gray. These clerks had their own desk just outside Gray's library on the second floor of his home in the District of Columbia, and when called in to him on Saturday mornings, they shared their views on the cases that session. (The clerks, like the justices, did not have offices at

---

6 Horace Gray Jr., *A Legal Review of the Case of Dred Scott* (Boston: Crosby, Nichols, 1857), 8.

7 John E. Semonche, "Horace Gray," in *Oxford Companion to the Supreme Court of the United States*, ed. Kermit Hall (New York: Oxford University Press, 1992), 345–46; Robert M. Spector, "Horace Gray Jr.," in *The Yale Dictionary of American Law*, ed. Roger K. Newman (New Haven, CT: Yale University Press, 2009), 229–30.

8 Robert M. Spector, "Legal Historian on the United States Supreme Court: Justice Horace Gray Jr. and the Historical Method," *American Journal of Legal History* 12 (1968): 181–210.

the court.) The exchanges were remarkably egalitarian, in that he asked for and genuinely wanted their views. The clerk for the 1886–87 session was William H. Dunbar, a graduate of Harvard College from Roxbury, Massachusetts. Dunbar would go into private practice after his clerkship years and then join Louis Brandeis's firm until Dunbar's death in 1916.[9]

Viterbo gave Gray the opportunity to discourse on the differences between Anglo-American common law of rentals and the same subject in the code of Louisiana, itself based on French law, and that going back to the Institutes of Justinian. It was a chance to demonstrate his erudition. The suit could have been resolved without extensive use of quotations from original sources of French law or the Institutes of Justinian for that matter. He could have simply reviewed the state court's decisions on lease law. After all, a Louisiana code provision, 2697 (1870), made absolute the lessee's right to abrogate (cancel the lease) when the use of the "thing" was "destroyed in part." But state courts had in previous years followed old Napoleonic Code provisions giving courts leeway "according to the nature of the case." These precedents protected the interest of the landowners. Gray's footnotes showed that the state courts had read their own law incorrectly. His opinion corrected them in favor of the foreign renter.

The precise issues in *Viterbo* were both simple and complex, simple as a matter of "choice of law" and complex to explain what those choices entailed. Choice of law, sometimes rendered as conflict of laws, was a set of rules determining which of two jurisdictions' laws would apply in a particular case. American common law and Louisiana civil law regarded the obligations of those who leased land and those who held those leases in very different light. The civil code of Louisiana derived from Spanish and French law, they in turn resting on the civil law of ancient Rome. The origin of this law was the code of Byzantine emperor Justinian in the sixth century. It saw a lease for years as a temporary transfer of real estate or other property and held the owner bound to keep that leasehold in good repair, fit for its original purpose. The lessee must pay the rent, of course. But even when the property is damaged or made unfit for its original use through no negligence of the owner, he must repair

---

9 Melvin Urofsky, *Louis D. Brandeis: A Life* (New York: Pantheon, 2009), 54–55; Todd C. Peppers, "Birth of an Institution: Horace Gray and the Lost Law Clerks," *Journal of Supreme Court History* 32 (2007): 241.

and restore it—or the renter can have the lease terminated, and the rent need not be paid.

Interpretation of the law of leases required comparing translations of Louisiana code provisions from French into English. That is, although the code was written in both languages, "In construing those articles of the Civil Code of Louisiana, which were originally enacted both in French and in English, the French text may be taken into consideration for the purpose of clearing up obscurities or ambiguities in the English text." One could not just cite code provisions. With this in mind, Gray tackled the facts of the case. "The breaking of a crevasse in the levees by the waters of the Mississippi River is a fortuitous or unforeseen event within the meaning of the Civil Code of Louisiana, and if in consequence thereof, the plantation is partially destroyed, or ceases to be fit for the use for which it was leased, within the meaning of articles 2697 (2667) and 2699 (2669) of that code, and the lessee is entitled to have the lease annulled."[10]

Here the case got a little more complex. Bear in mind that in the original case before the circuit federal court sitting in Louisiana, the lessee had wanted the court to order the rescinding of the five-year contract (that is, to annul the lease). The lessee did not want damages from the owner (lessor). To repeat, the remedy the lessee wanted was an order ending the lease. This was an "equitable" remedy rather than a legal one. At the time (before the equity and law dockets in federal courts were joined, in 1938), the case had to be refiled on the equity docket. There, the federal judge appointed a master to review the facts based on the depositions of the two sides and to recommend to the judge whether he should issue the equity decree (the injunction) that the lessee wanted. There was no jury and no trial of facts. The master found that the land had been damaged by the break in a levee on a neighboring piece of land, but the petitioner could still bring in a crop. The judge then declined to order the annulment of the lease. It was this denial that the lessee appealed to the Supreme Court.[11]

---

10 120 U.S. at 708 (Gray, J.).

11 On the difference between legal and equitable remedies in federal courts and the impact of the Federal Rules of Civil Procedure of 1938 joining the two kinds of proceedings, see Peter Charles Hoffer, Williamjames Hull Hoffer, and N. E. H. Hull, *The Federal Courts: An Essential History* (New York: Oxford University Press, 2016), 64–65, 298–304.

Gray did accept the master in equity's restatement of the facts but rejected the judge's reading of the law: "This was a petition, filed October 2, 1884, by a citizen of France against a citizen of Louisiana to annul a lease of a sugar plantation from the defendant to the petitioner for five years, and alleging that by an extraordinary rise of the Mississippi River, which could not have been foreseen, and without any fault of the lessee, a crevasse was made in the levees of a neighboring plantation, the leased plantation overflowed, all the cane destroyed, and the plantation rendered wholly unfit for the purpose for which it had been leased." Next, the lessee asked the owner "as soon as the water from the crevasse should have withdrawn, to put back the plantation in the same condition as when leased, and to replace the plant cane and stubble, and the defendant refused to do so." The "thing" was thus unusable. The master in equity thought that "the field were still suitable for the purpose of growing sugar. Some repairs would be necessary." This would have shifted the burden of the repairs to the lessee, and the court agreed. The lessee could not break the lease.[12]

Gray began his own analysis of the applicable law by explaining the difference between the common law (as it existed in the rest of the United States) and the civil code of Louisiana: "The common law regards such a lease as the grant of an estate for years which the lessee takes a title in, and is bound to pay the stipulated rent for, notwithstanding any injury by flood, fire, or external violence at least unless the injury is such a destruction of the land as to amount to an eviction, and by that law the lessor is under no implied covenant to repair, or even that the premises shall be fit for the purpose for which they are leased." Citations followed to cases in various US state courts: "The civil law, on the other hand, regards a lease for years as a mere transfer of the use and enjoyment of the property, and holds the landlord bound, without any express covenant, to keep it in repair and otherwise fit for use and enjoyment for the purpose for which it is leased, even when the need of repair or the unfitness is caused by an inevitable accident, and, if he does not do so, the tenant may have the lease annulled, or the rent abated." Suitable citations to various civil law sites followed. But the opinion did not end here.[13]

---

12 120 U.S. at 709, 710 (Gray, J.).
13 120 U.S. at 712, 713 (Gray, J.).

The next pages of the opinion presented a miniature essay on civil codes, beginning with, "It is accordingly laid down in the Pandects, on the authority of Julian, 'if anyone has let an estate, that, even if anything happens by *vis major*, [a superior or irresistible force, an act of God] he must make it good, he must stand by his contract,'" followed by the Latin version from the *Digest*, "and, on the authority of Ulpian, that 'a lease does not change the ownership,'" again followed by the terminology in the *Digest*. And "that the lessee has a right of action, if he cannot enjoy the thing which he has hired," followed by more Latin, from the *Digest*, followed by a list of the goods, lands, chattels, olives, birds, and just about everything else that the petitioner had or might have had according to the rental agreement. Each item was followed by the Latin text from the *Digest* of Ulpian.

The heavy-handed pedantry concealed what Gray was doing. He was importing a source, and the concepts in it, that were not part of US law. American law nowhere received the code of Justinian. Gray might use it as a reference or even think it was binding, but his use and his thinking did not make ancient Roman law part of US law. Citing the *Digest*, a compendium of fifty books of Roman precepts composed in 530 CE, was nevertheless a bold demonstration of judicial freedom. Where in American law did Gray find permission to plant Justinian in a Supreme Court opinion? Nowhere. He simply did it. True, according to the Judiciary Act of 1789, federal courts were to use the law of the state when deciding civil cases from that state, and Louisiana had received (adopted) some parts of Roman law from its French and Spanish colonizers. But as Gray would concede later in his opinion, Louisiana judges had departed from that code in the very areas that Gray cited. What exactly was going on here would be revealed by the footnotes.[14]

The footnotes demonstrated the reach and sweep of judicial discretion. Gray did not equivocate, hesitate, or qualify—he simply discoursed. To his aid, he summoned two modern commentators on the code. Their work was not incorporated in Louisiana law, so Gray could not argue in defense of his wide ranging analysis that he was merely reciting Louisiana law. The first was Jean Domat's *Civil Laws in their Natural Order* (1689), and the second was Joseph Pothier's *Treatise on Contracts* (1761).

---

14 120 U.S. at 713 (Gray, J.).

So Domat says, "If the tenant is expelled by the act of the sovereign, by *vis major*, or by some other accident, or if the property is destroyed by an inundation, by an earthquake, or other event, the lessor, who was bound to give the property, cannot demand the rent, and will be bound to restore so much of it as he has received, but without any other damages, for no one ought to answer for accidents. Droit Civil, pt. 1, lib. 1, tit. 4, sec. 3, No. 3." And then on to Pothier:

> Pothier brings out the same principles more fully, as applicable to cases resembling the case at bar, saying: "When the thing leased, which the lessor offers to deliver to the lessee, is found not to be entire, the lessor having lost a part of it since the contract, or when it is not in the same condition in which it was at the time of the contract; when what is wanting in the thing, or when the change that has happened in the thing, is such that the lessee would not have been willing to hire this thing if it had been such as it has since become—in that case, the lessee has the right to refuse to receive the thing, and to demand the annulment of the contract. This takes place even if it is by a *vis major*, occurring since the contract, that the thing is no longer entire, or is destroyed, as for example if, since the contract, lightning has burned a considerable part of the house that you have leased to me, and the rest is not sufficient for me to dwell in with my family, or if a field that you have leased to me has been inundated by an overflow of a river which has left a hurtful deposit that has spoiled the grass, but in this case I can only demand the annulment of the bargain, without being able to claim any damages for its nonexecution." Contrat de Louage, no. 74.[15]

Then the footnote: "Pothier Contrat de Louage [rental contract], nos. 139–163. *See also* nos. 309, 477; Introduction aux Coutumes d'Orleans, tit. 19, nos. 17–22." The footnote shifted the reader's attention from what appeared to be an account of binding law to what appeared to be scholarship, explaining the law. Gray could not call on these civil law sources as law, compelling his decision, but he could treat them as scholarly aids to understand the law. And that is what the footnote accomplished.

The next three pages went through the various code sections of the civil law of Louisiana to demonstrate how they embodied the principles

---

15 120 U.S. at 714 (Gray, J.).

that Domat and Pothier had codified. Gray explained very briefly, after (not before) his borrowing, "All the articles, already cited, except perhaps those regarding tenant's repairs, clearly apply to farms and plantations as well as to houses." The externalities—the treaty that brought Louisiana into the United States, the translation of the French code into English, and other matters of context—were ignored. Gray had collapsed context.[16]

But he could not wholly ignore facts or precedent. Facts: the defendants pleaded that the overflow of the Mississippi River was predictable, and so abating resulting damage from it was included in the rental agreement. It was true that in its lower reaches, the river was tidal, and one might predict that it would overflow its banks periodically or "seasonally." Even in the modern era, with the Army Corps of Engineers trying to prevent flooding along the riverbanks, heavy rainfall overflows the levees periodically. In this case, it was a breach in the levee of a neighboring planation that allowed the river waters to flood Friedlander's land. Precedent: If only a crop was destroyed, according to Louisiana case law, there were no grounds for annulling the contract, but if the water damage was so great that the renter could not put in a new crop without great expense, there were grounds to end the contract.

From his reading of the authorities, Gray nevertheless concluded that "the general purpose and the common rule of the civil law, as expressed in the code of Louisiana, are that the lessor shall secure to the lessee the possession, use, and enjoyment of the thing leased, against everything but the fault of the latter, and that any loss of the thing, or deprivation of its use or enjoyment, by accidents or fortuitous events, shall be borne by the lessor, and not by the lessee." Note that instead of line and verse from the civil code, Gray had switched, aided by the footnote, to "general purpose" and "common rule." His reading of Domat and Pothier, rather than the Louisiana judges, determined the rule, which he then regarded as controlling: "This appears from the general provisions in the articles above quoted, by which the lessor is bound, from the very nature of the contract of lease, and without any clause to that effect, not only to deliver the thing leased to the lessee, but also to maintain it in such a condition as to serve the purpose for which it is leased, to cause the les-

---

16 120 U.S. at 720, 728 (Gray, J.).

see to be in peaceable possession of the thing during the continuance of the lease; to make, during its continuance, all repairs."[17]

To repeat, the Louisiana courts believed, and had ruled, that such water damage was foreseeable, and thus the burden fell on the renter to suffer the loss or make good the repairs. Gray summarized that precedent: "The learned counsel for the defendant much relied on some dicta of Louisiana judges to the effect that the law of the state does not favor the abrogation of a lease when the loss or inconvenience is not caused by the fault of the lessor." By applying it rather than the Louisiana code (which, apparently, only Gray understood), the owner was thus protected from such suits. In short, such decisions favored the Louisiana owners over the foreign leaseholders. It was a home-field advantage.[18]

Gray was not convinced by the defendant's counsel:

> The breaking of a crevasse in the Louisiana levees by the waters of the Mississippi River, causing a plantation to be overflowed, must therefore be considered as a *cas fortuit*, a fortuitous or unforeseen event, within the meaning and scope of articles 2697 (2667) and 2699 (2669), entitling the lessee, if thereby the plantation is wholly or partly destroyed or is rendered unfit for the purpose for which it was leased, to have the lease annulled, although it is not a *cas fortuit extraordinaire*, an extraordinary as well as an unforeseen accident, within the meaning of article 2743 (2714), so as to justify an abatement of rent if the crop only is destroyed.[19]

At the conclusion of his opinion, having moved from citing civil law as controlling to using commentary and accompanying footnotes to regard the civil law as persuasive, Gray returned to where he wanted to go in the first place. The footnotes allow us to follow him. Under the Louisiana law, borrowed from French law, adapted from the Roman law, whose clauses Gray cited at length, "the thing leased is a sugar plantation, with the buildings, mules, and implements necessary for the cultivation and making of sugar, and the growing crop of sugar cane." The renter has to plant the crop as part of the obligation of the contract; it is part of the thing leased to the renter. "But they are parts and incidents

---

17 120 U.S. at 719 (Gray, J.).
18 120 U.S. at 720 (Gray, J.).
19 120 U.S. at 733 (Gray, J.).

of the principal contract of lease into which the parties have entered, and that contract is the lease of one entire thing, a sugar plantation, with growing cane upon it, and otherwise fit for the cultivation of sugar, to be used and enjoyed as such by the lessee until the end of the lease, and then to be returned by him to the lessor in like condition, barring such accidents as may excuse the lessee from the performance of the contract on his part." Unable to plant a new crop without extensive repairs left the renter at a disadvantage, which abatement of the rent could not relieve.[20]

The renter did want abatement of rent, which he could have sought under Louisiana law. The property was so damaged that it was no longer useful for its intended purpose. He wanted the rental contract annulled. This was an equitable remedy—the court ordering a party to do something rather than a monetary settlement. That the break in the levee on the neighboring plantation had severely affected the utility of the Friedlander plantation was obvious to Gray:

> The plaintiff had hardly put the plantation in a condition suitable for the cultivation of sugarcane, which was the sole purpose of the lease, and planted one crop, when the inundation came, putting the plantation under water for three months, filling up the canals and ditches necessary for its drainage, sweeping away the bridges, and leaving a deposit from three to six inches deep over the whole land, and making it necessary, in order to cultivate the thing leased as a sugar plantation the following year, to spend large sums of money to open and dig out canals and ditches, and replace bridges, and also destroying all the stubble cane as well as all the plant cane, and leaving the plantation without any cane upon it, either to make sugar of or to cut seed cane from for planting in succeeding years.[21]

Gray concluded, as he believed the master in equity appointed by the circuit court should have concluded, that "the inundation left the thing leased in such a condition that it was unfit for the purpose of a sugar plantation." To remedy the damage, for which the renter was not responsible, would have cost thousands of dollars. "This was not a mere destruction of a crop for one year, like the destruction of a crop of wheat or

---

20 120 U.S. at 733 (Gray, J.).
21 120 U.S. at 736 (Gray, J.).

of grapes or of apples, but it was more like the destruction of the vines or the apple trees from which present and future crops are to be gathered." Who should bear the financial burden of restoring the plantation and future crops was not the issue. The renter wanted out of the contract. The conclusion was obvious to Gray:

> Upon the whole case, we are of opinion that the lease being of a sugar plantation for the purpose of being used to cultivate sugar cane, the injuries proved to the plantation, and to its capacity for producing cane and sugar, amounted to a partial destruction of the plantation, or, what is the same thing in legal effect, to making it cease to be fit for the purpose for which it was leased . . . and that, under articles 2697 (2667) and 2699 (2669) of the Revised Civil Code [of Louisiana], construed in the light of the other articles that we have cited, and of the principles of the civil law as established in Louisiana, the plaintiff was entitled to have the lease annulled.

The federal circuit had erred in imposing common law on a Louisiana case.[22]

Gray was quite capable of putting long string citations into the text. He had no hesitation of adding material from foreign treatises and cases in the body of his opinion. Why the exception with the footnote? Was the note really a footnote? It did not come at the end of the opinion, but it was prefaced by a number, followed by a period, so it was not a citation in the text. Gray's draft, followed by the reporter's printed text, did not separate the note out of the text. One clue is that, different from the other citations, it cited treatises of French law that were not incorporated in federal law until he wrote the note.

But did the note actually do that? Did it "receive" the civil law? Remember that the details in the long passages on the civil code in its various forms, the extended quotations from the civil code commentators, were unnecessary to reach a decision in the appeal. All that was necessary to reach a decision was to cite and explain the various provisions of the Louisiana code. The insertion of the scholarship in the text and the appending of the footnotes was a learned digression. It was not neces-

---

22 120 U.S. at 737 (Gray, J.).

sary to respond to dissents, as there was no dissent in the case. Gray was not anticipating or responding to dissent. The assortment of quotations and the footnotes constituted a display of erudition and was thus, in effect, an implicit footnote.

Did the footnoted material in *Viterbo* then become part of our constitutional law? In one sense, the answer is simple: yes, because it was already established in choice of law cases that the forum state's law, here Louisiana's code, would be the deciding law when there was a conflict with another jurisdiction. But there was a hitch. According to the Louisiana code provision, in article 2697 (1870), if the "thing," in this case the plantation, "be only destroyed in part, the lessee may either demand a diminution of the price or a revocation of the lease." That was an absolute guarantee of the right to abrogate. But the earlier French sources that Gray cited made the abrogation only possible "according to the nature of the case." The Louisiana courts' reading of the code, in light of the French sources, was at variance with the code itself. Ordinarily, in conflict of laws, the forum state (here Louisiana) could decide to use the other jurisdiction's law (i.e., the common law in force in the rest of the country) or stick to its own (French law). Gray overrode that rule, which he could because the case was in the federal courts. But had Gray's extensive quotation from French law made that law Supreme Court precedent? The answer could not lie in the case itself or in his opinion; it could reside only in the adoption of his views by the court in later cases.[23]

One of those cases was far more important than *Viterbo*. In his majority opinion in *Wong Kim Ark* (1898), an opinion ranging over British and American law to find that the Fourteenth Amendment applied to citizenship for anyone born in the United States (save the children of serving ambassadors), Gray added at the end of the opinion a footnote (denoted by an asterisk): "Acts of May 6, 1882, c. 126, 22 Stat. 58; July 5, 1884, c. 220, 23 Stat. 116; September 13, 1888, c. 1015, and October 1, 1888, c. 1064, 2 Stat. 476, 504; May 5, 1892, c. 60, 27 Stat. 25; August 18, 1894, c. 301, 28 Stat. 390." He had assumed, in passing, that *Viterbo's* adoption of foreign law was precedent, though the note only included pieces of the U.S. Statutes at Large."[24]

---

23 Lynn M. Allain, "The Rights of the Lessee in Louisiana vis-à-vis the Lessor," *Tulane Civil Law Forum* 3 (1975), 52, 54–55.

24 United States v. Wong Kim Ark U. S. 169, 649, 705 (1898) (Gray, J.).

In dissent, Justice Melville Fuller added his own footnote from the laws of China, to prove that Chinese law did not support Gray's view. In so doing, Fuller confirmed (I think inadvertently) that foreign law could become Supreme Court precedent. Again, the note was signaled by an asterisk:

> The fundamental laws of China have remained practically unchanged since the second century before Christ. The statutes have from time to time undergone modifications, but there does not seem to be any English or French translation of the Chinese Penal Code later than that by Staunton published in 1810. That code provided: "All persons renouncing their country and allegiance, or devising the means thereof, shall be beheaded, and in the punishment of this offence, no distinction shall be made between principals and accessories. The property of all such criminals shall be confiscated, and their wives and children distributed as slave to the great officers of State. . . . The parents, grandparents, brothers and grandchildren of such criminals, whether habitually living with them under the same roof or not, shall be perpetually banished to the distance of 2000 *lee* . . . Staunton's Penal Code of China 272, § 255."[25]

However one reads the footnotes in these opinions, their appearance made clear a fact that more modern courts have routinely accepted (though not all, and not always). American law is part of a legal tradition stretching back centuries and crossing oceans. The Constitution itself was part of international law, and constitutional opinions incorporate foreign law concepts.[26]

---

25 169 U.S. at 732 (Fuller, J. dissenting).
26 See, for example, Stephen J. Breyer, *The Court and the World: American Law and the New Global Realities* (New York: Alfred A. Knopf, 2015), 236.

[4]

FRIENDS OF THE COURT

Muller v. Oregon, 208 U.S. 412 (1908)

The new century brought many changes to the United States, but the most striking was a transformation of work and workplaces. The signs were everywhere on the landscape—farms now crossed by railroad lines, horizons dotted with oil derricks, the sky itself blackened by the smoke of steel factories. According to the US census, the country was still rural, but no one visiting the metropolises of New York City, Chicago, and their sister cities would have doubted that a rural landscape was becoming urbanized. The law for a post–Civil War country, with its emphasis on the free labor of individual workers and the domestic roles of women, would have to change. This was the lesson of the single footnote containing the so-called Brandeis brief in *Muller v. Oregon* (1908).[1]

* * *

A Gilded Age had arrived in America at the end of the nineteenth century, a time of striking transitions and highly visible contradictions. A few members of society accumulated great wealth and displayed it conspicuously, while many labored in soot-covered cities and ill-lit factories. Metropolises like New York City and Chicago warehoused millions of immigrants from foreign lands (over thirteen million entered the country during the Gilded Age) and nearby rural areas seeking jobs. Cities hosted giant corporations whose headquarters filled new "skyscraper" office buildings. At the same time, unrest and violence in the city pit newcomer against native born, rich against poor, and labor against capital in a witch's brew of poverty, illness, crime, and corruption.[2]

---

1 Muller v. Oregon, 208 U.S. 412 (1908).
2 Vincent P. De Santis, *The Shaping of Modern America, 1877–1920*, 3rd ed. (Wheeling, IL: Harlan Davidson, 2000), 96–106; Mark Wahlgren Summers, *The Gilded Age: Or, the Hazard of New Functions* (Upper Saddle River, NJ: Prentice-Hall, 1997), 247; Roger Daniels, "The Immigrant

Big was better, or so the giants of industry seemed to think. Labeled robber barons by some, celebrated as industrial statesmen by others, manufacturing and banking moguls brought the nation into the modern age of business organization. In 1860, the largest business enterprises employed thousands, were capitalized at $1 million, and served a national market. In the Gilded Age, behemoths like Standard Oil employed tens of thousands, were capitalized in the tens of millions, and reached global markets. The new middle-management corporation, with layers of general managers between different divisions of the corporation, and squadrons of middle managers reporting to the general managers, abetted by investment bankers and aided by corporate lawyers, came to dominate the country's economic development. The value of manufactured exports rose from $205 million in 1895 to $485 million in 1900, more than doubling in five years and increasing its share of total exports from 25.8 percent to 35.3 percent. By the end of the Gilded Age in the mid-1890s, American heavy industry stood alongside food production and staple crop enterprises as the leading sectors in the national economy, exceeding them in terms of capital investment and market value.[3]

But lawyer Louis Brandeis of Boston did not agree that bigger was better. Quite the opposite. He was one of the new breed of reformers called progressives. Leading progressives were educated urban professionals and businesspeople. They shared a moralizing absolutism and the ideal of clean, efficient government by professionals like themselves. To bypass city and state political machines, progressives pushed for and won the secret ballot, a constitutional amendment for the direct election of senators, changes to several state constitutions providing for referenda, ballot initiatives, and the recall of state officials. Some, like Theodore Roosevelt, accepted bigness as inevitable and sought to regulate it.

Experience in the Gilded Age," in *The Gilded Age: Perspectives on the Origins of Modern America*, ed. Charles William Calhoun (Lanham, MD: Rowman and Littelfield, 2007), 76. Conventional dating of the Gilded Age, from the period immediately after Reconstruction to sometime in the middle of the 1890s, is somewhat imprecise; see Elisabeth Israels Perry and Karen Manners Smith, *The Gilded Age and Progressive Era* (New York: Oxford University Press, 2006), 6.

3 Alfred D. Chandler, *The Visible Hand: The Managerial Revolution in American Business* (Cambridge, MA: Harvard University Press, 1977), 171, 177, 178, 333; Douglas A. Irwin, "Explaining America's Surge in Manufactured Exports, 1880–1913," *National Bureau of Economic Research Working Papers* 85, no. 2 (2001): 364–76.

Brandeis rejected this solution and argued for a "new freedom" from corporate monopolies and trusts.[4]

Brandeis was born on November 13, 1856, in Louisville, Kentucky, a slave trader's city and the first stop on the underground railroad. He was the scion of a successful extended family of Jewish merchants. The family was first-generation American, but his father favored abolitionism, and an uncle was a continuing source of liberal ideals. The son grew up in an atmosphere of culture, reading, and reformism. Louis attended Harvard Law School and reportedly had the highest grade average on record to that time. He entered law practice in St. Louis, then the legal center of lower midwestern business, and in 1879 relocated to a partnership in Boston with Harvard Law School classmate Samuel Warren. The partnership was very successful, but Brandeis's love of the law had mutated into a vision of the transformative power of law in the public sphere. As was typical of successful law practices of that day, many of his clients were railroads, and he was soon one of the most prominent of the railroads' corporate advisers.[5]

Brandeis believed in government by the people, wanted the little guy to get a fair shake, and battled for banking and insurance regulation and for public ownership of utilities. He truly hated corruption, not just in government but in businesses and unions, and the causes he adopted (often uncompensated for his labors) were on behalf of the victims of this corruption. As he wrote to Massachusetts state assemblyman Norman Hill White on July 6, 1907, during the campaign to establish savings bank life insurance there, "We have before us the work of putting the law into successful practice." He believed in small government free of corruption, and he feared a powerful central government beholden to great industrial interests. Power, according to Brandeis, must always be supervised and checked by democratic means.[6]

---

4 Richard Hofstadter, *The Age of Reform* (New York: Random House, 1955), 5; Walter Nugent, *Progressivism: A Very Short Introduction* (New York: Oxford University Press, 2009), 54; Arthur Link, *Woodrow Wilson and the Progressive Era, 1910–1917* (New York: Harper, 1954), 69–72; Urofsky, *Brandeis*, 300–26.

5 Urofsky, *Brandeis*, 3–180.

6 Brandeis to Norman Hill White, July 6, 1907, in *Letters of Louis D. Brandeis*, ed. Melvin I. Urofsky and David W. Levy (Albany: State University of New York Press, 1971), 2:7; Woodrow Wilson, *The New Freedom, A Call for the Emancipation of the Generous Energies of the People* (Garden City, NY: Doubleday and Page, 1921), 3.

In 1903, the state of Oregon, following a progressive labor campaign, passed a law limiting the hours that women could work in factories, machine shops, and commercial laundries to sixty hours a week, in effect a ten-hour workday. A similar law had passed in the neighboring state of Washington. One Portland, Oregon, laundry owner, Curt Muller, forced a union representative named Emma Gotcher to work overtime. He was fined. The state courts upheld the fine and the statute. He and his fellow laundry owners decided to sue in federal court, appealing the Oregon Supreme Court decision to the US Supreme Court, relying on *Lochner v. New York* (1905), in which the court had struck down a state law limiting the hours that bakers could work.[7]

Brandeis's participation in what became *Muller v. Oregon* was first a matter of family ties. He often agreed to act as an adviser to reform groups. In this case, his sister-in-law Pauline Goldmark was one of a group of women progressives who had formed the private nonprofit National Consumers League (NCL) to protect consumers from fraud and tainted products. Led by Jane Addams and Florence Kelley, the NCL became an important lobbying group, and by the 1900s, it had turned its attention to the conditions of working women. When Muller sued, they turned to Brandeis to assist the attorney general of Oregon in defending the statute.[8]

Like many of the progressives, Brandeis was enamored of facts. He believed that when presented fully and fairly, facts would lead all people of good faith to practical reform. Without fee, he took the case that the NCL offered him. Working-hours limitations, one of the progressives' reform projects to improve the lives and safeguard the health of American workers, had been upheld by courts when the industry was inherently dangerous to the public or to the health and welfare of its laborers. But in industries that were not inherently dangerous or when the state could not convince the courts that the limitation of hours was within the state's police power, the courts struck down the legislation. That was what happened when New York tried to defend its hours limitation legislation in *Lochner*. The statute concerned men working in bakeries, whom the court found had the right to contract for their labor, including

---

7 Ruth Bader Ginsburg, "*Muller v. Oregon*: One Hundred Years Later," *Willamette Law Review* 45 (2009): 360; Lochner v. New York, 198 U.S. 45 (1905).
8 Urofsky, *Brandeis*, 201–29.

the hours they worked. The doctrine, based on the due process clause of the Fourteenth Amendment, was termed "freedom of contract."[9]

Did the women laundresses of Oregon have the same freedom of contract (even when everyone knew that the laundresses came from the poorest class of labor, had little freedom to choose their hours, and did not work under contracts anyhow)? Brandeis's one stipulation was that the state of Oregon, defending its own legislation, allow him to participate as cocounsel. The state agreed. Kelley and Goldmark assembled a team of ten researchers to scour libraries to find statistics on women's work and health. The aim was to show that the women suffered from excessive work hours. There was little of this in American records other than statutes, but in western European nations' publications, there was a treasure trove. Data was extracted from reports of factory inspectors, physicians, trade unions, economists, and social workers.[10]

The resulting Brandeis brief was an example of the amicus curiae (friends of the court) brief by a third party with an interest in the litigation, admitted by the discretion of the court for its consideration. "An *amicus curiae* brief that brings to the attention of the Court relevant matter not already brought to its attention by the parties may be of considerable help to the Court. An *amicus curiae* brief that does not serve this purpose burdens the Court, and its filing is not favored." The first of these briefs was the work of Henry Clay in 1821. From a trickle at the start of the twentieth century, in some controversial cases, these documents have become a flood. In abortion suits, the number of briefs for both sides often topped two dozen. In *Webster v. Reproduction Health Services* (1989), there were seventy-eight friends of the court briefs. But the best known amicus brief remains Brandeis's in *Muller*.[11]

The Brandeis brief ran 113 printed pages. Only the first three argued the law. There, Brandeis used *Lochner* against itself, drawing from the majority opinion's concessions an alternative opinion stressing the way

---

9 Landon Y. R. Storrs, *Civilizing Capitalism: The National Consumers League, Women's Activism, and Labor Standards in the New Deal Era* (Chapel Hill: University of North Carolina Press, 2000), 3–4; 98 U. S. at 54 (Peckham, J.).

10 Nancy Woloch, *Muller v. Oregon, A Brief History with Documents* (Boston: Bedford St. Martins, 1995), 28–29.

11 Rule 37, US Supreme Court Rules. There are other restrictions as well. Webster v. Reproduction Health Services, 492 U.S. 490 (1989); Jeffrey Scott, "You Got a Friend in Me: Facts and Supreme Court Amicus Briefs," *Georgetown Journal of Legal Ethics* 29 (2016): 1355, 1356.

in which state action to protect the health and welfare of workers was allowable. If the state act had no substantial or real relation to those powers, then it would fail, but the Oregon statute fell within the legitimate activity of the states. Each of the claims in these pages was followed by citations from *Lochner*. Following a list of states with similar regulations to Oregon's, the "argument" of the first part of the Brandeis brief reads as follows:

> The legal rules applicable to this case are few and are well established, namely: *First:* The right to purchase or to sell labor is a part of the "liberty" protected by the Fourteenth Amendment of the Federal Constitution. . . . *Second:* This right to "liberty" is, however, subject to such reasonable restraint of action as the State may impose in the exercise of the police power for the protection of health, safety, morals, and the general welfare. *Third:* The mere assertion that a statute restricting "liberty" relates, though in a remote degree, to the public health, safety, or welfare does not render it valid. The act must have a "real or substantial relation to the protection of the public health and the public safety." It must have "a more direct relation, as a means to an end, and the end itself must be appropriate and legitimate." *Fourth:* Such a law will not be sustained if the Court can see that it has no real or substantial relation to public health, safety, or welfare, or that it is "an unreasonable, unnecessary and arbitrary interference with the right of the individual to his personal liberty or to enter into those contracts in relation to labor which may seem to him appropriate or necessary for the support of himself and his family." But "If the end which the Legislature seeks to accomplish be one to which its power extends, and if the means employed to that end, although not the wisest or best, are yet not plainly and palpably unauthorized by law, then the Court cannot interfere. In other words, when the validity of a statute is questioned, the burden of proof, so to speak, is upon those" who assail it. *Fifth:* The validity of the Oregon statute must therefore be sustained unless the Court can find that there is no "fair ground, reasonable in and of itself, to say that there is material danger to the public health (or safety), or to the health (or safety) of the employees (or to the general welfare), if the hours of labor are not curtailed.[12]

---

12 Muller v. Oregon, brief for the Defendant in Error, U.S. Supreme Court (1907), 9–11.

The first part of the brief concluded that the Oregon statute was obviously enacted for the purpose of protecting public health, safety, and welfare. Standing alone, however, it did not do what the NCL and Brandeis wanted—to prove that working long hours was detrimental to the laundress's health.

The materials in the rest of the brief were not original. The use of medical evidence to support legislative relief for women laborers was well established in England—and Brandeis's researchers quoted from it. The first, in fact, came in 1833; the brief quoted the opinion of a Leeds surgeon who held that "males and females, whose work obliges them to stand constantly, are more subject to varicose veins of the lower extremities, and to a larger and more dangerous extent, than ever I have witnessed even in foot soldiers." Courts in England accepted it when businesses challenged the connection between long hours and debilities of female workers. The scope of the brief, in particular its volume and its comparative sweep, gave it a force that even conservatives on the United States Supreme Court could not gainsay.[13]

About as different from Brandeis as one could find in the ranks of practicing lawyers, Justice David J. Brewer wrote the opinion for a unanimous court in *Muller v. Oregon*. He had voted with the majority in *Lochner*, voiding a state law limiting the working hours of bakers. Here he found an even more stringent Oregon regulation to be constitutional. The difference lay less in the distinction between the two laws than in Brewer's own complicated social attitudes. Whether these belonged in a constitutional opinion, they reflected the views of all his brethren.[14]

Born in 1837 of missionary parents in Turkey, raised in Kansas, educated in New England at Yale, Brewer earned his law degree at Albany Law School in 1858. His thinking was thus reflective of the prewar, Northern ideals of free labor—and aligned him with those who favored "freedom of contract" ideology. Deeply conservative but not antipathetic to some kinds of reform, he served as a local Kansas judge, then on its elective Supreme Court. Indeed, as he told his state's bar association

---

13 See, for example, Noga Morag-Levine "Facts, Formalism, and the Brandeis Brief: The Origins of a Myth," *University of Illinois Law Review* (2013): 65–71, quotation from page 65.

14 See, for example, the discussion in Katie L. Gibson, *Ruth Bader Ginsburg's Legacy of Dissent: Feminist Rhetoric and the Law* (Tuscaloosa: University of Alabama Press, 2018), 23–24 ("all women treated as though they will be mothers").

in 1893, "There is scarcely any judicial position which I have not filled, scarcely any service in the profession which I have not been called upon to discharge." Perhaps without realizing it, Brewer had conceded that he was a man for all seasons in his profession. Friendship and patronage aided his advance. For his loyalty to the Republican Party, President Chester Alan Arthur named Brewer to the eighth circuit, and then President Benjamin Harrison elevated Brewer to the US Supreme Court in 1889, where his uncle, David J. Field, already sat.[15]

Brewer's views of legal reform were a complicated mix of conservative and liberal. He wrote and spoke widely on the need for world peace, and in 1905, two years before he wrote for the court in *Muller*, he published a 115-page book explaining why the United States was a "Christian Nation." After reviewing the early history of the colonies, their charters, and their laws, he concluded, "These various declarations in charters, constitutions and statutes indicate the general thought and purpose. In no charter or constitution is there anything to even suggest that any other than the Christian is the religion of his country." He was economically conservative, but the conservatism was not a love of bigness or corporate property. When given the choice, he defended the rights of women and immigrants but not African Americans. He was no friend to labor unions, but he was not antipathetic to workers. If he did not share the liberal sympathies of counsel for the laundresses in *Muller v. Oregon*, he recognized the value of protecting future generations by limiting the hours that the mothers of that generation worked. This was a Victorian view of the weaker sex and the connection between morals and working hours—giving support to a doctrine of special treatment and protective laws for women.[16]

Brewer opened his *Muller* opinion with his reservations about legislatively imposed conditions on employment, an echo of *Lochner*: "It thus appears that, putting to one side the elective franchise, in the matter of personal and contractual rights, they stand on the same plane as the other sex. Their rights in these respects can no more be infringed than the equal rights of their brothers." Then he pivoted: "But this assumes

---

15 Michael J. Brodhead, *David J. Brewer, The Life of a Supreme Court Justice, 1837–1910* (Carbondale: Southern Illinois University Press, 1994), xi, 52, 73, 78.

16 Michael J. Brodhead, "David J. Brewer," in Newman, ed., *Biographical Dictionary*, 73–74; David J. Brewer, *The United States a Christian Nation* (Philadelphia: Winston, 1905), 31; Woloch, *Muller*, 71.

that the difference between the sexes does not justify a different rule respecting a restriction of the hours of labor."[17]

Next came a preface to the footnote: "It may not be amiss, in the present case, before examining the constitutional question, to notice the course of legislation, as well as expressions of opinion from other than judicial sources. In the brief filed by Mr. Louis D. Brandeis for the defendant in error is a very copious collection of all these matters, an epitome of which is found in the margin.*" Brewer noted that the Brandeis materials were not actually "judicial sources." They were, however, legal sources—legislative findings. Thus, they had to be included, but severed from the opinion itself by the asterisk. "The legislation and opinions referred to in the margin may not be, technically speaking, authorities, and in them is little or no discussion of the constitutional question presented to us for determination, yet they are significant of a widespread belief that woman's physical structure, and the functions she performs in consequence thereof, justify special legislation restricting or qualifying the conditions under which she should be permitted to toil."[18]

In what can be regarded as dicta—that is, material in the opinion not relevant to the holding of the court—Brewer added his view of the weaker sex. He actually favored giving women the right to vote, but this extension of legal equality did not mean that he believed in the equality of the sexes:

> That woman's physical structure and the performance of maternal functions place her at a disadvantage in the struggle for subsistence is obvious. This is especially true when the burdens of motherhood are upon her. Even when they are not, by abundant testimony of the medical fraternity, continuance for a long time on her feet at work, repeating this from day to day, tends to injurious effects upon the body, and, as healthy mothers are essential to vigorous offspring, the physical wellbeing of woman becomes an object of public interest and care in order to preserve the strength and vigor of the race.

Protecting the future of the white race, one of the features of both the immigration restriction movement and the eugenics movement, were

---

17 Muller v. Oregon, 208 U.S. 412, 418 (1908) (Brewer, J.).
18 408 U.S. at 420 (Brewer, J.).

no more judicially cognizable than Chief Justice Roger Taney's dicta in *Dred Scott v. Sandford* (1857) that African Americans could never be citizens. But Brewer pressed on with further dicta: "Still again, history discloses the fact that woman has always been dependent upon man."[19]

The full "epitome" of the Brandeis brief Brewer attached at the end of the opinion with an asterisk, making it into a true footnote, unlike the hybrid in *Viterbo*.

* The following legislation of the states imposes restriction in some form or another upon the hours of labor that may be required of women: Massachusetts: 1874, Rev.Laws 1902, chap. 106, § 24; Rhode Island: 1885, Acts and Resolves 1902, chap. 994, p. 73; Louisiana: 1886, Rev.Laws 1904, vol. 1, § 4, p. 989; Connecticut: 1887, Gen.Stat.Revision 1902, § 4691; Maine: 1887, Rev.Stat. 1903, chap. 40, § 48; New Hampshire: 1887, Laws 1907, chap. 94, p. 95; Maryland: 1888, Pub.Gen.Laws 1903, art. 100, § 1; Virginia: 1890, Code 1904, title 51A, chap. 178A, § 3657b; Pennsylvania: 1897, Laws 1905, No. 226, p. 352; New York: 1899, Laws 1907, chap. 507, § 77, subdiv. 3, p. 1078; Nebraska: 1899, Comp.Stat. 1905, § 7955, p. 1986; Washington: Stat. 1901, chap. 68, § 1, p. 118; Colorado: Acts 1903, chap. 138, § 3, p. 310; New Jersey: 1892, Gen.Stat. 1895, p. 2350, §§ 66. 67; Oklahoma; 1890, Rev.Stat. 1903, chap. 25, art. 58, § 729; North Dakota: 1877, Rev.Code 1905, § 9440; South Dakota: 1877, Rev.Code (Penal Code § 764), p. 1185; Wisconsin: 1897, Code 1898, § 1728; South Carolina: Acts 1907, No. 233.

In foreign legislation, Mr. Brandeis calls attention to these statutes: Great Britain, 1844: Law 1901, 1 Edw. VII. chap. 22. France, 1848: Act Nov. 2, 1892, and March 30, 1900. Switzerland, Canton of Glarus, 1848: Federal Law 1877, art. 2, § 1. Austria, 1855; Acts 1897, art. 96a, §§ 1–3. Holland, 1889; art. 5, § 1. Italy, June 19, 1902, art. 7. Germany, Laws 1891.

Then follow extracts from over ninety reports of committees, bureaus of statistics, commissioners of hygiene, inspectors of factories, both in this country and in Europe, to the effect that long hours of labor are dangerous for women, primarily because of their special physical organization. The matter is discussed in these reports in different aspects, but all agree as to the danger. It would, of course, take too much space to give these reports in detail. Following them are extracts from similar reports

---

19 408 U.S. at 421–422 (Brewer, J.).

discussing the general benefits of short hours from an economic aspect
of the question. In many of these reports, individual instances are given
tending to support the general conclusion. Perhaps the general scope and
character of all these reports may be summed up in what an inspector for
Hanover says:

> The reasons for the reduction of the working day to ten hours—(a) the
> physical organization of women, (b) her maternal functions, (c) the rear-
> ing and education of the children, (d) the maintenance of the home—are
> all so important and so far-reaching that the need for such reduction
> need hardly be discussed.[20]

Note that the brief included the law and the findings of fact of foreign governments alongside those of domestic jurisdictions. Like Gray,
Brewer has assumed that these foreign "facts" were not only relevant to
the case, they also belonged in the precedent. In 1908, with President
Roosevelt's Great White Fleet circling the globe and the United States
arbitrating a peace between czarist Russia and imperial Japan, no one
could doubt that the US was a world power. In this situation, foreign law
did not look so foreign anymore.[21]

The opinion established a regime of protective treatment of working
women that Kelley and Goldmark wished, and the case became precedent for similar legislation throughout the country. In *Bunting v. Oregon* (1916), for example, the ten-hour day was extended to all workers.
In retrospect, later critics of the decision, and in particular of Brewer's
dicta, found *Muller* "a roadblock" to fuller equality, but this may be too
retrospectively harsh. In a narrower sense, it proved that imaginative
lawyering could change the world.[22]

Had Brewer's reference to the Brandeis brief made the content of
that brief, or even Brewer's "epitome" of that brief, a part of American

---

20 408 U.S. at 425 (Brewer, J.).

21 Again, the question of where "foreign" or "comparative" law belongs in the opinion. If it
appeared in the text, it was obviously part of the rationale for the decision, but putting it in the text,
no more than putting it in the footnote, incorporated or received foreign law into American law.
The issue is fully discussed in the majority and dissenting opinions in Medellín v. Texas 552 U.S. 491
(2008); and Alan Mygatt-Tauber, *Medellín v. Texas, International Justice, Federalism, and the
Execution of José Medellín* (Lawrence: University Press of Kansas, 2022), 102–15.

22 Ginsburg, "*Muller v. Oregon*," 359, 370; Martha Minow, "Foreword: Justice Engendered," *Harvard
Law Review* 101 (1993), 88; Urofsky, *Brandeis*, 219–20.

law? The answer is yes and no. Brewer wanted the opinion to recognize Brandeis's contribution, and a precedent had been set for the inclusion of social science findings in later opinions (as will be seen in subsequent chapters of this book), but the permissive inclusion of such findings did not make them law—unless the court later cited them. Still more important, the precedent had been set for inclusion of friends of the court briefs in the body of legal opinions. Isolated as footnotes, the briefs were not law, but regarded like the briefs of parties to the suit, the material in amicus briefs could become law. In this case, insofar as state legislatures or Congress (for example, in child labor statutes) were influenced by social science and relied on the social science to pass laws, social science was absorbed into American lawmaking through the medium of amicus briefs cited in footnotes.[23]

* * *

But returning to the brief and to the case, as a matter of equal protection under the Fourteenth Amendment, the Oregon law plainly gave to women a benefit that was not extended to men who worked long hours in laundries, factories, and other arduous occupations. Presumably, this was because, according to the brief, such labor would not harm their role bearing and raising children. The first part of that assumption is still true; men do not bear children, and they do not raise them as women do. Whether pregnancy imposes certain burdens on future fathers, as some briefs in post-*Roe* cases have argued, is not on point. Would or should the Oregon statute fail before an equal protection challenge? Can one conceive of such a challenge in a constitutional regime that denied

---

23 Brandeis was not done. Before he joined the court in 1916, he prepared amicus briefs in four more state cases. Perhaps the most impressive one was the 529-page brief in support of a New York law barring the nighttime factory employment of women. The legislation carried the day, but his brief was not cited in the opinion of the court of appeals. See *People v. Charles Schweinler Press*, 295 NY 402 (1915). The number and importance of friends of the court briefs have skyrocketed in the later years of the twentieth century and into the twenty-first. Briefs were especially numerous in abortion rights cases. In *Roe v. Wade* (1973), there were twenty-three amicus briefs. In *Dobbs v. Jackson Women's Health* (2023), there were 140. On reproductive rights and amicus briefs, see chapter 8 herein. How important amicus briefs were to the justices' opinions is discussed in William H. Manz, "Citations in Supreme Court Opinions and [Amicus] Briefs," *Law Library Journal* 94 (2002): 267–300 (cases cited in amici made it into opinions more often than not); and Frederick R. Parker Jr., "*Washington v. Glucksburg* and *Vacco v. Quill*: An Analysis of the Amicus Curiae Briefs and the Supreme Court's Majority and Concurring Opinions," *Saint Louis Law Journal* 43 (1999): 469–542 (amici had little impact on the opinions in assisted suicide cases).

women even more basic equality than hours of work? One must not forget that in 1908, in almost all of the states, women could not vote. They did not hold elective public office, or indeed work in government offices except as secretaries, librarians, and janitorial staff. Their numbers were few in academe, medicine, and law. As George Washington University Law School dean Alan B. Morrison has argued, "It is hard to accept the notion that facts are irrelevant, but it is equally hard to argue that courts should be free to second-guess legislatures by making unfavorable findings of fact whenever there is a claim that a group has been treated less favorably than others."[24]

In 1916, Brandeis would join the Supreme Court bench. There he would find himself in the minority defending the kind of reform state and federal legislation to which he had devoted his earlier career. *Muller's* promise of social justice for the worker was not forgotten, but the underlying premise of the Brandeis brief seemed lost in the "return to normalcy" of the 1920s. Yet what is put aside in law is never really lost, and the essence of Brandeis's contribution reappeared in arguably the greatest of all Supreme Court footnotes—number 4 in *United States v. Carolene Products* (1938), to which we now turn.[25]

---

24 Alan B. Morrison, "The Brandeis Brief and 21st Century Litigation," *Lewis and Clark Law Review* 18 (2014): 719.

25 Of course, no victory is without its naysayers. Advocates of feminism in later years argued that the Brandeis brief was a defeat for women's equal rights. See, for example, Phillipa Strum, *On Account of Sex: Ruth Bader Ginsburg and the Making of Gender Equality Law* (Lawrence: University Press of Kansas, 2022), 17.

[5]

DISCRETE AND INSULAR MINORITIES

United States v. Carolene Products, 304 U.S. 144 (1938)

The progressive movement of the early twentieth century found new life in the New Deal of the Franklin Delano Roosevelt administration. While *Muller* was an exception to the pro-business, laissez-faire jurisprudence of the 1920s, the New Deal brought what some constitutional scholars have called a great transformation in law. According to Yale Law School's Bruce Ackerman, the court's later permissive attitude toward New Deal welfare state reforms was a moment equivalent in some ways to the original framing of the Constitution. For while the first response of the Charles Evans Hughes court to hastily imposed congressional legislation was less than welcoming, by 1937, a majority of the court was willing to allow Congress and state legislatures great latitude to intervene in economic and commercial activities. Left out of this sea change in the law were discrete and insular minorities. The problem with the rational-basis reading of legislation was that it permitted great latitude to states' racially discriminatory legislation. The court would find an answer to that dilemma in footnote 4 to *United States v. Carolene Products*.[1]

* * *

Footnote 4 to Justice Harlan Fiske Stone's opinion in *Carolene Products* is considered by many court experts to be "*the* footnote." Not only introducing the concept of "strict scrutiny" of state legislation when it

---

1 Bruce Ackerman, *We The People: Foundations, vol.* 1 (Cambridge, MA: Harvard University Press, 1991), 59–60, 118–20; William E. Leuchtenburg, *The Supreme Court Reborn: The Constitutional Revolution in the Age of Roosevelt* (New York: Oxford University Press, 1995), 316. Rational basis is the least restrictive reading of a state law under the due process clause of the Fourteenth Amendment. According to the conventional description of the test, a prudential or judicially invented doctrine, the statute or ordinance (state or local) must address a legitimate state interest, and there must be a rational connection between the statute's/ordinance's means and goals.

adversely affected discrete and insular minorities, it moved footnotes from the bottom of the page to the top of courts' considerations. It is acclaimed as the magna carta of "the relation between judges and other agencies of government," and for some, it is the most famous footnote in constitutional law. Whether the placement of the doctrinal novelty in the note was sly, the opinion in a mocking discussion with itself, moving the "discussion of the impurities of the democratic process to the (impure) footnote," or whether the footnote "commenced a new era on constitutional law" that saved the reputation of a court recently "discredited" by its opposition to the New Deal, no one can doubt that it belongs in any essay on Supreme Court footnotes.[2]

The style of the footnote is not particularly elegant. It is the doctrinal implications of the footnote that mattered. "There may be narrower scope for operation of the presumption of constitutionality when legislation appears on its face to be within a specific prohibition of the Constitution, such as those of the first ten Amendments, which are deemed equally specific when held to be embraced within the Fourteenth . . . whether prejudice against discrete and insular minorities may be a special condition, which tends seriously to curtail the operation of those political processes ordinarily to be relied upon to protect minorities, and which may call for a correspondingly more searching judicial inquiry." The note, escorted by an armada of citations, had no legitimate purpose in the opinion, as it regarded cases not yet before the court and set out a rule for those cases that did not derive from *Carolene Products*. Stone admitted as much: "It is unnecessary to consider now whether legislation that restricts those political processes which can ordinarily be expected to bring about repeal of undesirable legislation, is to be subjected to more exacting judicial scrutiny." Number 4 was a statement of future intent that Justice Stone had no real justification making in the context of the case at hand, except to make the rule in the footnote into law. Such

2 Owen M. Fiss, "Forward: The Forms of Justice," *Harvard Law Review* 93 (1979): 6; Michael C. Dorff and Samuel Isacharoff, "Can Process Theory Constrain Courts," *University of Colorado Law Review* 72 (2001): 926; J. M. Balkin, "The Footnote," *Northwestern University Law Review* 275 (1988–89): 284; Lewis F. Powell Jr., "*Carolene Products* Revisited," *Columbia Law Review* 82 (1982): 1087; Bruce Ackerman, "Beyond *Carolene Products*," *Harvard Law Review* 98 (1985): 714. The "strict scrutiny" test is another prudential (judicially invented) measure of the constitutionality of a state law. It required that the state legislature must have passed the law to further a "compelling governmental interest," and must have narrowly tailored the law to achieve that interest.

judicial legerdemain was worthy of a Chief Justice John Marshall, and Stone must have known it.[3]

The origin of the footnote, according to one source, lay in the vagueness of a celebrated case immediately preceding, *Palko v. Connecticut* (1937), and its author, the aging but still brilliant Justice Benjamin Cardozo. In *Palko*, Cardozo performed a feat that can only be compared to Chief Justice John Marshall's in *Marbury v. Madison* (1803). He stated a new rule of "ordered liberty" for incorporation of portions of the Bill of Rights in the Fourteenth Amendment and then protected the intervention by denying Palko's plea for relief. Palko claimed that Connecticut's subjecting him twice to trial was double jeopardy, barred by the Fifth Amendment. Cardozo opined that double jeopardy was not part of the regime of ordered liberty.[4]

An old Connecticut statute allowed the court of errors to give the prosecution permission to retry a convict for a more serious crime than that for which he or she had been convicted. Palko was convicted of murder in the second degree by a jury, and the state asked and gained permission from the court to retry him, upon which he was convicted of murder in the first degree, a capital crime. Palko appealed. His counsel claimed that the Fourteenth Amendment incorporated the portion of the Fifth Amendment against double jeopardy. On its face, this incorporation would have voided the Connecticut law. The state argued that the first trial had not heard his confession. While the jury panel was being assembled for the second trial, he made his appeal. It was overruled, and the second trial jury found him guilty of the more serious offense. The state's court of errors affirmed the second jury verdict.[5]

But Palko's counsel had not stopped there. He argued that the entirety of the guarantees (amendments one through eight) was incorporated. Cardozo was adamant: "There is no such general rule." So what? If the

---

3 The entire footnote is much longer. United States v. Carolene Products. 304 U.S. 144, 155 (Stone, J.).

4 Palko v. Connecticut, 302 U.S. 319, 325 (1937) (Cardozo, J.). In Marbury v. Madison (1803) Chief Justice Marshall found that Marbury was entitled to the commission given him by President John Adams, but the court could not provide relief sought because the case was improperly brought to the court. Hence, the pronouncement of judicial review in his opinion was unchallengeable. This and the following passages derived from Peter Charles Hoffer, *Reading Law Forward: The Making of a Democratic Jurisprudence from John Marshall to Stephen G. Breyer* (Lawrence: University Press of Kansas, 2023), 194–98.

5 302 U.S. at 322 (Cardozo, J.).

expansive argument was not justified (because incorporation was, after all, prudential), did that rule out the narrower argument about double jeopardy? *Hurtado v. California* (1884) found that trial for capital crimes need not be by indictment. An "information" would suffice. As the court had found in *Twining v. New Jersey* (1908), the Fifth Amendment barred self-incrimination. Trial by jury had similarly been omitted from the list of incorporated rights. As poorly reasoned and offensive to modern law as one may find these decisions today, they were sufficient precedent should the court apply them in *Palko*. Had Cardozo merely done that, the case would have been of little interest and his opinion far shorter. But then, what would happen to the court's incorporation of other parts of the Bills of Rights?

> On the other hand, the due process clause of the Fourteenth Amendment may make it unlawful for a state to abridge by its statutes the freedom of speech which the First Amendment safeguards against encroachment by the Congress—or like freedom of the press—or the free exercise of religion—or the right of peaceable assembly, without which speech would be unduly trammeled—or the right of one accused of crime to the benefit of counsel.

What made these rights different? They had been found, according to Cardozo, "to be implicit in the concept of ordered liberty, and thus, through the Fourteenth Amendment, become valid as against the states."[6]

Now he looked to the future of incorporation: "So it has come about that the domain of liberty, withdrawn by the Fourteenth Amendment from encroachment by the states, has been enlarged by latter-day judgments to include liberty of the mind as well as liberty of action." Again, by what means or process? "The extension became, indeed, a logical imperative when once it was recognized, as long ago it was, that liberty is something more than exemption from physical restraint, and that, even in the field of substantive rights and duties, the legislative judgment, if oppressive and arbitrary, may be overridden by the courts." Due process became ordered liberty, those "fundamental

---

6 302 U.S. at 325 (Cardozo, J.).

principles of liberty and Justice which lie at the base of all our civil and political institutions." Individual liberty prevails when it is part of the foundations of the polity.[7]

The problem for Stone and others who wanted to extend the realm of ordered liberty beyond criminal procedure was the vagueness of the term itself. Was there any way to make ordered liberty more specific? *Carolene Products* provided an opportunity, not in terms of criminal justice subject matter but in mere propinquity. In short, it came at the right time.

The case itself was something of an overreach by the whole-milk lobby against its much smaller rival, the filled, or skim, or condensed milk companies. The battle began in the first decade of the century, as evaporated milk came on the market. Various state legislatures, pressed by the dairy industry, barred the filled milk as unhealthy. These laws were sometimes upheld by state supreme courts. Whether the filled milk was an adulterated product or simply a cheaper version of milk was debated in these state cases, with the dairy industry experts gradually winning the day.[8]

The Filled Milk Act of Congress of March 4, 1923, defines the term *filled milk* as meaning any milk, cream, or skimmed milk, whether condensed, dried, or otherwise processed, to which has been added or which has been blended or compounded with any fat or oil other than milk fat so that the resulting product is in imitation or semblance of milk, cream, or skimmed milk, whether condensed, dried, or otherwise processed. In short, this was canned milk with low or no milk fat. Today, it is familiar as Carnation or other brands (as the Filled Milk Act was held unconstitutional in 1972). In 1923, the federal government stepped in with the Filled Milk Act banning interstate commerce in the product as "an adulterated article of food, injurious to the public health, and its sale constitutes a fraud upon the public." The defendant, Carolene, shipped one of its products, Millnut, "a compound of condensed skimmed milk and coconut oil made in the imitation or semblance of condensed milk or cream" across a state line.[9]

---

7 302 U.S. at 328 (Cardozo, J.).
8 Geoffrey P. Miller, "The True Story of Carolene Products," *Supreme Court Review* (1987): 397–428.
9 United States v. Carolene Products, 304 U.S. 144, 145 (1938).

The defense fell back on the tried-and-true line (at least before 1937) that the "the statute was beyond the power of Congress over interstate commerce, and hence an invasion of a field of action said to be reserved to the states by the Tenth Amendment." This was the argument in a wide variety of cases during the Taft court. "Appellee also complains that the statute denies to it equal protection of the laws and, in violation of the Fifth Amendment, deprives it of its property without due process of law, particularly in that the statute purports to make binding and conclusive upon appellee the legislative declaration that appellee's product 'is an adulterated article of food injurious to the public health and its sale constitutes a fraud on the public.'"[10]

Stone dismissed the defendant's constitutional argument as if this were the first, rather than the last, in a long line of cases over the past year in which the court deferred to the federal government. For the overturning of the reign of the conservatives on the court who opposed legislation like the Filled Milk Act was now complete. Justice Owen Roberts was finally on board with Stone and the other liberal justices, Justice Willis Van Devanter had been replaced by Justice Hugo Black, Justice James McReynolds was ill, and Justice George Sutherland was near retirement. The victory for the New Deal Democrats in Congress was almost too easy, and Stone treated it as a foregone conclusion. The logical steps in his opinion were easily explained: the power to regulate interstate commerce extended to the prohibition of certain goods. "The power "is complete in itself, may be exercised to its utmost extent, and acknowledges no limitations other than are prescribed by the Constitution." Medical and other expert evidence provided by the dairy industry and accepted by Congress proved that adulterated milk products were inherently dangerous. Deferring to these findings, "Congress is free to exclude from interstate commerce articles whose use in the states for which they are destined it may reasonably conceive to be injurious to the public health, morals or welfare."[11]

---

10 304 U.S. at 147 (Stone, J.).

11 304 U.S. at 148 (Stone, J.). Note how expert testimony or expert opinion in briefs from science, medical authorities, and other nonlegal sources was entering mainstream constitutional writing. Christopher M. Milroy, "A Brief History of the Expert Witness," *Academic Forensic Pathology* 7 (2017): 516–26. The current standard is to be found in Daubert v. Merrell Dow Pharmaceuticals, Inc., 509 U.S. 579 (1993).

Stone was not quite finished. There came next one of those tangled passages of legal writing that today still bewilders the lay reader and must have left even members of the bar scratching their heads: "There is no need to consider it here as more than a declaration of the legislative findings deemed to support and justify the action taken as a constitutional exertion of the legislative power, aiding informed judicial review, as do the reports of legislative committees, by revealing the rationale of the legislation." The sentence featured two dangling participles clinging perilously to the initial clause. The sentence started out with a simple example of deference to legislative findings and spun into judicial review and the rationale of the legislation. One had to presume that Stone was restating the "rational basis test"—if the purpose of the legislation were legitimate (here, the health of milk users) and the statute rationally related to the purpose, then it passed constitutional muster. But while readers were trying to untangle this sentence, Stone hit them with an even more dense proposition: "Even in the absence of such aids, the existence of facts supporting the legislative judgment is to be presumed, for regulatory legislation affecting ordinary commercial transactions is not to be pronounced unconstitutional unless, in the light of the facts made known or generally assumed, it is of such a character as to preclude the assumption that it rests upon some rational basis within the knowledge and experience of the legislators." The operative phrase was "is to be presumed." That was a lot of discretion to hand to state and federal legislators, and Stone realized it had to be curbed. Hence the twist in the case—grant the discretion in the body of the opinion, and then limit it in the footnotes. So here appeared footnote 4.[12]

Footnote 4, with the embedded citations removed:

---

12 304 U.S. at 149 (Stone, J.). Compare S. C. v. Barnwell Brothers, 303 U.S. 177 (1938), decided a few weeks earlier: "That since the adoption of one weight or width regulation, rather than another is a legislative not a judicial choice, constitutionality is not to be determined by weighing in the judicial scales the merits of the legislative choice and rejecting it if the weight of evidence presented in court appears to favor a different standard" 303 U.S. 191 (Stone, J.). Stone suggested that the state regulation of weight and width of trucks on its highways had a rational basis and did not trigger a more stringent constitutional test. Its footnote 2 hinted that something more on the "different standard" was coming. "Underlying the stated rule has been the thought, often expressed in judicial opinion, that, when the regulation is of such a character that its burden falls principally upon those without the state, legislative action is not likely to be subjected to those political restraints which are normally exerted on legislation where it affects adversely some interests within the state."

[part 1] There may be narrower scope for operation of the presumption of constitutionality when legislation appears on its face to be within a specific prohibition of the Constitution, such as those of the first ten amendments, which are deemed equally specific when held to be embraced within the Fourteenth.

[2] It is unnecessary to consider now whether legislation which restricts those political processes which can ordinarily be expected to bring about repeal of undesirable legislation is to be subjected to more exacting judicial scrutiny under the general prohibitions of the Fourteenth Amendment than are most other types of legislation. On restrictions upon the right to vote . . . on interferences with political organizations, . . . as to prohibition of peaceable assembly . . .

[3] Nor need we enquire whether similar considerations enter into the review of statutes directed at particular religious . . . or national . . . or racial minorities . . . whether prejudice against discrete and insular minorities may be a special condition, which tends seriously to curtail the operation of those political processes ordinarily to be relied upon to protect minorities, and which may call for a correspondingly more searching judicial inquiry.[13]

The cases cited after the first part were *Stromberg v. California* (1931) and *Lovell v. Griffin* (1938). Both cases featured Chief Justice Charles Evans Hughes's opinions for the court. In the first, Hughes reversed the conviction of Yetta Stromberg, a member of the Young Communist League, under a California law making it a crime to display a red flag in a public place. The place was a summer camp that was run by the league. Hers was symbolic speech protected by the First Amendment. In the second case, Alma Lovell was distributing Jehovah Witness pamphlets door to door in Griffin, Georgia, in violation of a city ordinance requiring prior permission. Chief Justice Hughes's opinion for the court found that the ordinance was in violation of the First Amendment, and he reversed her conviction. With these two cases as support, the first part of the footnote implied that some "specific" rights under the Constitution infringed by the states triggered greater scrutiny by the court.[14]

---

13 304 U. S. at 155 (Stone, J.).
14 Stromberg v. California, 283 U.S. 350 (1931); Lovell v. Griffin, 303 U.S. 444 (1938).

But the next two parts were of a different order. They were negatively phrased, the court declining to say "which legislation" is to fall under the rubric of the first part of the footnote. According to the second part of the footnote, some categories of legislation, in particular "right to vote . . . on interferences with political organizations, . . . as to prohibition of peaceable assembly," seemed to belong to the category. The third part, again proceeding by negation (it is not necessary to say at this time, but . . .), added, "statutes directed at particular religious . . . or national . . . or racial minorities." When "prejudice against discrete and insular minorities . . . curtail the operation of those political processes ordinarily to be relied upon to protect minorities," then heightened scrutiny "may" be appropriate.

What had happened? A footnote that began as an attempt to rein in deference to legislatures would end as something very different. To understand this transformation, one needs to realize that it had not one but three authors: Justice Stone, his clerk, Louis Lusky, a native of Louisville, Kentucky, and Chief Justice Hughes. Stone was another New Englander on the court, but he was far more liberal than Gray and Brewer. Named to the court in 1925 by President Calvin Coolidge, Stone, intellectually inclined (he was a professor and then dean of Columbia Law School) and capable of great warmth and friendship (Coolidge had been his classmate at Amherst), was then the US attorney general. On the court, Stone demonstrated time and again that he could hold his own with any of his brethren, sometimes driving Chief Justice William Howard Taft to distraction. Expected to be as conservative as his predecessor, Justice Joseph Mckenna, Stone would instead join with Justices Louis Brandeis and Oliver Wendell Holmes Jr. to form a liberal minority on the court. His opinions would become the bedrock of a new kind of substantive due process based not on property but on democratic empowerment.[15]

Like Gray, Stone had been a law professor, and by this time, the justices were hiring law "clerks" from prestigious law schools to assist them in research. Since 1937, a majority of the court had become willing to allow federal and state regulation of the economy, but looming on the horizon was another kind of state case for the court, the civil rights case. These had periodically appeared since the Civil War, and the court had routinely, though not always, deferred to state legislators. Stone and

---

15 Alpheus T. Mason, *Harland Fiske Stone: Pillar of the Law* (New York: Viking, 1956), 184f.

Lusky took this occasion to differentiate deference in economic regulation from deference when minority individual rights were concerned.
Note that the original version cited cases as though the precepts of the
footnote were already established—a stricter scrutiny of legislation
when fundamental rights were at stake.[16]

Lusky, who later claimed to have written a first version of parts two and
three of the note and put it into the draft (or would have, before a fellow
clerk urged caution), insisted that he never drafted something that Stone
did not want. An honor graduate of Columbia Law School, where Stone
had taught, and was for a time dean, Lusky was one of Stone's clerks in
the new 1937 term. Stone accepted some of the note but revised it. Lusky
claimed that he was the author of the "discrete and insular minorities" terminology, which might explain why that part of the note read awkwardly.
Whether he or Stone added the note to the opinion, in another twist of the
note's status, what they had done amounted to a "caveat"—an objection to
the holding of the opinion itself. Stone admitted this: "I wish to avoid the
possibility of having what I have written in the body of the opinion about
the presumption of constitutionality in the ordinary run of due process
cases applied as a matter of course to those other more exceptional cases.
For that reason it seemed to me desirable to file a caveat in the note, without, however, committing the Court to any proposition contained in it."
Recall that the opinion deferred to Congress. Now came a note that suggested exceptions to that deference. For this, Lusky gave credit to Stone,
however. "About four months later [after *Palko*] Justice Stone, writing for
the Court in *United States v. Carolene Products*, undertook to articulate a
more satisfactory justification" for not deferring.[17]

Hughes wanted Stone to think about that footnote. Lusky recalled,
"Hughes sent back a [memo] proposing a different approach for the Foot-
note. 'Are the 'considerations' different,' asked the Chief Justice, 'or does
the difference lie not in the test but in the nature of the right invoked?'"
Here was an idea quite foreign to the original submission. Some rights,
Hughes was suggesting, deserve more judicial attention than others be-

---

16 Williamjames Hull Hoffer, *Schechter v. U.S. and the New Deal* (Lawrence: University Press of
Kansas, 2024), passim.
17 Louis Lusky, *Our Nine Tributes: The Supreme Court in Modern America* (New York: Preager,
1993), 177–78, 180; Milner S. Ball, "The Judicial Protection of Powerless Minorities," *Iowa Law
Review* 59 (1974), 1061–62n5; Louis Lusky, *By What Right: A Commentary on the Supreme Court's
Power to Revise the Constitution* (Charlottesville, VA: Michie, 1975), 108–9.

cause they are mentioned in the text of the Constitution, even though the text, on any fair interpretation, had fallen short of affording the protection the court was now asked to provide. Lusky provided further explanation: "The implicit assumption is that this recognition of their special significance by the revered Framers will legitimize extraordinarily intrusive judicial review as implementing the intent of the Framers themselves. The dynamics of government play no part in the calculus." This was Lusky acting as another author of the footnote:

> I shall take a moment to reflect on the ease with which Stone responded to the Hughes proposal. One might suppose that Stone would have received with consternation, or with distaste, or at least with regret, the news that little dictum had evoked a rival rationale for preservation of the landmark civil liberties precedents. One might suppose that he must have thought himself confronted with a Hobson's choice-to win the Chief to his own rationale; or to accept the Chief's; or to see the Chief follow the example of [Justice Hugo] Black and Butler, which would have left Stone with only three of the seven sitting justices. That he saw no need for any of these responses reveals a basic fact (to be identified presently) that commentators have overlooked with virtual unanimity, though it ought to be plain on the face of the published Footnote.

To wit: the first part of the note was pure Hughes, while the second and third parts were revised versions of Stone.[18]

Hughes had served on the court from 1910 to 1916, when he unsuccessfully ran for president. He then served as US secretary of state when President Herbert Hoover named Hughes to replace the retiring William Howard Taft. Hughes's nomination sparked acrimonious debate in the Senate. On February 24, 1930, eleven days after he was confirmed, liberal senators like William Borah, George Norris, Robert La Follette, and Burton Wheeler denounced Hughes for representing oil companies and other major corporations. None of these critics doubted Hughes's integrity or ability, but all worried that another conservative chief justice would only continue in Taft's path. By contrast, conservative south-

---

18 Louis Lusky, "Footnote Redux: A *Carolene Products* Reminiscence," *Columbia Law Review* 82 (1982): 1097–98.

ern senators were concerned that Hughes might be too liberal. Hughes proved all the doubters wrong. His patrician bearing and personal dignity, along with a sense of his own historical importance, added gravity to the court. Louis Brandeis in particular appreciated the new chief's evenhandedness. Hughes moved the conference along expeditiously, cutting off tangential comments, something that Taft, for all his businesslike manner, could not manage. Hughes did not hold private conferences at home with a select few of the members, a practice that Taft adopted. At oral argument, Hughes was at his best, keeping counsel on their toes and turning the occasion into a genuinely informative event.[19]

According to Lusky, Stone thought that he was elucidating settled doctrine. Perhaps Hughes did not think the same way, so the conjoining of their views was responsible for the awkward structure of the footnote. It seemed to be both a promise and a done deal. Lusky concluded that the footnote tried to do too much and had been a failure. So a third twist of fate is added to the reputation of "the footnote." It was not Stone's at all but a collaborative effort. Which makes a final twist so ironic. There were only seven members of the court who took part in the case. Newly appointed Justice Stanley Forman Reed had argued the case for the government as its solicitor general, and Justice Cardozo was too ill to participate. James McReynolds dissented. Justice Pierce Butler did not agree to the opinion but only the result. Justice Hugo Black signed on, but not to part 3, which had the footnote. Thus Stone had only Justices Brandeis, himself nearing retirement, Owen Roberts, who had lately voted with the more conservative justices, and the chief justice concurring in the entire opinion.[20]

* * *

Whoever was ultimately credited, the note is famous not just for its presumption but because it raised still unanswered questions about judicial activism and restraint, deference, minimalism, and the role of judges and the anti-majoritarian dilemma. Stone himself relied on the first part of the footnote in his dissents in *Minersville School District v. Gobitis*

---

19 Timothy L. Hall, *Supreme Court Justices* (New York: Facts on File, 2001), 247–51; William G. Ross, *The Chief Justiceship of Charles Evans Hughes: 1930–1941* (Columbia: University of South Carolina Press, 2007), 219–20; Lawrence Wrightsman, *Oral Arguments before the Supreme Court: An Empirical Approach* (New York: Oxford University Press, 2008), 39.
20 Lusky, "'Reminiscence,'" 1099. Also see Bruce Ackerman, "Beyond *Carolene Products*," 713–46.

(1940) and *Jones v. Opelika* (1942). He did not see the protection of Jehovah Witnesses freedom of speech as judicial activism.[21]

Long after Hughes and Stone had passed from the scene, the battle over the meaning and use of the footnotes continued in law reviews. Indeed, one of the most striking features of the law reviews' accounts of footnote 4 is the compelling need to retell its story. Every generation of law professors, Supreme Court justices, and court watchers seems compelled to revisit the authorship and meaning of the footnote. One thinks of the injunction at the Passover seder to retell the story of the Exodus every year, but with new commentary from the meal's participants.

Lusky, by now himself a law professor at Columbia Law School, saw the two parts of the footnote introducing the "germs" of both the "preferred freedoms" and the "process" doctrines. The first he found in part 1 and the second in the remainder. In later years, he worried that the footnote may have sent the court on unjustified activist forays. He even suggested that Stone's concession to Hughes made the footnote internally inconsistent. Bruce Ackerman found the parts of the footnote at war with one another, for some minorities have more than their share of political influence, or at least an "enormous bargaining advantage" in a system where many interest groups compete for favorable treatment. What was more, the footnote never did define minority. In 1991, Daniel Farber and Philip Frickey wondered if *Carolene Products* was "dead"—not the filled milk issue but the question of minorities' lack of political clout. For real- world evidence rather than a public choice or other abstract model that Ackerman adopted did not conform to the continuing debility of some minorities. But if this was so, then was not the footnote an empty vessel for social change? In 1995, Peter Linzer worried that Lusky, and even more so John Hart Ely, were wrong to narrow the implications of the footnote, seeing it as a "representation reinforcing" doctrine rather than what it was to Stone and his cohort, a misrepresentation curbing doctrine. Then, Barry Cushman reminded all of us that the holding of *Carolene* was about very broad deference to congressional acts.[22]

---

21 Minersville School District v. Gobitis, 310 U.S. 586 (1940); Jones v. Opelika, 316 U.S. 584 (1942); Peter Linzer, "The *Carolene Products* Footnote and the Preferred Position of Individual Rights: Louis Lusky and John Hart Ely vs. Harlan Fiske Stone," *Constitutional Commentary* 12 (1995): 302.
22 Lusky, *By What Right?* 111, 353. The "process school" or legal process doctrine, most associated with Harvard Law School and the teachings of Henry Hart and Albert Sacks there, argued that decisions of government institutions ought to be assigned to each branch according to its

Over time, the reputation of the footnote has waxed and waned. While a Lusky 2000 essay progressively revealed his authorship, Lusky himself backed away from the strongest claims of the footnote's originality. In effect, his recollections added another caveat to those in the footnote itself. If, as he finally implied, he had been the originator of the footnote, Lusky's increasingly fulsome accounts of his own role in the footnote had not clarified Stone's or Hughes's positions, at least not for later commentators; they still debated whether the footnote was a starting point or a settled point. In an example of original intent interpretation (for more on which, see chapter 7), observers tried to answer the question by asking what Stone and Hughes had in mind. Was Stone the originator of the concept of preferred rights, or was Hughes? Although part 1 of footnote 4 came from Hughes, he stood with the majority in *Gobitis*, when Stone, citing part 1 of the footnote, dissented. Curiouser and curiouser. Stone believed in judicial restraint, but that did not restrain his dissent in *Gobitis*.[23]

While the scholars were having a field day with the footnote, the court, after Stone had departed, did not often cite the case or its footnote 4. But whatever one thinks of the unending inquiry into which constitutional theory the footnote best fits or can be made to fit, one cannot find *Carolene Products* without its footnote 4. The amount of commentary it has occasioned truly makes it "the footnote." This is significant. For there is no better proof that a footnote can become law, even when the precedent is amended or discarded.[24]

---

constitutional function and the decisions of courts within that system and ought to be based on neutral principles and reasoned elaboration. Herbert Wechsler, "Toward Neutral Principles of Constitutional Law," *Harvard Law Review* 73 (1959): 1–35. The best and most comprehensive account of the school is G. Edward White, *The Law in American History* (New York: Oxford University Press, 2019), 3:352–66.

23 Mathew Perry, "Justice Stone and Footnote 4," *George Mason University Civil Rights Law Journal* 6 (1996): 48–49; Felix Gilman, "The Famous Footnote Four: A History of the *Carolene Products* Footnote," *South Texas Law Review* 46 (2004): 163–244; Ackerman, "Beyond *Carolene Products*," 723; Daniel A. Farber and Philip P. Frickey, "Is *Carolene Products* Dead?: Reflections on Affirmative Action and the Dynamics of Civil Rights Legislation," *California Law Review* 79 (1991): 701, 704; John Hart Ely, *Democracy and Distrust* (Cambridge, MA: Harvard University Press, 1980), 73–77; Barry Cushman, "Carolene Products and Constitutional Structure," *Supreme Court Review* (2122): 322–23.

24 Dan T. Coenen, "The Future of Footnote Four," *Georgia Law Review* 41 (2007): 825–26. An exception: Cushman, "Carolene Products and Constitutional Structure," 322, 376, on the importance of the case to deference in interstate commerce.

[6]

SOCIAL PSYCHOLOGY

Brown v. Board of Education of Topeka, 347 U.S. 483 (1954)

Footnote 4 to *Carolene* is celebrated, even if it is rarely cited today. By contrast, no footnote caused and has continued to cause as much commotion in the ranks of academic jurisprudents as footnote 11 to *Brown v. Board of Education*. In 1954, that footnote contended with the foremost social, economic, and political dilemma of post–World War II America—racial discrimination and segregation. Although Jim Crow, as it was called, predated the war years, it surely was out of step with the four freedoms for which the country had entered, and had won, the war. But Congress, dominated by long-serving members from segregationist states, could not or would not give force to Reconstruction era civil rights statutes. While President Harry Truman did what he could to relieve segregation in federal workplaces, it fell to the federal courts to hear and decide cases of the unconstitutionality of segregation.[1]

* * *

When the lawyers of the National Association for the Advancement of Colored People Legal Defense Fund (LDF) summoned social scientists like Kenneth Clark to aid in the dismantling of Jim Crow education, there was nothing new in social science evidence in federal litigation. The Brandeis brief had set the precedent; *Carolene Products* rested on allegedly expert evidence that filled milk was dangerous for children. What could have been especially noteworthy about including that evidence as a footnote in the opinion striking down segregated schools? After all, as Chief Justice Earl Warren, the author of the opinion put it,

---

1 Peter Charles Hoffer, *The Search for Justice: Lawyers in the Civil Rights Revolution 1950–1975* (Chicago: University of Chicago Press, 2019), 14–24.

"It was just a note." Why would a different jurist later call it "the most inflammatory English ever in fine print"?[2]

Some footnotes seem to fit nicely into the text, like the Brandeis brief in *Muller*. Some stand out, like footnote 4, gaining the status of a miniature opinion. Some seem stuck to an opinion like a Post-it, asking for but not providing more detailed inquiry. Such was the case with footnote 11 to *Brown v. Board of Education* (1954). The text to which the footnote was attached was plain and persuasive: "A sense of inferiority affects the motivation of a child to learn. Segregation with the sanction of law, therefore, has a tendency to [retard] the educational and mental development of negro children and to deprive them of some of the benefits they would receive in a racial integrated school system. Whatever may have been the extent of psychological knowledge at the time of Plessy v. Ferguson, this finding is amply supported by modern authority."[3]

It's safe to say of footnote 11 that never had a note attracted so much adverse commentary or that a note in an otherwise luminous and sensible decision had suffered so much denunciation. If Chief Justice Warren had anticipated such a response, might he have omitted the note? Hardly, for the material in the note was a vital collateral support to the decision.[4]

On its face, the note does look hastily composed—a list of authorities without any rule for their inclusion (or the exclusion of others) nor any attempt to link their content together in logical fashion. As social science, which relies on the linkage of studies to one another, on replication, and on peer authentication, the note as a whole was not very scientific looking. Moreover, none of the items in it rested on law (although they had been deployed in earlier litigation), much less settled law. Here is the entire text of the footnote:

---

2 Earl Warren quoted in Richard Kluger, *Simple Justice: The History of Brown v. Board of Education and Black America's Struggle for Equality* (New York: Alfred A. Knopf, 1976), 706; J. Harvey Wilkinson, *From Brown to Bakke: The Supreme Court and School Integration, 1945–1978* (New York: Oxford University Press, 1979), 31.

3 Brown v. Board of Education of Topeka 347 U.S. 483, 494 (1954) (Warren, C. J.).

4 Sanjay Mody, "Brown Footnote Eleven in Historical Context: Social Science and the Supreme Court's Quest For Legitimacy," *Stanford Law Review* 54 (2002): 794 (the court did not rely on the studies in the footnote); and Michael Heise, "Brown v. Board of Education, Footnote 11, and Multidisciplinarity," *Cornell Law Review* 90 (2005): 293 (the footnote was "much maligned").

K.B. Clark, "Effect of Prejudice and Discrimination on Personality Devel-
opment" (Mid-century White House Conference on Children and Youth,
1950); Witmer and Kotinsky, *Personality in the Making* (1952), c. VI;
Deutscher and Chein, "The Psychological Effects of Enforced Segrega-
tion A Survey of Social Science Opinion," 26 *J.Psychol.* 259 (1948); Chein,
"What are the Psychological Effects of Segregation Under Conditions of
Equal Facilities?," 3 *Int.J.Opinion and Attitude Res.* 229 (1949); Brameld,
"Educational Costs," in *Discrimination and National Welfare* (MacIver,
ed., 1949), 44–48; Frazier, *The Negro in the United States* (1949), 674–681.
And see generally Myrdal, *An American Dilemma* (1944).

Were the items just citing one another, reinforcing what had become
something of an orthodoxy among liberal social psychologists and so-
ciologists, or were the studies in the note independent confirmations of
a central point, that all other variables being held constant, segregation
was bad for children? A closer reading of the content of the notes suggests that they did align. The entries in the list reinforced one another;
that is, they were a survey of the field, although later commentary from
social psychologists and educational specialists raised questions about
the methodology of the studies, and even about their validity.[5]

The Clark study was the best known of the individual experiments
and the one that LDF lawyers presented during the litigation. Kenneth
and Marie Clark worked closely with the LDF to prepare, replicate, and
testify to the evidence, and their conclusions and served as a liaison to
other social scientists. Their findings were the easiest for nonspecialists
to understand. For example, in preparation for the *Briggs v. Elliott* case
in South Carolina, attorney Thurgood Marshall asked Drs. Kenneth and
Mamie Clark to repeat experiments with school children from Clarendon County, South Carolina. Both psychologists, Kenneth and Mamie
had conducted studies in New York City in the 1930s. In the experiment,
the Clarks handed Black children four dolls. The dolls were the same
except two had a dark skin and two had light skin. The Clarks asked
the children questions such as which dolls were "nice" and which were
"bad" and "which doll is most like you?" The results showed that the

---

5 See, for example, the giant (a page of single spaced references) footnote 9 in John Hart Ely, "If at
First You Don't Succeed, Ignore the Question Next Time: Group Harm in in *Brown v. Board of
Education* and *Loving v. Virginia*," *Constitutional Comment* 15 (1998): 21–218n9.

majority of Black children preferred the white dolls to the Black dolls. The children would say the Black dolls were "bad" and the white dolls looked most like them. To the Clarks, these tests provided proof that segregation gave African American children a sense of inferiority. That sense of inferiority would last the rest of their lives.[6]

In 1949, Helen L. Witmer and Ruth Kotinsky had edited a collaborative report on children's personality, the official fact-finding report of the Midcentury White House Conference on Children and Youth, the fifth in a series that began in 1909. It "differs from the preceding conferences in that it takes into account the 'children's feelings,' their emotional health." It was a supplement to these earlier conferences, "putting to use what is currently known about conditions favoring or obstructing the healthy development of personality." Employing recent findings in social psychology, "It not only seeks to take inventory but also to point towards possible areas of research. The basic assumption of these conferences is that a sound personality is commensurate with a strong democracy." The essays had a strongly negative view of segregation. "Segregation has detrimental psychological effects on members of the segregated groups even if equal facilities are provided."[7]

Max Deutscher and Isidor Chein, with the assistance of Natalie Sadigur (omitted from the note), surveyed other professional authorities on education. The "subjects" thus were the opinions of other experts in the field: "The present report is an attempt to gather the current opinions of social scientists about one aspect of the problem: namely, the psychological effects of enforced segregation, both on the group which enforces the segregation and on the group which is segregated. Since the purpose of the study was to gather material which would be

---

6 Paul L. Rosen, *The Supreme Court and Social Science* (Urbana: University of Illinois Press, 1972), 137–38; Kenneth B. Clark and Mamie P. Clark, "Racial Identification and Preference in Negro Children," in *Readings in Social Psychology*, ed. T. M. Newcomb and E. L. Hartley (New York: Holt, Rinehart & Winston, 1947), 602–11. Later accounts faulted the Clark study for too small a sample (of children, not of dolls). Even at the time, not all of the LDF lawyers wanted to include the doll study. Jack M. Balkin, "*Brown v. Board of Education*: A Critical Introduction," in *What Brown v. Board of Education Should Have Said: The Nation's Top Legal Experts Rewrite America's Landmark Civil Rights Decision*, ed. Jack M. Balkin (New York: New York University Press, 2001), 51. A doll from the study is preserved by the National Park Service, in the Brown v. Board of Education National Park in Topeka, Kansas, along with the commentary herein; see www.nps.gov.
7 H. L. Witmer and R. Kotinsky, eds., *Personality in the Making: The Fact-Finding Report of the Midcentury White House Conference on Children and Youth* (New York: Harper, 1952), 139.

relevant to a court decision, the focus was on aspects pertinent to the legal questions involved." The authors were aware that defenders of segregation argued that were the separate schools truly equal, there would be no detrimental effects of segregation. "It was focused on the effects of enforced segregation when equal facilities are provided for the segregated groups. This qualification may seem unrealistic since there is ample reason for believing that 'equal facilities' represents, at best, a social fiction." Worried about bias in the responses, in particular the fear that they were "leading" the polling group toward a desired response, they "asked the respondents to indicate the bases on which they formed their opinions as to the psychological effects of enforced segregation under conditions of equal facilities." The responses were striking. Among them, "Quite a few respondents refer to the development of submissiveness, martyrdom, feelings of persecution, withdrawal tendencies, self-ambivalence, and so on." At the same time, "A small number of respondents indicate their belief that some individuals gain psychologically from being members of segregated groups while others are harmed thereby. Generally, as in the following instance, these respondents indicate that, in balancing the gains against the losses, the larger number suffer from segregation."[8]

E. Franklin Frazier's pioneering study of Black families in America appeared in 1939 as *The Negro Family in the United States*, a revised version of his 1931 PhD dissertation at the University of Chicago. Expanded in 1949 as *The Negro in the United States*, it was a classic sociology of prejudice. Born and bred in the Jim Crow South, Frazier knew personally the toxic effects of segregation in education. In 1937, the Carnegie Corporation commissioned a study of segregation from the Swedish social scientist Gunnar Myrdal, who traveled through the South and conducted interviews that revealed much of what Frazier had encountered as a native. Published in 1944 as *An American Dilemma: The Negro Problem and American Democracy*, the work located the problem not with people of color but with deeply entrenched

---

8 Max Deutscher, Isidor Chein, and Natalie Sadigur, "The Psychological Effects of Enforced Segregation: A Survey of Social Science Opinion," *Journal of Psychology*, 26 (1948): 260, 269, 274, 276. Note that one of the findings, that some respondents preferred segregated settings, would be the basis for criticism of *Brown* in some quarters. See, for example, Derrick Bell, "Dissenting," in Balkin, *What Brown v. Board of Education Should Have Said*, 185–200.

racism. The two works constituted an indictment of social and economic oppression that could not be ignored.[9]

* * *

To understand why footnote 11 was not only apposite but necessary in
Brown, one has to return to the immediately preceding history of the
"school cases" in the federal courts and then turn to Warren's opinion for
the court in *Brown*. The LDF had won in a series of graduate school cases,
but in 1951, the LDF, led by Thurgood Marshall, changed its strategy: it
would try to end segregation in public school K–12 cases. It was in this
context of limited expectations of support from the state and federal judiciary in the South that the LDF nevertheless moved its focus from the area
of graduate and professional education to the instruction of the young
and impressionable. Jack Greenberg recalled that the LDF called these the
"school cases," and Thurgood Marshall was somewhat hesitant to bring
them. He wanted to win, for losing gave a foothold to the segregation-
ists. But the odds looked long. "The old dilemma reappeared: to fight for
equalization or for an end to segregation." Members of the Black communities were divided, reckoning that white resistance to desegregation
would be immediate and violent or that true equalization was better for
minority interests than desegregation. Local Black lawyers were similarly
of two minds. Some lagged behind the LDF decision, but Marshall convinced them to join the battle for desegregation. It was important to lead
but not to go "so far ahead" that the local lawyers would not follow.[10]

In a second change of strategy, the South Carolina, Virginia, and
Kansas cases went not to state courts, then on constitutional grounds
to the federal courts, but directly to federal district courts in which the
LDF directly attacked "separate but equal." State courts were unlikely to
overturn state constitutions or state statutes on federal constitutional
grounds, although they could apply federal law if they wished. Federal

---

9 E. Franklin Frazier, *The Negro Family in the United States* (Chicago: University of Chicago Press,
1939); Gunnar Myrdal, *An American Dilemma: The Negro Problem and American Democracy* (New
York: Harper and Brothers, 1944). The impact of the two books within the social sciences and the
media was immense. See, for example, Andrea G. Hunter, "Teaching the Classics in Family Studies: E.
Franklin Frazier's *The Negro Family in the United States*," *Family Relations* 55 (2006): 90; William J.
Barber, *Gunnar Myrdal: An Intellectual Biography* (New York: Palgrave Macmillan, 2008), 64–74, 79.
10 Jack Greenberg, *Crusaders in the Courts* (New York: Basic Books, 1994), 116–32. Additional
material in this section derived from Hoffer, *Search for Justice*, 53–84.

courts were only slightly more amenable to voiding state law on federal grounds, but because the LDF sought injunctive relief against the state, federal civil procedure required the empaneling of a three-judge court. One or more of those judges might be willing to rule in favor of the plaintiffs. Even if the panel upheld the state law, appeal from the three-judge panel went directly to the US Supreme Court, and that is exactly where Marshall wanted to go.[11]

In the school cases, lower federal courts in South Carolina, Virginia, and Kansas upheld state-mandated separation of the races. All but one of the judges in these courts, J. Waties Waring of South Carolina, averred that they were bound by earlier Supreme Court decisions. They had no discretion to rule otherwise. Only the Supreme Court could overrule its own precedents. In the Kansas case, *Brown v. Board of Education of Topeka*, the state permitted school districts to segregate or integrate. Topeka chose to segregate its elementary schools. The three-judge federal court, assembled under the Three-Judge Court Act, that heard *Brown* would not override the state law and would not order white schools to admit Black students. As Tenth Circuit judge Walter Huxman, a former Democratic governor of the state, wrote for his brethren on the *Brown* district panel, "As a subordinate court in the federal judicial system, we seek the answer to this constitutional question in the decision of the Supreme Court when it has spoken on the subject and do not substitute our own views for the declared law by the Supreme Court." In a later interview, Judge Huxman revealed that "there was no way around" *Plessy*, but he hoped that the Supreme Court would find a way. Petitioners appealed his decision to the Supreme Court. *Brown* was the lead case, joined by the court with three other cases, from South Carolina, Virginia, Delaware, and another from the District of Columbia decided at the same time.[12]

---

11 The requirement that only a three-judge panel could enjoin a state from obeying its own laws originated in the Progressive Era, part of the complex effort to regulate railroad freight rates. When states passed various acts creating commissions to do this, railroad companies sought injunctive relief in federal courts against the imposition of the state laws. The Mann-Elkins Act (Three Judge Panel Act of 1910), 36 Stat. 557, was a response. Later cases limited its application in criminal matters, deferring to state court interpretations of state law. Note, "The Three-Judge Court Act of 1910 Purpose, Procedure and Alternatives," *Journal of Criminal Law, Criminology, and Police Science* 62 (1971): 205–19.

12 Brown v. Board of Education of Topeka, 98 F. Supp. 797, 798 (D.C. D. Kans. 1951) (Huxman, J.); Kluger, *Simple Justice*, 424.

The three-judge district court that heard and decided *Briggs v. Elliott*, with an opinion by circuit judge John J. Parker, found that the facilities for Black students in South Carolina's rural Clarendon County schools were not equal, but the reason was not discrimination so much as the economic deficiencies of the Clarendon County region. Marshall—along with Robert Carter, Spottswood Robinson, and local attorney Harold R. Boulware of Columbia, South Carolina—led the plaintiff's case, relying on the expert witness testimony that Marshall had helped pioneer in the graduate school cases. Kenneth Clark, for example, repeated his Black dolls/white dolls test with children from the Clarendon district and found that the Black children once again thought the white dolls were good and the Black dolls were bad.

On the other side of the aisle, Robert McCormick Figg—a longtime Charleston, South Carolina, politician representing the state alongside its attorney general, T. C. Callison—insisted that the outside academic experts were not qualified to speak to the conditions or the attitudes of a rural South Carolina county. Instead, the court should listen to the county's former school superintendent, E. R. Crow, currently the director of the South Carolina Educational Finance Commission. Marshall cross-examined, seeking to know whether the state would actually close its public schools rather than desegregate them. Would the government refuse to obey an order to desegregate if such were issued? No answer. Marshall won the day but not the case.[13]

Judge John J. Parker, joined by district judge George Bell Timmerman, was not persuaded to order desegregation. Parker was a distinguished jurist, had served on the Fourth Circuit Court of Appeals from 1925 to 1958, the last ten years of which he was its chief judge, and had been nominated for a seat on the Supreme Court in 1930. There is some evidence that President Eisenhower had considered Parker for the center seat of the high court when Chief Justice Fred Vinson died. A born and bred North Carolinian, he did not hide his sympathy for the defeated South, telling one gathering of Georgia lawyers, "When I think of the lawyers of Georgia . . . whom I know and love and respect, . . . I think also of the great figures who have added glory to this bar in the

---

13 Material here and after adapted from Hoffer, Hoffer, and Hull, *The Federal Courts*, 352–64; and Hoffer, *Search for Justice*, 52–84.

past . . . Judge [T. R. R.] Cobb . . . and Alexander H. Stephens. . . . I feel
that their spirits still linger here and that their presence add to the dignity of all your deliberations." Cobb had written the Confederate States
of America Constitution and Stephens had served as the vice president
of the CSA. Parker's opinion rested on local knowledge, a set of supposed facts that he shared with judges like McClendon and Timmerman. "The defendants contend, however, that the district is one of the
rural school districts which has not kept pace with urban districts in
providing educational facilities for the children of either race, and that
the inequalities have resulted from limited resources." Governor James
F. Byrnes and the state legislature had promised in the future to make
up the difference, although no positive steps had been taken. Nevertheless, as equity presumed good faith on the part of the defendant state
(petitioners sought injunctive relief), Parker continued, "How this shall
be done is a matter for the school authorities and not for the court, so
long as it is done in good faith and equality of facilities is afforded."
Petitioners had asked the federal courts to provide appropriate relief.
Parker replied, "One of the great virtues of our constitutional system is
that, while the federal government protects the fundamental rights of
the individual, it leaves to the several states the solution of local problems. . . . Local self-government in local matters is essential to the peace
and happiness of the people in the several communities." The "peace
and happiness" Parker cited referred to the potential for white violence
against Black people if the court should order the end of segregation,
an argument that would be repeated by southern officials for the next
twenty years. He did, however, order the state to equalize facilities in
Clarendon County. A few years earlier, the LDF might have counted this
as a victory. When, six months later, the state reported tentative financial
steps toward compliance, Judge Parker was content that the state had
fulfilled its constitutional obligations: "There can be no doubt that as a
result of the program in which defendants are engaged the educational
facilities and opportunities afforded Negroes within the district will, by
the beginning of the next school year in September 1952, be made equal
to those afforded white persons."[14]

---

14 Briggs v. Elliott, 98 F. Supp. 529, 531, 532 (E.D. S.C. 1951) (Parker, J.); Briggs v. Elliott, 103 F. Supp.
920, 922 (E.D. S.C. 1952) (Parker, J.).

None of this persuaded the dissenter on the panel, district judge Waring. He was educated in Charleston, the descendant of Confederate leaders, a son of the South deeply wedded to its traditions. He practiced law
in Charleston for nearly forty years before Franklin D. Roosevelt named
him to the District Court of the Eastern District in 1942. By the time
the case came to the district court, he recalled that he had become frustrated by the injustice of separate and invariably unequal laws. After listening to Thurgood Marshall argue the case for the petitioners, Waring
grew impatient with Judge Parker's temporizing, and his dissent hinted
what everyone in the courtroom and on the bench knew or should have
known—South Carolina had no more intention of equalizing its educational facilities for the two races than it did of abolishing segregation
itself. "If this method of judicial evasion be adopted, these very infant
plaintiffs now pupils in Clarendon County will probably be bringing
lawsuits for their children and grandchildren decades or rather generations hence in an effort to get for their descendants what are today denied to them." In effect, he was accusing his brethren of conspiring with
the state government to deny the petitioners their long overdue rights.
Waring did not agree with Parker when the state reported its plan for
equalization, writing to Parker that he would not sign off on anything
short of the end of segregated schools. For his courage, Waring was ostracized by polite society and threatened by racist terrorists, ultimately
leaving the court and the city for northern climes. In the meantime,
plaintiffs appealed to the Supreme Court.[15]

Prince Edward County in Virginia exhibited much the same socioeconomic and demographic characteristics as Clarendon County, South
Carolina. Fifty miles west of Richmond, today the county is still largely
rural and poor. Race relations there were not as hostile as in Clarendon,
but in 1951, Black students refused to attend schools admittedly inferior
in physical plant, curricula, and transportation to local white schools. In
Dorothy E. Davis, et al. v. County School Board of Prince Edward County
(1952), the district court ordered the defendants forthwith to provide
substantially equal curricula and transportation but would not order the

---

15 Christopher W. Schmidt, "J. Waties Waring," in *The Yale Biographical Dictionary of American
Law*, ed. Roger K. Newman (New Haven, CT: Yale University Press, 2009), 570–71; Tinsley
Yarbrough, *A Passion for Justice: J. Waties Waring and Civil Rights* (New York: Oxford University
Press, 1987), 195–97, 208; 98 F. Supp., at 540 (Waring, J.).

end of the discriminatory system itself. The petitioner's attorney, Spottswood Robinson III (later a judge in the District Court and then the Court of Appeals for the District of Columbia) argued that "Virginia's separation of the Negro youth from his white contemporary stigmatizes the former as an unwanted, that the impress is alike on the minds of the colored and the white, the parents as well as the children, and indeed of the public generally, and that the stamp is deeper and the more indelible because imposed by law." Robert L. Carter led the examination of expert witnesses, including Kenneth Clark, that segregation stigmatized Black children. Arguing for the state, Attorney General J. Lindsay Almond disparaged such witness testimony. He had attended the *Briggs* hearing and seen how South Carolina had failed to undermine the LDF experts' credentials. He did not make the same mistake. He "led the fight" for segregation, he later recalled, but "mine was not a spirit of defiance." After all, he was a lawyer and, as such, tried to "find some legal avenue of accommodation." In his three-page opinion for the defendants, Judge Albert Bryan did not find that Robinson's argument or Carter's witnesses' testimony compelled a desegregation order. To his thinking and that of the other members of the three-judge court, Armistead Dobie and C. Sterling Hutcheson, there was sufficient evidence from "distinguished and qualified educationists and leaders in the other fields" that separate and truly equal would not stigmatize Black students. Custom trumped any disparity in expert evidence. "Separation of white and colored 'children' in the public schools of Virginia has for generations been a part of the mores of her people. To have separate schools has been their use and wont." Bryan, a Truman nominee in 1947, knew whereof he spoke. He was born, bred, and educated in eastern Virginia. President Kennedy would name him in 1961 for the Fourth Circuit, where he sat until his death in 1984.[16]

* * *

When the cases came to the high court, Chief Justice Warren had the four cases from Delaware, Kansas, South Carolina, and Virginia

---

16 Davis v. County Sch. Bd., 103 F. Supp. 337, 338, 339 (D.C. E.D. Va. 1952) (Bryan, J.); Peter Irons, *Jim Crow's Children: The Broken Promise of the Brown Decision* (New York: Viking, 2002), 88, 90, 93; J. Lindsay Almond, "Oral History," February 7, 1968, John F. Kennedy Library, Boston, Massachusetts, 4.

joined, while a fifth, concerning the District of Columbia, was included in the decision under the Fifth rather than the Fourteenth Amendment. The decision in *Brown v. Board of Education* was unanimous, the lobbying efforts of Chief Justice Warren bringing on board all of his colleagues. That story is remarkably well told in Richard Kluger's *Simple Justice*, and it needs no elaboration here. But the role of the chief was central. When Chief Justice Vinson, Warren's predecessor, presided over the first round of arguments in 1952, he was not entirely persuaded by the LDF arguments. His death opened the way to Warren's storied career as chief justice, the opinion in *Brown* heralding the Warren era.

Warren was born in 1891 in Los Angeles and raised in Bakersfield, California. After graduating from the University of California, Berkeley School of Law, he began a legal career in Oakland. He was hired as a deputy district attorney for Alameda County in 1920 and was appointed district attorney in 1925. He emerged as a leader of the state Republican Party and won election as the attorney general of California in 1938. In that position, he supported, and was a firm proponent of, the forced removal and internment of over one hundred thousand Japanese Americans during World War II. In the 1942 California gubernatorial election, Warren defeated incumbent Democratic governor Culbert Olson. He served as governor of California until 1953, presiding over a period of major growth for the state. Warren is the only governor of California to be elected for three consecutive terms. Warren served as Thomas E. Dewey's running mate in the 1948 presidential election, but Dewey lost the election to incumbent Harry S. Truman. Warren sought the Republican nomination in the 1952 presidential election, but the party nominated General Dwight D. Eisenhower. After Eisenhower won election as president, he appointed Warren as chief justice. Little did anyone expect that Warren had moved so firmly to the liberal side of civil rights jurisprudence, but he had.[17]

The decision was controversial in some ways, as older precedent seemed to lie on the other side, and it reversed the rulings of four of the five lower appeals courts. But the message was clear enough—

---

17 Peter Charles Hoffer, Williamjames Hull Hoffer, and N. E. H. Hull, *The Supreme Court: An Essential History*, 2nd ed. (Lawrence: University Press of Kansas, 2018), 335–37. G. Edward White, *Earl Warren, A Public Life* (New York 1982), 9–158.

segregation of elementary schools violated the Fourteenth Amendment. In a recent assessment, legal historian G. Edward White has called the opinion "short on legal analysis." Perhaps, but the opinion did not rest on the notes. Warren had delegated to one of his clerks, Earl F. Pollock, to add the notes, in a manner similar to Stone's delegation to his clerk in *Carolene*. The placement of footnote was not a critical matter. Pollock recalled, "The only reason to have to include footnote #11 was as a rebuttal to the cheap psychology of *Plessy* that said inferiority was only the in the mind of the Negro." But Pollock made it clear that it was the decision of the chief justice to add the note. The only real pushback on the court was concern that the inclusion of Myrdal's work would ruffle the feathers of some southerners. Why did the opinion need the note anyhow? Pollock's explanation was not included, of course. But the note was part of Warren's thinking.[18]

Chief Justice Warren's relatively brief opinion for a unanimous court may be the most cited and certainly the nearly canonical text in the court's literature. He keenly felt the burden of history, for precedent seemed to lie in the other direction. He could not ignore it. But the claim of the petitioners lay in the future. An examination of the operative parts of the opinion shows how the footnote served to bridge the chasm between past and future:

> In each of the cases, minors of the Negro race, through their legal representatives, seek the aid of the courts in obtaining admission to the public schools of their community on a nonsegregated basis. In each instance, they had been denied admission to schools attended by white children under laws requiring or permitting segregation according to race. This segregation was alleged to deprive the plaintiffs of the equal protection of the laws under the Fourteenth Amendment. In each of the cases other than the Delaware case, a three-judge federal district court denied relief to the plaintiffs on the so-called "separate but equal" doctrine announced by this Court in *Plessy v. Ferguson*, 163 U. S. 537. Under that doctrine, equality of treatment is accorded when the races are provided substantially equal facilities, even though these facilities be separate.

---

18 White, *Law in American History*, 3:358; Kluger *Simple Justice*, 705–6.

Looking at the past, "The plaintiffs contend that segregated public schools are not 'equal' and cannot be made 'equal,' and that hence they are deprived of the equal protection of the laws."[19]

The burden of history lay not only in the law but in the practice of elementary education in the South, where "the movement toward free common schools, supported by general taxation, had not yet taken hold. Education of white children was largely in the hands of private groups. Education of Negroes was almost nonexistent, and practically all of the race were illiterate. In fact, any education of Negroes was forbidden by law in some states." Then, Warren leaped to the present and the future. Assumptions about the natural abilities of Blacks that may have underlaid the ill treatment of the race as a whole had been dispelled. "Today, in contrast, many Negroes have achieved outstanding success in the arts and sciences, as well as in the business and professional world."[20]

Next, back he went to the time of the ratification of the Fourteenth Amendment, as the pro-segregation counselors had argued that segregation then was understood to be permissible. That attitude, counsel for the segregated school systems insisted, should control present and future schools. Times were different then, Warren countered, and in any case, there was little evidence that the issue of segregation was on the minds of the drafters or ratifiers of the amendment:

> It is true that public school education at the time of the [Fourteenth] Amendment had advanced further in the North, but the effect of the Amendment on Northern States was generally ignored in the congressional debates. Even in the North, the conditions of public education did not approximate those existing today. The curriculum was usually rudimentary; ungraded schools were common in rural areas; the school term was but three months a year in many states, and compulsory school attendance was virtually unknown. As a consequence, it is not surprising that there should be so little in the history of the Fourteenth Amendment relating to its intended effect on public education.[21]

---

19 347 U.S. at 487 (Warren, C.J.).
20 347 U.S. at 489, 490 (Warren, C.J.).
21 347 U.S. at 491 (Warren, C.J.).

Warren's opinion remained in the past, following the course of the rise of Jim Crow in the schools with the appearance of Jim Crow in the courts. "The doctrine of 'separate but equal' did not make its appearance in this Court until 1896 in the case of *Plessy v. Ferguson, supra,* involving not education but transportation. American courts have since labored with the doctrine for over half a century. In this Court, there have been six cases involving the 'separate but equal' doctrine in the field of public education." All of these precedents were supportive of the doctrine of separation.[22]

Then came the more recent cases of segregation of law schools and graduate schools. Here the outcome was different, although the doctrine survived the challenge. The schools were not equal and could not be made equal. Warren's travel through the history of separate but equal finally brought him to the present. That present was profoundly and irreversibly different from the past. Warren's conclusion was that "in approaching this problem, we cannot turn the clock back to 1868, when the Amendment was adopted, or even to 1896, when *Plessy v. Ferguson* was written. We must consider public education in the light of its full development and its present place in American life throughout the Nation. Only in this way can it be determined if segregation in public schools deprives these plaintiffs of the equal protection of the laws." The problem was how to make constitutional law follow the leap that attitudes had already made, at least in most of Americans' minds.[23]

The answer was to link law to related disciplines, education, and its allied fields, social psychology and sociology. A functional theory of law (after all, Warren was a politician as well as a judge) would serve—look at the job that law does rather than the barren words of the law:

Today, education is perhaps the most important *function* of state and local governments [italics added]. Compulsory school attendance laws and the great expenditures for education both demonstrate our recognition of the importance of education to our democratic society. It is required in the performance of our most basic public responsibilities, even service

---

22 Plessy v. Ferguson, 163 U.S. 537 (1896). The Fourteenth Amendment equal protection clause could not force "comingling of the races on terms unacceptable to either." 163 U.S. at 544 (Brown, J.).
23 347 U.S. at 492, 493 (Warren, C. J.).

in the armed forces. It is the very foundation of good citizenship. Today it is a principal instrument in awakening the child to cultural values, in preparing him for later professional training, and in helping him to adjust normally to his environment. In these days, it is doubtful that any child may reasonably be expected to succeed in life if he is denied the opportunity of an education. Such an opportunity, where the state has undertaken to provide it, is a right which must be made available to all on equal terms.[24]

Thus, when Warren returned to the present time, to ask, "Does segregation of children in public schools solely on the basis of race, even though the physical facilities and other 'tangible' factors may be equal, deprive the children of the minority group of equal educational opportunities?," the footnote pulled its weight. "We believe that it does. . . . [citing the cases of graduate schools and law schools]. Such considerations apply with added force to children in grade and high schools. To separate them from others of similar age and qualifications solely because of their race generates a feeling of inferiority as to their status in the community that may affect their hearts and minds in a way unlikely ever to be undone." The last sentence looked to a future in which the impact of segregated education was permanent. Nothing in the legal pleadings did or could prove this. But social psychology findings did exactly that. Which is why footnote 11, or something like it, was essential.[25]

One sees how the need for evidence for the tortious effect of segregation in the hearts and minds of the children had to be part of the opinion. Social psychology and sociology bound present and future harms together:

> Segregation of white and colored children in public schools has a detrimental effect upon the colored children. The impact is greater when it has the sanction of the law, for the policy of separating the races is usually interpreted as denoting the inferiority of the negro group. A sense of inferiority affects the motivation of a child to learn. Segregation with the sanction of law, therefore, has a tendency to [retard] the educational

---

24 347 U.S. at 493 (Warren, C.J.).
25 347 U.S. at 494 (Warren, C.J.).

and mental development of negro children and to deprive them of some
of the benefits they would receive in a racial[ly] integrated school system. . . . Whatever may have been the extent of psychological knowledge
at the time of *Plessy v. Ferguson*, this finding is amply supported by modern authority. Any language in *Plessy v. Ferguson* contrary to this finding
is rejected.

And this is where, in the opinion, footnote 11 appeared.[26]

Putting the social psychology citations in the footnote protected
them as well as the text of the opinion. They were not exiled so much as
quarantined. Separate, they provided evidence for what Warren argued,
without being part of the argument or subject to any of its weaknesses.
That is, after all, what footnotes do best.

The excursus through social science complete, Warren retuned to
the purely legal conclusion: "We conclude that, in the field of public
education, the doctrine of "separate but equal" has no place. Separate
educational facilities are inherently unequal. Therefore, we hold that the
plaintiffs and others similarly situated for whom the actions have been
brought are, by reason of the segregation complained of, deprived of
the equal protection of the laws guaranteed by the Fourteenth Amendment. This disposition makes unnecessary any discussion whether such
segregation also violates the Due Process Clause of the Fourteenth
Amendment."[27]

* * *

In retrospect, there is one part of the footnote that deserves a little more
attention. It is not the citations themselves but the "and see generally."
Although it looks like a boilerplate introduction to the Myrdal book,
linked to that particular book it functions very differently. It is a reminder
about the moral purpose of the footnote. For Myrdal had argued that
segregation undermined the very foundations of American democracy.
Written in 1944, when white and Black Americans fought against tyranny
throughout the world, Myrdal's point was clear: democracy could not
survive long in a nation divided against itself by racism. How much more

---

26 347 U.S. at 494 (Warren, C.J.).
27 347 U.S. at 495 (warren, C.J.).

potent was that observation in a world fragmented by the Cold War. Segregation was the strongest tool that Soviet communists had against democracies. "And see generally" turned Myrdal's warning into a brooding omnipresence that overshadowed all the other references.[28]

All this said, one must remember that unlike the social science testimony deployed throughout the litigation, the footnote itself was added at the very end of the drafting process of the opinion after the May 1954 court vote on the cases. It was not quite an afterthought as we have seen, but it was also not central to Warren's manufacturing of unanimity. That is, he had everyone on board before he asked Pollock to add the footnote. It cannot be said, thus, that it had a great deal to do with the vote by the members. If for no other reason, this was grounds to call Warren the "super chief."[29]

But many court watchers thought that Warren had overstepped by including footnote 11. In *The Supreme Court and Social Sciences*, Paul L. Rosen collected these criticisms. South Carolina governor James F. Byrnes, a former member of the court himself, whose support for segregated schools was manifest in *Briggs v. Elliott* (1952), questioned the "loyalty to the United States" of the authors of the dolls findings. Neighboring Georgia's governor Herman E. Talmadge, like Byrnes a lawyer, sneered, "Who are these authorities? What is their background?" Others were more responsible, for example political scientist Alpheus Mason, in decrying the absence of judicial precedents and the reliance on "two of the flimsiest of all our disciplines—sociology and psychology—as the basis for the decision." Ten years later, Paul Freund of Harvard Law School, an acolyte of Felix Frankfurter, found that the use of "sociological writings is open to question." As a statement of fact, that certainly was true—many had questioned it. The complaint would reappear in the Declaration of Constitutional Principles, the so-called Southern Manifesto of 1956.[30]

28 See, for example, John Minor Wisdom, "Random Remarks on the Role of Social Science in the Judicial Decision-Making Process in School Desegregation Cases," *Law and Contemporary Problems*, 39 (1975): 139.

29 See, for example, Dennis Hutchinson, "Unanimity and Desegregation: Decisionmaking in the Supreme Court, 1948–1958," *Georgia Law Journal* 68 (1979): 40–42, 87 (it was Warren's assembling of a unanimous court rather than the opinion that was critical); Bernard Schwartz, "Chief Justice Earl Warren: Super Chief in Action," *Tulsa Law Journal* 33 (1997): 483–84.

30 Rosen, *Social Science*, 175, 177. See also Robin Bernstein, *Racial Innocence: Performing American Childhood from Slavery to Civil Rights* (New York: New York University Press, 2011), 197 ("deep flaws" in the tests); and James R. Acker, "Thirty Years of Social Science in Supreme Court Opinions

The Southern Manifesto's implicit sociological theory was the antithesis of the explicit sociological theory in *Brown*, proving that the manifesto's authors' dismissal of the social science in *Brown* did not deter them from resorting to social factoids when these supported their views. "[Our] interpretation, restated time and again, became a part of the life of the people of many of the States and confirmed their habits, traditions, and way of life. It is founded on elemental humanity and commonsense, for parents should not be deprived by Government of the right to direct the lives and education of their own children." The invocation of both local autonomy and tradition was not especially southern; one could find it in the customs and culture of the many regions of the nation. It often elided the suppression of minorities, however, as the "life of the people" was not inclusive and diverse but exclusive and homogeneous. The opposite view was characteristic of urban localities, where many different cultures met. The South, however, was at this time still not heavily urbanized and, more important, its politics retained a rural character. It was this view of the world, and the law, that had no place for footnote 11.[31]

---

in Criminal Cases," *Law and Policy* 12 (1994): 1–24 (social science rarely used in Supreme Court opinions).

31 *Congressional Record*, 84th Congress, Second Session, vol. 102, part 4 (March 12, 1956) (Washington, DC: Governmental Printing Office, 1956), 4459–60; on the origins, see E. L. Forrester to Richard Russell, August 5, 1955, Richard Russell Collection, box 21, folder 1, Russell Library for Political Research and Studies, University of Georgia Libraries, Athens. For the comments on sociology, see Hoffer, *Search for Justice*, 114.

[7]

ORIGINALISM

District of Columbia v. Heller, 554 U.S. 570 (2008)

The first time the court heard *Brown* in 1952 it asked counsel to research segregation in the era of the Fourteenth Amendment but later decided that the historical record was not useful. "We cannot turn back the clock to 1868," Chief Justice Warren explained. The arrival on the docket of *District of Columbia v. Heller* (2008) marked a reversal of the *Brown* approach, a commitment to historical evidence that the court in *Brown* explicitly declined to adopt. The issue in *Heller* was not civil rights but gun control, as violence in the cities had replaced state-mandated segregation as one of the most pressing issues for federal and local government. The reliance on historical research had gained a name— originalism—and the project was perfectly aligned with the growing importance of footnotes, for footnotes contained the evidence to support originalist constitutionalism. "The *Brown* Court did not employ originalism." The *Heller* court wallowed in it. Indeed, *Heller*'s many footnotes seemed to signal a new era when footnoting on the court would determine the outcome of litigation.[1]

* * *

Originalism, not surprisingly, has a history of its own. In one sense, it goes back to the authors of the *Federalist Papers*, a series of newspaper op-ed pieces that James Madison, Alexander Hamilton, and John Jay wrote to convince members of the New York State constitutional Ratification Convention to vote yea. Their eighty-one essays examined the

---

1 483 U.S. at 492 (Warren, C.J.); Ronald Turner, "On Brown v. Board of Education and Discretionary Originalism," *Utah Law Review* (2015): 1144; Jamal Green, "*Heller* High Water?: The Future of Originalism," *Harvard Journal of Law and Policy* 3 (2009): 325. The decision not to rely on the history of the Fourteenth Amendment in *Brown* is traced in Richard Kluger, *Simple Justice: The History of Brown v. Board of Education and Black America's Struggle for Equality* (New York: Random House, 1975), 614–16, 654–55, 679–80.

draft federal Constitution and gave meaning to its clauses using evidence from history. Two of the authors were the original originalists; having taken part in the drafting of the Constitution, they could speak to both the intent of the framers (which in the main, they had concealed) and the public meaning of the document. The important point for today's student of these essays is that they were not unbiased originalists; they advocated at the same time as they interpreted. This has been true of their heirs. Political scientists, historians, journalists, politicians, and, yes, judges who return to historical texts are not always disinterested in their findings. Or in their method.[2]

Originalism is not another version of "neutral principles." It has never been neutral in the way that Herbert Wechsler or others defined that doctrine. First came law professor Robert Bork, whose "Neutral Principles and Some First Amendment Problems" sounded the alarm of a missing interpretive doctrine: "A persistently disturbing aspect of constitutional law is its lack of theory, a lack which is manifest not merely in the work of the courts but in the public, professional and even scholarly discussion of the topic. The result, of course, is that courts are without effective criteria and, therefore we have come to expect that the nature of the Constitution will change, often quite dramatically, as the personnel of the Supreme Court changes." Candidates for that doctrine flocked to his standard. They warned about a judiciary unrestrained by fidelity to original texts. Attorney General Edwin Meese, in 1985, suggested that "the text of the document and the original intention of those who framed it should be the judicial standard in giving effect to the Constitution." Critics on the left and supporters on the right joined ranks as original intent became public meaning. The rest is (law office) history.[3]

Naked originalism, termed original intent, that lawyers and judges could somehow divine the minds of the framers, has been exploded so thoroughly by historians that even its original advocates had to retreat to

---

2 The *Federalist Papers* are by far the most frequent outside evidence the Supreme Court cites, 34 percent of the total of from 1955 to 1984. Pamela C. Corley, Robert M. Howard, and David C. Nixon, "The Supreme Court and Opinion Content: The Use of the Federalist Papers," *Political Research Quarterly* (2005): 330.

3 Lawrence B. Solum, "District of Columbia v. Heller and Originalism," *Northwestern Law Review* 103 (2009): 927–33; Robert Bork, "Neutral Principles and some First Amendment Problems," *Indiana Law Review* 47 (1971), 1; Edwin Meese, "Toward a Jurisprudence of Original Intent" *Public Administration Review*, 45 (1985): 701–4.

an alternative—the plain meaning or public versions of originalism. One looked at the text the way that contemporaries looked at it, and their understanding should be the understanding of lawyers and judges two hundred years later. The problem remained that plain meaning still required historical investigation. The lawyers and judges were, in the main, ill trained and inexperienced in that sort of investigation, although the lack of expertise did not stop some of them from trying. In general, they turned to historians and political scientists hired by one or the other party. The history these hirelings (apologies, but this term is the most appropriate one) produced, familiar to anyone who watched the expert witnesses in tobacco and other mass products liability cases, always supported the hiring parties' position. Derided as law-office history by those not in the pay of the law firms, it is still a staple of litigation.[4]

Originalism at present has many followers and many formulas, but central to all of them is strict fidelity to constitutional text. Critics ask whether this is ever possible when the intent of the text's authors cannot be determined with certainty. Defenders reply that contemporary understandings of the language of the texts suffice to fix their meaning. Whichever position one adopts, precedent—the authority of older cases—is central to common-law jurisprudence; reading the law forward is unorthodox, but actually part of the common-law tradition. That is, the common law has proven itself capable of growth from within. This tension is present in constitutional adjudication.[5]

The authority of the originalist jurisprudent, like that of the historian, comes from the search through primary sources. These were the texts of journals, newspapers, diaries, court records, and wills. The originalist does not just present evidence; they must interpret it. That is, it

---

4 See, for example, Paul Brest, "The Misconceived Quest for the Original Understanding," *Boston University Law Review* 60 (1980): 214–17; Laura Kalman, "Border Patrol: Reflections on the Turn to History in Legal Scholarship," *Fordham Law Review* 66 (1997): 87–124; Saul Cornell, "Heller, New Originalism, and Law Office History: Meet the New Boss, Same as the Old Boss," *University of California Law Review* 56 (2009): 1095–1126.

5 The literature on originalism is explored in Jack M. Balkin, *Living Originalism* (Cambridge, MA: Harvard University Press, 2011). Balkin's work was reviewed by Lawrence Solum in "Construction and Constraint," *Jerusalem Review of Legal Studies* 7 (2013): 17–34. In a sophisticated linguistic essay, Solum sees originalism as a "family" of theories, although the term *clade* might be more appropriate, all of which concern (but none settle) the vexing question of constraining the discretion of judges. A new start on the problem is William Baude, "Is Originalism Our Law?," *Columbia Law Review* 115 (2015): 2349–2408.

must be compared, contextualized, and synthesized to find meaning. No one could deny that historical study was vital to understanding the gun control issue. Insofar as the constitutional right to own and bear arms rests on a 1789 proposed amendment to the Constitution that was included in the Bill of Rights ratified by the states in 1791, the interpretation of the text of the Second Amendment is crucial to the adjudication of gun ownership cases. That interpretative doctrine is nowhere found in the Constitution, and certainly not in the Second Amendment itself. In other words, there has to be a rubric or rule for reading the text. And the source of that rule is the court itself. Originalism is a "prudential" doctrine, that is, the doctrine adopted by some members of the court in the gun control case, among others.[6]

Observers, including law professors and political scientists, agree that *Heller* was a supernova of originalist analysis. All the opinions in it engaged in careful and thorough historical argument, as did the subsequent academic literature. "Never had the Court considered in such depth the question of how historical sources should be used in constitutional interpretation." What was more, *Heller* was "the most explicitly and self-consciously originalist opinion in the history of the Supreme Court." None of the scholarly or popular accounts focused on the unique role of the footnotes to the opinions, however. This and the following chapter undertake that enterprise. Note that this and the subsequent chapter do not focus on a single footnote. Instead, it is the structure of a series of footnotes, appearing in two different but related opinions, that concerns us.[7]

---

6 See, for example, Saul Cornell, "Right to Carry Firearms outside of the Home: Separating Historical Myths from Historical Realities," *Fordham Urban Law Journal* 39 (2012), 1695–1726.

7 A close second, in my opinion, would be Chief Justice Roger Taney's flawed review of history of citizenship in *Dred Scott v. Sandford*, 60 U.S. 393 (1857). *Heller* was also the catalyst for law review articles on originalism. See, for example, Rory K. Little, "*Heller* and Constitutional Interpretation: Originalism's Last Gasp," *Hastings Law Journal* 60 (2008), 1414–30; Cass R. Sunstein, "Second Amendment Minimalism, *Heller* as *Griswold*," *Harvard Law Review* 122 (2008): 246–74; Mark Tushnet, "*Heller* and the New Originalism," *Ohio State Law Journal* 69 (2008): 609–24; Marc Spindelman, "Some Early Views on *District of Columbia v. Heller*," *Ohio State Law Journal* 69 (2008), 603–8; Saul Cornell "Originalism on Trial: The Use and Abuse of History in *District of Columbia v. Heller*," *Ohio State Law Journal* 69 (2008): 625–40; Reva B. Siegal, "*Heller* and Orignalism's Dead Hand—In Theory and Practice," *UCLA Law Review* 56 (2009): 1399–1424; Jeffrey M. Shaman, "The End of Originalism," *San Diego Law Review* 47 (2010), 83–108. *MacDonald v. City of Chicago*, 561 U.S. 742 (2010), spurred a second burst of articles. See, for example, Saul Cornell, "Meaning and Understanding in the History of Constitutional Ideas: The Intellectual History

* * *

While various states and municipalities have legislated on handgun ownership, carry, and licensing, the ultimate source of the right is the Second Amendment to the US Constitution. The Fourteenth Amendment is assumed by the court, under its prudential doctrine of incorporation, to impose the Bill of Rights, of which the Second Amendment is a part, on the states. The District of Columbia is not a state, so the Second Amendment, presumably, applies directly to it. For the originalist, the meaning of the language of the amendments dictates the resolution of litigation on gun ownership and its allied issues. But who is to determine meaning of the constitutional texts, and by what rules? Is the right a collective one, relating to membership in the militia (that is, some organized and official military body of the state) or an individual right? If the latter, who are the individuals who may assert this right? Need they be citizens? Adults? Can they be former felons? Mentally ill? These questions were not all answered by *Heller*, where the court majority relied on originalism to affirm for the first time that the Second Amendment guarantees an individual right to possess firearms.[8]

Predictably, the academic literature on the history of gun control anticipating *Heller* was voluminous. The footnotes in the case captured the vigorousness of the prior scholarly debate. The notes also showed that the justices very selectively read (and cited) the history. In other words, the only history that mattered was that supporting the justices' own, sharply divergent, views. Thus, only a small part of the articles, books, op-eds, and official reports made it into the briefs of counsel, the amicus briefs, and the justices' opinions. These secondary sources quoted from primary sources—contemporary eighteenth- and early nineteenth-century accounts of gun use and gun control. They were genuine—the historians who joined the briefs and even those who just signed on believed that what they wrote was true—the

---

Alternative to Originalism," *Fordham Law Review* 82 (2013): 721–56; Joshua Stein, "Historians before the Bench: Friends of the Court, Foes of Originalism," *Yale Journal of Law & the Humanities* 25 (2013): 359–90; Rebecca Piller, "History in the Making: Why Courts Are Ill-Equipped to Employ Originalism," *Review of Litigation* 34 (2015), 187–212; and Lorianne Updike Toler, J. Carl Cecere, and Don Willett, "Pre-Originalism," *Harvard Journal of Law and Public Policy* 36 (2013): 279.
8 District of Columbia v. Heller, 554 U.S. 570 (2008).

paradox of which is that the majority of historians these days don't believe in the objective truth of historical accounts.[9]

No one was more associated with the doctrine of originalism on the court than Justice Antonin Scalia. He had been a law professor before he joined the court, and one sees all the skills of the law professor in his fashioning of the footnotes in *Heller*. But his oftentimes adversary on the court, Justice John Paul Stevens, was also an able footnoter, and to his aid had come scholarly briefs in support of gun control. The justices saw one another's drafts, and so their footnotes referred to each other's text and footnotes. Scalia often drafted his own opinions, and Stevens almost always did. The result was a running contest within the court, much as one might see in actual trials, but this time the stakes were might higher.[10]

Scalia was born in Trenton, New Jersey, the only child in a devoutly Roman Catholic Italian family. He carried that fidelity to the church throughout his life. He won scholarships to parochial school and to Georgetown University and was a brilliant law student at Harvard Law School. In the early 1970s, he served in the Richard Nixon and Gerald Ford administrations. During the presidency of Jimmy Carter, Scalia taught at the University of Chicago Law School, where he helped to found the Federalist Society. The Ronald Reagan administration was looking for bright conservative law professors for judicial slots, and in 1982, Scalia was named to the US Court of Appeals for the District of Columbia Circuit. In 1986, he was confirmed for a seat on the US Supreme Court by a vote of ninety-eight to zero. On the court, he was a fierce controversialist, an often compelling writer, who never hesitated

---

9 See, for example, Stein, "Historians before the Bench," 362f. On the gun historians in recent news, see, for example, Shawn Hubler, "In the Gun Law Fights of 2023, a Need for Experts on the Weapons of 1791," *New York Times*, March 14, 2023, www.nytimes.com.

10 On Stevens's opinion writing, see Todd C. Peppers, *In Chambers: Stories of Supreme Court Law Clerks and Their Justices* (Charlottesville: University of Virginia Press, 2013), 396; On Scalia's opinions, see Paul D. Clement, "Why We Read the Scalia Opinion First," *Judicature* 101 (2017), https://judicature.duke.edu: "Although he did ask his law clerks to provide first drafts, he was routinely handed a stone and returned a sculpture. Indeed, his revision was so transformative, and the final product so distinctly Scaliaesque, that I wondered why he bothered asking for a draft at all." On Scalia and originalism, see Scalia, "Originalism: The Lesser Evil," *University of Cincinnati Law Review* 57 (1989): 864: Originalism "establishes a historical criterion that is conceptually quite separate from the preferences of the judge himself. And the principal defect of that approach-that historical research is always difficult and sometimes inconclusive-will, unlike nonoriginalism, lead to a more moderate rather than a more extreme result."

to dissent or to challenge his fellow justices. Intellectually, he was a worthy opponent.[11]

In 1970, President Richard Nixon appointed John Paul Stevens to the United States Court of Appeals for the Seventh Circuit. Five years later, President Gerald Ford appointed Stevens to the Supreme Court to fill the vacancy caused by the retirement of Justice William O. Douglas. Stevens served on the court from 1975 to 2010. His long tenure saw him write for the court on most issues of American law, including civil liberties, the death penalty, government action, and intellectual property. Unlike Scalia, who tended to defer to the executive branch, Stevens wrote that even presidents were to be held accountable to law. Despite being a registered Republican who throughout his life identified as a conservative, Stevens was considered to have been on the liberal side of the court at the time of his retirement.[12]

Pause here for a moment as these two heavy hitters square up against one another over gun control in the District of Columbia. Scalia's opinion's text will be replete with citations. So will Stevens's. Therein one finds precedent, treatise, and historical account. Then ask, Why would they need footnotes? What did the footnotes do that the authorities in the text did not? As one reads the footnotes and sees how many references there were to the other man's views, the need for footnotes, and the purpose of the footnotes, becomes clearer.

Circulation of draft opinions among the justices after the conference, when they reveal their votes on the case, is commonplace. The drafts are then revised according to the justices' responses to one another. It is not quite a collaborative effort, but it is a collective one. The footnotes, added at or near the end of the exchange, constitute a written version of the conversation among the justices. One should start with Scalia's opinion, the draft of which was clearly read in Stevens's chambers. One should remember that the justices' clerks have a hand in finding citations for the footnotes and even writing them, but the result always reflects the views of the justices.[13]

---

11 Peter Charles Hoffer, Williamjames Hull Hoffer, and N. E. H. Hull, *The Supreme Court: An Essential History*, 2nd ed. (Lawrence: University Press of Kansas, 2018), 409–10.

12 Hoffer, Hoffer, and Hull, *Supreme Court*, 375–76.

13 Mark C. Miller, "Law Clerks and Their Influence at the US Supreme Court: Comments on Recent Works by Peppers and Ward," *Law and Social Inquiry* (2014): 1–17; Stephen J. Choi and G. Muti Gulati, "Which Judges Write Their Opinions (and Why Should We Care?)," *Florida State*

＊ ＊ ＊

Scalia began his opinion with the facts of the case: "We consider whether a District of Columbia prohibition on the possession of usable handguns in the home violates the Second Amendment to the Constitution." The District of Columbia had very strict handgun controls. Carrying an unregistered firearm was a crime. Registering handguns without a license to carry was a crime. Lawfully owned long guns (rifles and shotguns) had to be kept home under lock and key. Dick Heller was a special police officer allowed an exception while on duty at the Federal Judicial Center. He wished to register the firearm for personal protection in his home. The district refused, and he sued in federal court (the district has its own federal courts) under the Second Amendment. He lost in the district court but the court of appeals reversed. It was this reversal that the district (the District of Columbia, not the federal district court for DC) appealed to the US Supreme Court.[14]

Scalia turned then to the most important primary (historical) source—the Second Amendment itself. The amendment reads: "A well-regulated Militia, being necessary to the security of a free State, the right of the people to keep and bear Arms, shall not be infringed." Scalia offered a simple formula for interpreting this text—the public usage test. He did not use his own credentials to justify employing this test of meaning, however, but cited prior case law. Why not just say that the court should be guided by what everyone, at the time of the drafting of the Constitution, understood its meaning to be? The answer was that he had read Stevens's opinion, in particular Stevens's footnote 4 (on

---

University Law Review 32 (2005): 1078n3; but see Stephen J. Choi and G. Mitu Gulati, "Choosing the Next Supreme Court Justice: An Empirical Ranking of Judge Performance," *Southern California Law Review* 78 (2004): 52 (judges who rely on their clerks may not have a consistently high quality output of opinions).

In the 2007–08 term of the court, Scalia's clerks were Aditya Bamzai, John F. Bash III, Bryan M. Killian, and Rachel Kovner. Stevens's clerks in that term were Todd Jason Gluth, Sarah J. Klein, Kate Shaw, and Abby C. Wright. In a *New York Times* op-ed piece, on May 31, 2022, Bash and Shaw revealed their roles: "We each assisted a boss we revered in drafting his opinion, and we're able to acknowledge that work without breaching any confidences." Justice Scalia had a practice of signing one opinion for a clerk each term, which permitted the clerk to disclose having worked on that case, and for John, that was Heller; Justice Stevens noted in his 2019 autobiography, *The Making of a Justice: Reflections on My First 94 Years* (New York: Little, Brown, 2019), cccxliv, that Kate Shaw was the Heller clerk in his chambers.

14 544 U.S. at 573 (Scalia, J.).

which see below), and he knew that Stevens's dissent was going to rely on a particular view of public meaning—the meaning that prior courts had given to the amendment and that historians in friends of the court briefs had given to the it. Scalia had to base his reading of the amendment on original sources. From the outset, then, the footnotes heralded a war over the use of history, Scalia relying on his reading of the primary sources, Stevens relying on later interpretations of the primary sources *in* histories and court precedent.[15]

Back to Scalia. We are guided by the principle that "the Constitution was written to be understood by the voters; its words and phrases were used in their normal and ordinary as distinguished from technical meaning. For which, see *United States* v. *Sprague*, 282 *U. S. 716*, 731 (1931); see also *Gibbons* v. *Ogden*, 9 Wheat. 1, 188 (1824)." Scalia used the precedent to support his rule for reading the primary sources rather than his own voice—a nice twist to Stevens's argument, although one would have to read the two opinion's footnotes side by side to appreciate the poke. Then Scalia returned to his preferred use of history in the plain meaning version of originalism: "Normal meaning may of course include an idiomatic meaning, but it excludes secret or technical meanings that would not have been known to ordinary citizens in the founding generation."[16]

---

15 544 U.S. at 576 (Scalia, J.). From the outset, most of the friends of the court briefs were about policy; they were not from historians. Also, not every historian who weighed in on gun control disagreed with Scalia. The preponderance of the historians who did take part supported the Stevens view of the amendment, however. There were nineteen briefs for the district and forty-eight for the challengers to the handgun ban. The so-called historians' brief, drafted by Stanford historian Jack Rakove, an expert in early constitutional history, in particular James Madison's contributions, provided support to Stevens. It was signed by fifteen historians. The "interest" of the signers, required in all acceptable friends of the court briefs, was "Amici curiae have an interest in the Court having an informed understanding of the history that led to the adoption of the Second Amendment." The signers continued: "Historians can best assess these claims by reconstructing the context within which the adopters of the Amendment acted." "Brief of Amici Curiae Jack N. Rakove, Saul Cornell, David T. Konig, William J. Novak, Lois G. Schwoerer et al. in Support of Petitioners," 1, 2. The other signers were Fred Anderson, Carol Berkin, Paul Finkelman, R. Don Higginbotham, Stanley N. Katz, Pauline Maier, Peter S. Onuf, John Shy, and Alan Taylor. None had law degrees. On the other side, historians like Joyce Lee Malcolm offered support to Heller. For a list of the briefs, see Ilya Shapiro, "Friends of the Second Amendment: A Walk through the Amicus Briefs in D. C. v. Heller," *Journal on Firearms and Public Policy*, 20 (2008): 1–27, available through the Cato Institute, www.cato.org. Assuming, for argument's sake, that Rakove, a Pulitzer Prize–winning historian on Madison and the Constitution, knew more about Madison's thinking and that Madison was the driving force behind the Second Amendment, should Rakove's reading of the amendment be more persuasive than Scalia's? Stevens thought so.
16 544 U.S. at 576–577 (Scalia J.).

The conflicting views of the amendment on the court were certainly important then and remain important, but for the purposes of the present essay, it is the way the footnotes interlaced with the text of the opinions to carry the argument beyond the amendment that matters. Scalia knew this. "The two sides in this case have set out very different interpretations of the Amendment. Petitioners and today's dissenting Justices believe that it protects only the right to possess and carry a firearm in connection with militia service. Respondent argues that it protects an individual right to possess a firearm unconnected with service in a militia, and to use that arm for traditionally lawful purposes, such as self-defense within the home."[17]

How to parse the disagreement? Scalia: treat the amendment's words as *the* governing source: "The Second Amendment is naturally divided into two parts: its prefatory clause and its operative clause. The former does not limit the latter grammatically, but rather announces a purpose." If Scalia could find a way to sever the document's two parts, the second could stand scrutiny without the first. But is the amendment "naturally" divided into two parts? Effecting that division (after all, it was not separated by a full stop—a period) would require a lot of parsing. The amendment was not phrased in such a way that the second part automatically depended on the first part. That left an opening, but what could fill it? Scalia tried. "Although this structure of the Second Amendment is unique in our Constitution, other legal documents of the founding era, particularly individual-rights provisions of state constitutions, commonly included a prefatory statement of purpose." Scalia has found an answer in the concept of a preamble. Conventionally, preambles set out the purpose of a resolution but are not part of the command. They are not self-effectuating.[18]

Scalia continued the project of separating the amendment into two parts. The first was the purpose of the amendment, the second

---

17 544 U.S. 577 (Scalia J.).
18 544 U.S. at 577 (Scalia, J.). Scalia cited Eugene Volokh, "The Commonplace Second Amendment," *New York University Law Review* 73 (1998): 814–21, to support his view of the first clause. Volokh was a Scalia law clerk. But see Richard Epstein, "A Structural Interpretation of the Second Amendment: Why *Heller* Is (Probably) Wrong on Originalist Grounds," *Syracuse Law Review* 59 (2008): 173: "The decision of Justice Scalia to treat the [first] phrase as entirely prefatory rests upon his appeal to general canons of statutory construction, which do not hone [*sic*] in on this particular case. This critical move leaves us with two obvious questions. Why put it [the first phrase] in at all?" (9).

was its command. "Logic demands that there be a link between the stated purpose and the command," but logic did not trump language, and the language of the amendment indicated to him that the first clause was purposive and the second was mandatory. Various commentators on the Constitution agreed that a prefatory clause (note how the first part of a single sentence had become a preface) "does not limit or expand the scope of the operative clause." Scalia's sources for this distinction were three nineteenth-century treatises on interpreting statutes; their full identity appeared in the footnote 3. They were not law; they were commentary on how to read law. Nevertheless, he treated them as authorities, and they were crucial to his argument. "Therefore, while we will begin our textual analysis with the operative clause, we will return to the prefatory clause to ensure that our reading of the operative clause is consistent with the announced purpose." How the "therefore" followed from the three secondary sources might not be persuasive. After all, they were not concerned with the federal Constitution, and two of them were English. Hence they were banished to the footnotes.[19]

To respond to Justice Stevens's concerns (and the concerns of others, no doubt) about this linguistic two-step, he added footnote 4: "Justice Stevens criticizes us for discussing the prologue last. But if a prologue can be used only to clarify an ambiguous operative provision, surely the first step must be to determine whether the operative provision is ambiguous." This was circular—the first step would ordinarily be to examine the first clause. Scalia recognized the danger. "It might be argued, we suppose, that the prologue itself should be one of the factors that go into the determination of whether the operative provision is ambiguous—but that would cause the prologue to be used to produce ambiguity rather than just to resolve it." That concern was not sufficient to allay Stevens's criticism. "In any event, even if we considered the prologue *along with* the operative provision we would reach the same result we do today, since (as we explain) our interpretation of

---

19 544 U.S. at 578 (Scalia, J.); "See F. Dwarris, *A General Treatise on Statutes*, 268–69 (P. Potter ed., 1871) (hereinafter Dwarris); T. Sedgwick, *The Interpretation and Construction of Statutory and Constitutional Law* 42–45 (2nd ed. 1874). [*Footnote 3*] "'It is nothing unusual in acts . . . for the enacting part to go beyond the preamble; the remedy often extends beyond the particular act or mischief which first suggested the necessity of the law.'" J. Bishop, *Commentaries on Written Laws and Their Interpretation* § 51, p. 49 (1882) (quoting *Rex* v. *Marks*, 3 East, 157, 165 (K. B. 1802)."

'the right of the people to keep and bear arms' furthers the purpose of an effective militia no less than (indeed, more than) the dissent's interpretation."[20]

Lurking in the background of this decision to sever the parts of the amendment and treat them separately was the rule of interpretation of legal texts originally advanced by Francis Lieber in his *Legal and Political Hermeneutics*. As taught in every law school class on statutory interpretation, it is simply this: read the meaning of any part of a legal document (or constitutional text, one presumes) in the light of the purpose of the entire document. If, as Scalia conceded, the first clause of the amendment was preface, was not the purpose of prefaces to indicate the purpose of the subsequent text? Thus the preamble to the federal Constitution was purposive, not operative, without specific instructions from the body of the Constitution. But one should let this observation remain in the shadows until Stevens threw light on it in his dissent.[21]

Following Scalia through the rest of his opinion was like riding a whirlwind with Scalia holding the reins. On every word in every part of the "Operative Clause" and then the "Prefatory Clause," he imposed his powerful interpretive schema. Go back to the originals, he told the reader, and use evidence from the time to see what the common, public meaning of the words was. Look at comparable, corresponding documents to find similarities. Contemporary dictionaries helped; so did a naïve realist linguistics. His result: one finds individual rights, not collective rights. "We the people" is collective, but it refers to the powers exercised by the government (a collectivity), not to rights. The militia was collective, but it was a separate topic. The meaning of terms like *keep, bear,* and *arms* was similarly easy to find in contemporary sources. Arms were weapons, not just military equipment. For "keep arms," Scalia had to reach out to contemporary English sources. "To bear" meant to carry. Evidence for this was included in the text and spilled over into the footnotes. "From our review of founding-era sources, we conclude that this natural meaning was also the meaning

---

20 544 U.S. at 578–579, fn 4 (Scalia).
21 Francis Lieber, *Legal and Political Hermeneutics, or Principles of Interpretation and Construction in Law and Politics*, 3rd ed. (St. Louis: F. H. Thomas, 1880), 8; first published 1839, C. C. Little and J. Brown (Boston).

that 'bear arms' had in the 18th century. In numerous instances, 'bear arms' was unambiguously used to refer to the carrying of weapons outside of an organized militia."[22]

Routinely, Scalia cited as evidence for his interpretation the terms from contemporary sources in the body of his opinion. What need did he have of footnotes at all? Even when he nitpicked against Stevens, the nits fit inside the opinion. So, for example, "the phrase 'bear Arms' also had at the time of the founding an idiomatic meaning that was significantly different from its natural meaning: 'to serve as a soldier, do military service, fight' or 'to wage war.' Then a citation, in the text: "See Linguists' Brief 18; *post*, at 11 (Stevens, J., dissenting)." Then followed Scalia, commenting on Stevens's comment on Scalia: "But it *unequivocally* bore that idiomatic meaning only when followed by the preposition 'against,' which was in turn followed by the target of the hostilities." He read through the dissents and through the amicus briefs and concluded, "Every example given by petitioners' *amici* for the idiomatic meaning of 'bear arms' from the founding period either includes the preposition 'against' or is not clearly idiomatic."[23]

In the text of the majority opinion, Scalia tore at Stevens's dissent with eager aggression. "In any event, the meaning of 'bear arms' that petitioners and Justice Stevens propose is *not even* the (sometimes) idiomatic meaning. Rather, they manufacture a hybrid definition, whereby 'bear arms' connotes the actual carrying of arms (and therefore is not really an idiom) but only in the service of an organized militia." It was a bravura performance, though hardly one exhibiting the collegiality one might expect of "the brethren." Scalia concluded that parts of the dissent were absurd, incoherent, and "grotesque."[24]

An occasional law review piece from friendly academics graced Scalia's opinion. But the opinion never rested on the citation. It was

---

22 544 U.S. at 584 (Scalia, J.). Linguistic realism is a belief that words are the world. "The basis of linguistic realism is the rejection of words as a means, and the acceptance of them, and other forms of representation, as an end in themselves." Bruce Fleming, "Dogma of the Day," *Montréal Review* (September, 2016), www.themontrealreview.com. Naïve linguistic realism, my own term, is that one need not probe the controversies around linguistic realism to adopt it. If one did not want to adopt this approach, one might read the essays in Christina Behme and Martin Neef, eds., *Essays on Linguistic Realism* (Amsterdam: John Benjamins, 2018).
23 544 U.S. at 586 (Scalia, J.).
24 544 U.S. at 587 (Scalia, J.).

window dressing. Such inclusions are a way of acknowledging support from the academic community. For example, calling up "Barnett, 'Was the Right to Keep and Bear Arms Conditioned on Service in an Organized Militia?', 83 Tex. L. Rev. 237, 261 (2004) and Cramer & Olson, 'What Did "Bear Arms" Mean in the Second Amendment?,' 6 Georgetown J. L. & Pub. Pol'y (forthcoming Sept. 2008), online at http://papers.ssrn.com/abstract=1086176 (as visited June 24, 2008, and available in Clerk of Court's case file)" were gratuitous, actually much like a gratuity. Scalia had already made the point himself. More indicative of his method was "See, *e.g.*, 30 Journals of Continental Congress 349–351 (J. Fitzpatrick ed. 1934)," a barebones historical source—no interpretation necessary.[25]

When Scalia agreed with Stevens, it was to skewer the dissent for making some common logical error. For example, Stevens "points to a study by *amici* supposedly showing that the phrase 'bear arms' was most frequently used in the military context. Of course, as we have said, the fact that the phrase was commonly used in a particular context does not show that it is limited to that context, and, in any event, we have given many sources where the phrase was used in nonmilitary contexts." So the battle of citations amounted, as so many battles do, to the size of the forces engaged. Scalia's army of citations was larger than Stevens's.[26]

According to Scalia, who had by now wandered from his own argument to a relentless engagement with Stevens's, even the latter's particular pieces of evidence were misread. "Justice Stevens places great weight on James Madison's inclusion of a conscientious-objector clause in his original draft of the Second Amendment: 'but no person religiously scrupulous of bearing arms, shall be compelled to render military service in person' [citation omitted]. He argues that this clause establishes that the drafters of the Second Amendment intended 'bear Arms' to refer only to military service: [but] It is always perilous to derive the meaning of an adopted provision from another provision deleted in the drafting process." That telling point was worth elucidation, or, in reality, further pounding on the

---

25 544 U.S. at 587, 588 (Scalia, J.).
26 544 U.S. at 588 (Scalia, J.).

other side. "In any case, what Justice Stevens would conclude from the deleted provision does not follow. It was not meant to exempt from military service those who objected to going to war but had no scruples about personal gunfights." The tone was as derogatory as the correction. But Scalia did not need a footnote to hammer it home. The text of the majority opinion served that function perfectly well.[27]

Last, but hardly least:

> Finally, Justice Stevens suggests that "keep and bear Arms" was some sort of term of art, presumably akin to "hue and cry" or "cease and desist." (This suggestion usefully evades the problem that there is no evidence whatsoever to support a military reading of "keep arms.") Justice Stevens believes that the unitary meaning of "keep and bear Arms" is established by the Second Amendment's calling it a "right" (singular) rather than "rights" (plural). See *post*, at 16. There is nothing to this. State constitutions of the founding period routinely grouped multiple (related) guarantees under a singular "right," and the First Amendment protects the "right [singular] of the people peaceably to assemble, and to petition the Government for a redress of grievances."

The conclusion was, or should have been, obvious: "Putting all of these textual elements together, we find that they guarantee the individual right to possess and carry weapons in case of confrontation."[28]

At this point, and thereafter, Scalia turned to historical examples to show that "the Second Amendment, like the First and Fourth Amendments, codified a *pre-existing* right. The very text of the Second Amendment implicitly recognizes the pre-existence of the right and declares only that it "shall not be infringed." The parade of examples began in England, in 1660, and continued into the twentieth century. In it, primary sources marched in lockstep. Newspaper articles from the eighteenth century passed by the reviewing stand shoulder to shoulder with William Blackstone's *Commentaries* and St. George Tucker's commentaries on the *Commentaries*. "There

---

27 544 U.S. at 589, 590 (Scalia, J.).
28 544 U.S. at 591 (Scalia, J.).

seems to us no doubt, on the basis of both text and history, that the Second Amendment conferred an individual right to keep and bear arms."[29]

This was the easy part. Had the amendment included only the second clause, Scalia would have had to deal only with the limitations on the right. He did this in the last portion of his opinion, in many ways the most important part. For the exceptions he allowed, though vague, were significant, and would have allayed much of the criticism of his opinion had they come at the beginning. If the amendment had been broken in two completely separate parts—two full sentences—then the problem of the prefatory clause would have disappeared. The statement that a well-regulated militia was vital to the security of the country would have stood on its own bottom. But the awkward connection of the two clauses was a source of confusion, an example of poor draftsmanship, and of packing too much into too small a space. In any case, Scalia's prose, so sharp and clear up to now, stumbled in his account of the prefatory clause. He conceded that the definition rested on contemporary usage, and he summarized it in a confused compilation of source materials.

> Although we agree with petitioners' interpretive assumption that "mili-
> tia" means the same thing in Article I and the Second Amendment, we
> believe that petitioners identify the wrong thing, namely, the organized
> militia. Unlike armies and navies, which Congress is given the power to
> create ("to raise . . . Armies"; "to provide . . . a Navy," Art. I, § 8, cls. 12–13),
> the militia is assumed by Article I already to be *in existence.* Congress is
> given the power to "provide for calling forth the militia," § 8, cl. 15; and
> the power not to create, but to "organiz[e]" it—and not to organize "a"
> militia, which is what one would expect if the militia were to be a federal
> creation, but to organize "the" militia, connoting a body already in exis-
> tence, *ibid.,* cl. 16.[30]

---

29 544 U.S. at 592 (Scalia, J.). Had Scalia violated "an elementary rule of any sound historical inquiry" by substituting his own views of the motivations for those of historical actors? Saul Cornell, "Meaning and Understanding in the History of Constitutional Ideas: The Intellectual History Alternative to Originalism," *Fordham Law Review* 82 (2013), 744. In short, was Scalia's review of the history of the second, operative clause, just more law office history? History is common sense, according to many historians, and nothing in Scalia's account of the desire of elite Americans to insure their right to own and bear arms violates common sense.
30 544 U.S. at 596 (Scalia, J.).

Scalia found himself trying to fit military history into an interpretive essay on constitutional law. Why? Because Stevens had done it. The dissent had dragged Scalia into the morass. Thus, because Stevens had explored the term *well-regulated*, Scalia had to mention it. "Finally, the adjective 'well-regulated' implies nothing more than the imposition of proper discipline and training. See Johnson 1619 ('Regulate': 'To adjust by rule or method'); Rawle 121–122; cf. Va. Declaration of Rights § 13 (1776), in 7 Thorpe 3812, 3814 (referring to 'a well-regulated militia, composed of the body of the people, trained to arms')."[31]

Finally, mercifully, "We reach the question, then: Does the preface fit with an operative clause that creates an individual right to keep and bear arms? It fits perfectly, once one knows the history that the founding generation knew and that we have described above." Scalia returned to England, whose "history showed that the way tyrants had eliminated a militia consisting of all the able-bodied men was not by banning the militia but simply by taking away the people's arms, enabling a select militia or standing army to suppress political opponents. This is what had occurred in England that prompted codification of the right to have arms in the English Bill of Rights." This is probably the worst historical summary of the Exclusion Movement, the Monmouth Rebellion, and the Glorious Revolution ever published.[32]

Wisely, Scalia skipped immediately to the American Revolution: "The debate with respect to the right to keep and bear arms, as with other guarantees in the Bill of Rights, was not over whether it was desirable (all agreed that it was) but over whether it needed to be codified in the Constitution." Realizing that his grip over the history of the militia was slipping (it was not the militia that won the War for Independence, it was the Continental Army's regulars and the French expeditionary force), Scalia jumped again (time travel being common in legal briefs and opinions), this time to 1788: "During the 1788 ratification debates, the fear that the federal government would disarm the people in order to impose rule through a standing army or select

---

31 544 U.S. at 597 (Scalia, J.).
32 544 U.S. at 598 (Scalia, J.).

militia was pervasive in Antifederalist rhetoric." But antifederalists did not write the Second Amendment.[33]

For this tangent, which really needed no proof, Scalia offered lots of evidence, although like the point, it was unnecessary. Still, instead of being banished to a footnote, it cluttered the body of the opinion: "It is therefore entirely sensible that the Second Amendment's prefatory clause announces the purpose for which the right was codified: to prevent elimination of the militia." But the point was easily made without any citation of primary sources. "The prefatory clause does not suggest that preserving the militia was the only reason Americans valued the ancient right." So, admit the amendment was poorly drafted and move on. (As a matter of fact, in a separate dissent—with no footnotes— Justice Stephen Breyer offered that individual self-defense is merely a "subsidiary interest" of the right to keep and bear arms. Scalia replied, "But he, like his fellow dissenter, was profoundly mistaken.")[34]

Scalia went on to explore the comparable passages in early state constitutions, cases from the antebellum-period cases after the Civil War, and more modern cases. There is no need to follow his narrative. The point is clear. There was enough in the body of the opinion without any footnotes to elide the need for footnotes entirely. Scalia had made his point. A final swipe at the dissent would have sufficed. "Justice Stevens relies on the drafting history of the Second Amendment—the various proposals in the state conventions and the debates in Congress. It is dubious to rely on such history to interpret a text that was widely understood to codify a pre-existing right, rather than to fashion a new one. But even assuming that this legislative history is relevant, Justice Stevens flatly misreads the historical record." Why belabor an already overstuffed opinion with more sources? Is the answer that, like Gray, Scalia was showboating? Whether or not he impressed his intended audience out of doors, he did not silence the dissenters. They wheeled up their own battery of authorities and blasted away. The real contention was only obliquely revealed by Scalia. "Justice Stevens' view thus relies on the proposition, unsupported by any evidence, that different people of the founding period had

---

33 544 U.S. at 598 (Scalia, J.).
34 544 U.S. at 598 (Scalia, J.).

vastly different conceptions of the right to keep and bear arms. That simply does not comport with our longstanding view that the Bill of Rights codified venerable, widely understood liberties."[35]

All the footnotes were implicit or explicit responses to Justice Stevens. All relied on originalist readings of primary historical sources. Some were directly confrontational. What is important for the present reading of the notes is how they assumed that the historical record could be understood without the implicit or explicit aid of historians. The rule for plain text originalism was that the modern judge was as able as any historical expert to understand what the historical record meant. This is a powerful theme in some versions of philosophy of history, to wit, that human nature has not changed, although the outer trappings of culture and language may have evolved. According to this view of history, judges today are able to cast themselves back in time, read old texts with old eyes, and then return to the present and explicate those texts for modern readers with perfect accuracy. This is what (without the explicit adoption of a philosophy of history to accompany the jurisprudence of plain meaning originalism) Scalia did in his footnotes. It enabled him to refute Stevens point by point.[36]

* * *

The footnotes to the majority opinion are embedded in the pages of the report corresponding to the text of Scalia's opinion. Here I extract them to illustrate how Scalia used them:

Footnote 3 Justice Stevens says that we violate the general rule that every clause in a statute must have effect. *Post*, at 8. But where the text of

---

35 544 U.S. at 603 (Scalia, J.). The dueling historical examples reflected something more complex in the way that modern Americans practiced history. It was a debate about American historiography, about consensus in American history versus diversity in American history. In the 1950s and early 1960s, historians stressed that a consensus of attitudes and values marked American culture. In later years, the very opposite proposition was advanced by a new generation of historians. The disagreement itself disproved the assumption of consensus historians, but the same disagreement challenged the new generation's faith in diversity. The we-know-more-than-you-do back and forth concealed a broader, and more genuine, disagreement about how to do history, hence about originalism.

36 See, for example. David Boucher, *The Social and Political Thought of R. G. Collingwood* (Cambridge, UK: Cambridge University Press, 1989), 13, 17, 39, quoting R. G. Collingwood, *The Idea of History* (1946) (one "reenacts" the ideas of the past in one's own mind; thus they are timeless).

a clause itself indicates that it does not have operative effect, such as "whereas" clauses in federal legislation or the Constitution's preamble, a court has no license to make it do what it was not designed to do. Or to put the point differently, operative provisions should be given effect as operative provisions, and prologues as prologues.

Footnote 5 Justice Stevens is of course correct, *post*, at 10, that the right to assemble cannot be exercised alone, but it is still an individual right, and not one conditioned upon membership in some defined "assembly," as he contends the right to bear arms is conditioned upon membership in a defined militia. And Justice Stevens is dead wrong to think that the right to petition is "primarily collective in nature.

Footnote 11 Justice Stevens contends, *post*, at 15, that since we assert that adding "against" to "bear arms" gives it a military meaning we must concede that adding a purposive qualifying phrase to "bear arms" can alter its meaning. But the difference is that we do not maintain that "against" *alters* the meaning of "bear arms" but merely that it *clarifies* which of various meanings (one of which is military) is intended. Justice Stevens, however, argues that "[t]he term 'bear arms' is a familiar idiom; when used unadorned by any additional words, its meaning is 'to serve as a soldier, do military service, fight.'" *Post*, at 11. He therefore must establish that adding a contradictory purposive phrase can *alter* a word's meaning.

Footnote 12 Justice Stevens finds support for his legislative history inference from the recorded views of one Antifederalist member of the House. *Post*, at 26 n. 25. [but] "The claim that the best or most representative reading of the [language of the] amendments would conform to the understanding and concerns of [the Antifederalists] is . . . highly problematic."

Footnote 14 Faced with this clear historical usage, Justice Stevens resorts to the bizarre argument that because the word "to" is not included before "bear" (whereas it is included before "petition" in the First Amendment), the unitary meaning of "to keep and bear" is established. *Post*, at 16, n. 13. We have never heard of the proposition that omitting repetition of the "to" causes two verbs with different meanings to become one. A promise "to support and to defend the Constitution of the United States" is not a whit different from a promise "to support and defend the Constitution of the United States."

Footnote 16 Contrary to Justice Stevens' wholly unsupported assertion, *post*, at 17, there was no pre-existing right in English law "to use weapons for certain military purposes" or to use arms in an organized militia.

Footnote 18 Justice Stevens says that the drafters of the Virginia Declaration of Rights rejected this proposal and adopted "instead" a provision written by George Mason stressing the importance of the militia. See *post*, at 24, and n. 24. There is no evidence that the drafters regarded the Mason proposal as a substitute for the Jefferson proposal.

Footnote 19 Justice Stevens quotes some of Tucker's unpublished notes, which he claims show that Tucker had ambiguous views about the Second Amendment. See *post*, at 31, and n. 32. But it is clear from the notes that Tucker located the power of States to arm their militias in the *Tenth* Amendment, and that he cited the Second Amendment for the proposition that such armament could not run afoul of any power of the federal government (since the amendment prohibits Congress from ordering disarmament). Nothing in the passage implies that the Second Amendment pertains only to the carrying of arms in the organized militia.

Footnote 21 Justice Stevens suggests that this is not obvious because free blacks in Virginia had been required to muster without arms. See *post*, at 28, n. 29 (citing Siegel, The Federal Government's Power to Enact Color-Conscious Laws, 92 Nw. U. L. Rev. 477, 497 (1998)). But that could not have been the type of law referred to in *Aldridge*, because that practice had stopped 30 years earlier when blacks were excluded entirely from the militia by the First Militia Act. See Siegel, *supra*, at 498, n. 120. Justice Stevens further suggests that laws barring blacks from militia service could have been said to violate the "right to bear arms." But under Justice Stevens' reading of the Second Amendment (we think), the protected right is the right to carry arms to the extent one is enrolled in the militia, not the right *to be in the militia*. Perhaps Justice Stevens really does adopt the full-blown idiomatic meaning of "bear arms," in which case every man and woman in this country has a right "to be a soldier" or even "to wage war." In any case, it is clear to us that *Aldridge's* allusion to the existing Virginia "restriction" upon the right of free blacks "to bear arms" could only have referred to "laws prohibiting blacks from keeping weapons," Siegel, *supra*, at 497–498.

Footnote 22 Justice Stevens' accusation that this is "not accurate," *post*, at 39, is wrong. It is true it was the indictment that described the right as "bearing arms for a lawful purpose." But, in explicit reference to the right described in the indictment, the Court stated that "The second amendment declares that it [*i.e.*, the right of bearing arms for a lawful purpose] shall not be infringed." 92 U. S., at 553.

Footnote 24 As for the "hundreds of judges," *post*, at 2, who have relied on the view of the Second Amendment Justice Stevens claims we endorsed in *Miller*: If so, they overread *Miller*. And their erroneous reliance upon an uncontested and virtually unreasoned case cannot nullify the reliance of millions of Americans (as our historical analysis has shown) upon the true meaning of the right to keep and bear arms. In any event, it should not be thought that the cases decided by these judges would necessarily have come out differently under a proper interpretation of the right.

The opinion of the majority of an appellate court is law. Putting a running rebuke of a fellow justice, by name, in the opinion adds that rebuke into the law. Even so veteran a controversialist as Scalia had to hesitate before he did that. At points in his opinion, he did allow his sharp wit to spill over the dissent. But the footnotes were another matter. Although attached to the opinion as an appendage, they were not law, and so directing an assault on Stevens in them insulated (for the most part) the assault from becoming law.[37]

---

37 In all fairness, one should add, as Scalia did at the very end of the opinion, that he was not arguing against all regulations. John Bash made this point in his op-ed defense of the opinion in 2022: "Justice Scalia—the foremost proponent of originalism, who throughout his tenure stressed the limited role of courts in difficult policy debates—could not have been clearer in the closing passage of Heller that 'the problem of handgun violence in this country' is serious and that the Constitution leaves the government with 'a variety of tools for combating that problem, including some measures regulating handguns.' Heller merely established the constitutional baseline that the government may not disarm citizens in their homes."

* * *

In many ways, Stevens's dissent was as originalist as the majority opinion. This was necessary if Stevens was going to refute Scalia's reading of the primary historical sources. But Stevens's originalism was different from Scalia's. First, Stevens tried to reset the issue from the outset by reconnecting the two parts of the amendment. If he could accomplish this, then the second clause did not entail an individual right to bear arms apart from militia duty. Stevens did not question that individuals could claim a right to own and bear arms: "The question presented by this case is not whether the Second Amendment protects a 'collective right' or an 'individual right.' Surely it protects a right that can be enforced by individuals." But where was the place to find an answer? There was one case on point: "Our decision in *United States* v. *Miller*, 307 U. S. 174 (1939), provide[s] a clear answer to that question." In *Miller*, the high court upheld, on interstate commerce clause grounds, a congressional act barring the transportation of sawed-off shotguns across state lines. That this was interstate traffic one could not doubt. Was it also commerce if the purpose was not sale or use of the shotguns? By 1939, the court has so broadened the definition of interstate commerce that the guns, even if intended for personal use, were commerce. The court, like Congress, was aware that the purpose was to carry out criminal activities. The sawed-off shotgun was not a hunting weapon—unless one walked right up to the prey. Nor was it particularly suitable for personal self-defense. The court thus did not spend time on the Second Amendment, save to remark that the shotgun was not likely part of the militia ordnance. Stevens concluded that it was clear from *Miller* that Congress could limit individuals' right to bear arms.[38]

This meant that the second part of the amendment could not stand alone. "The Second Amendment," Stevens insisted, "was adopted to protect the right of the people of each of the several States to maintain a well-regulated militia." The source of this was not a naïve realist linguistics but a reading of what expert historians in the subject matter said about the amendment. The consensus among the historians was that the amendment "was a response to concerns raised during the ratifica-

---

38 544 U.S. at 636, 637 (Stevens, J. dissenting); United States v. Miller, 307 U. S. 174, 178 (1939).

tion of the Constitution that the power of Congress to disarm the state militias and create a national standing army posed an intolerable threat to the sovereignty of the several States." What the historians had done, and Stevens credited, was to add historical context to the text. Read in context by the historians, and propounded by Stevens, was that neither the text of the amendment nor the arguments advanced by its proponents evidenced the slightest interest in limiting any legislature's authority to regulate private civilian uses of firearms. Specifically, there was no indication that the framers of the amendment intended to enshrine the common-law right of self-defense in the Constitution.[39]

Stevens then combined the court's interpretation of the amendment in *Miller* with the historians' interpretation of the amendment, collapsing the time between 1789, 1939, and 2008 as if the meanings of the amendment in them aligned: "The view of the Amendment we took in *Miller*—that it protects the right to keep and bear arms for certain military purposes, but that it does not curtail the Legislature's power to regulate the nonmilitary use and ownership of weapons—is both the most natural reading of the Amendment's text and the interpretation most faithful to the history of its adoption." Now came the interpretive passages that Scalia scathed.[40]

To his aid, he summoned history: "A review of the drafting history of the Amendment demonstrates that its Framers *rejected* proposals that would have broadened its coverage to include such [individual] uses." Did omission of the individual right in some quarters amount to proof that the individual right had been rejected? Can this evidence be effective against evidence that in some quarters, the individual right was sustained? "The opinion the Court announces today fails to identify any new evidence supporting the view that the Amendment was intended to limit the power of Congress to regulate civilian uses of weapons."[41]

At this point, Stevens's footnote 4 took over the assault on Scalia's originalism. Stevens was not so much concerned with primary sources of the past (although he paraded them past the reader) but

---

39 544 U.S. at 637 (Stevens, J. dissenting).
40 544 U.S. at 637–638 (Stevens, J. dissenting). Going back to the original text is sometimes called "textualism." "Intentionalism" is going back to the intentions of the framers of the text, The first requires a rule for reading text, and the second requires mind reading. Worse (or harder) the two terms are themselves subject to varying interpretations. Brest, "Misconceived," 207.
41 544 U.S. at 639 (Stevens J. dissenting).

with the way that earlier courts had disposed of cases. Thus, he preferred one kind of originalism—the plain meaning of earlier cases—to
the originalist reading of the primary sources that Scalia provided.
This is called precedent, and it has a particular bite in a common-
law system. His attack on Scalia's methods he clothed in doctrine:
"[Stare decisis] permits society to presume that bedrock principles are
founded in the law rather than in the proclivities of individuals, and
thereby contributes to the integrity of our constitutional system of
government, both in appearance and in fact." The individual was none
other than Scalia. Stevens was lecturing Scalia on basic common-law
doctrine. Case law, he believed, was explicitly historical. "While *stare
decisis* is not an inexorable command, the careful observer will dis-
cern that any detours from the straight path of *stare decisis* in our
past have occurred for articulable reasons, and only when the Court
has felt obliged 'to bring its opinions into agreement with experience
and with facts newly ascertained.'" Precedent thus brought history to
bear on present constitutional problems through a complex weighing of changing contexts rather than a simplistic process of looking
at primary sources and announcing their meaning. Again, the target
was Scalia. "Break down this belief in judicial continuity and let it be
felt that on great constitutional questions this Court is to depart from
the settled conclusions of its predecessors, and to determine them all
according to the mere opinion of those who temporarily fill its bench,
and our Constitution will, in my judgment, be bereft of value and
become a most dangerous instrument to the rights and liberties of
the people." Scalia's individualistic reading of evidence was downright
"dangerous."[42]

* * *

To this end, the preference for complexity and context differentiated
Stevens's footnotes from Scalia's. Thus, Stevens was more comfortable
with the amicus briefs than was Scalia. For example, in footnote 31:
"Moreover, it was the Crown, not Parliament, that was bound by the
English provision; indeed, according to some prominent historians,
Article VII is best understood not as announcing any individual right

---

42 544 U.S. at 640 fn 4 (Stevens, J. dissenting).

to unregulated firearm ownership (after all, such a reading would fly in the face of the text), but as an assertion of the concept of parliamentary supremacy." To which he added "See Brief for Jack N. Rakove et al. as *Amici Curiae* 6–9."[43]

Stevens felt compelled to answer Scalia point by point, and that is what his footnotes did. For example, what did the term *bear arms* mean? Was it to be read as two separate words meaning carrying something that happened in this case to be a weapon, or was it one term of two words? In 2021, armed with a new computer tool, scholars revisited the key terms in the debate. Absent this modern intervention, Stevens carried on the campaign in the footnotes.[44]

* * *

Footnote 9 offered evidence for Stevens's reading of the latter, an itemization of instances, as if they all had the same weight (like integers in a math equation). "*Amici* professors of Linguistics and English reviewed uses of the term "bear arms" in a compilation of books, pamphlets, and other sources disseminated in the period between the Declaration of Independence and the adoption of the Second Amendment . . . *Amici* determined that of 115 texts that employed the term, all but five usages were in a clearly military context, and in four of the remaining five instances, further qualifying language conveyed a different meaning." Scalia allowed that "bear Arms" did have as an idiomatic meaning, "'to serve as a soldier, do military service, fight,'" but Scalia asserted on his own authority "that it '*unequivocally* bore that idiomatic meaning only when followed by the preposition "against," which was in turn followed by the target of the hostilities.'" Stevens rejoined, "But contemporary sources make clear that the phrase 'bear arms' was often used to convey a military meaning without those additional words." The note contained a load of evidence, Stevens relying on the briefs of counsel:

---

43 544 U.S. at 664 fn 31 (Stevens, J. dissenting).

44 COFEA—Corpus of Founding Era American English is a searchable collation of one hundred thousand texts that permits analysis of frequency of certain terms. These included *bear arms*. James C. Philips and Josh Blackmun, "Decoding the Second Amendment: Corpus Linguistics and *Heller*," *Wake Forest Law Review* 56 (2021): 614: "On balance, a corpus linguistics analysis shows that the meaning of the operative clause of the Second Amendment is a much closer call than either the *Heller* majority or the dissent were willing to admit. In fact, we found linguistic evidence that supports both views."

See, *e.g.*, To The Printer, Providence Gazette, (May 27, 1775) ("By the common estimate of three millions of people in America, allowing one in five
to bear arms, there will be found 600,000 fighting men"); Letter of Henry
Laurens to the Mass. Council (Jan. 21, 1778), in Letters of Delegates to
Congress 1774–1789, p. 622 (P. Smith ed. 1981) ("Congress were yesterday
informed . . . that those Canadians who returned from Saratoga . . . had
been compelled by Sir Guy Carleton to bear Arms"); Of the Manner of
Making War among the Indians of North-America, Connecticut Courant
(May 23, 1785) ("The Indians begin to bear arms at the age of fifteen, and
lay them aside when they arrive at the age of sixty. Some nations to the
southward, I have been informed, do not continue their military exercises
after they are fifty"); 28 Journals of the Continental Congress 1030 (G.
Hunt ed. 1910) ("That hostages be mutually given as a security that the
Convention troops and those received in exchange for them do not bear
arms prior to the first day of May next"); H. R. J., 9th Cong., 1st Sess., 217
(Feb. 12, 1806) ("Whereas the commanders of British armed vessels have
impressed many American seamen, and compelled them to bear arms on
board said vessels, and assist in fighting their battles with nations in amity
and peace with the United States"); H. R. J., 15th Cong., 2d Sess., 182–183
(Jan. 14, 1819) ("[The petitioners] state that they were residing in the British province of Canada, at the commencement of the late war, and that
owing to their attachment to the United States, they refused to bear arms,
when called upon by the British authorities . . .").

Not content with this collection of friends of the court's reading of
primary sources, Stevens offered more evidence from case law:

Footnote 10 *Aymette* v. *State*, 21 Tenn. 154, 156 (1840), a case we cited
in *Miller*, further confirms this reading of the phrase. In *Aymette*, the
Tennessee Supreme Court construed the guarantee in Tennessee's 1834
Constitution that "the free white men of this State, have a right to keep
and bear arms for their common defence." Explaining that the provision
was adopted with the same goals as the Federal Constitution's Second
Amendment, the court wrote: "The words 'bear arms' . . . have reference
to their military use, and were not employed to mean wearing them about
the person as part of the dress. As the object for which the right to keep
and bear arms is secured, is of general and public nature, to be exercised

by the people in a body, for their *common defence*, so the *arms*, the right
to keep which is secured, are such as are usually employed in civilized
warfare, and that constitute the ordinary military equipment." 21 Tenn., at
158. The court elaborated: "[W]e may remark, that the phrase *'bear arms'*
is used in the Kentucky Constitution as well as our own, and implies, as
has already been suggested, their military use. . . . A man in the pursuit
of deer, elk, and buffaloes, might carry his rifle every day, for forty years,
and, yet, it would never be said of him, that he had *borne arms*, much less
could it be said, that a private citizen *bears arms*, because he has a dirk or
pistol concealed under his clothes, or a spear in a cane." *Id.*, at 161."

The court's error, to break the two-word term into two separate
words, did not escape Stevens's notice.
Footnote 14 explained:

The Court's [i.e. Scalia's] atomistic, word-by-word approach to construing
the Amendment calls to mind the parable of the six blind men and the
elephant, famously set in verse by John Godfrey Saxe. The Poems of John
Godfrey Saxe 135–136 (1873). In the parable, each blind man approaches
a single elephant; touching a different part of the elephant's body in iso-
lation, each concludes that he has learned its true nature. One touches
the animal's leg, and concludes that the elephant is like a tree; another
touches the trunk and decides that the elephant is like a snake; and so on.
Each of them, of course, has fundamentally failed to grasp the nature of
the creature.

Stevens could not be denied his bit of buffoonery, not only using the
story of the blind men, but finding the authority for it.

* * *

But what looked like a comic turn was in fact the serious key to all of
these footnotes. Never intended to be part of the decision, they were free
to be something else entirely. Scalia and Stevens had sat on the court for
many years. They were entitled, or at least believed they were entitled,
to show off their erudition. Hence the scope of the references. They did
have different styles of writing, including notes. "Some Justices, like . . .
the retired Justice John Paul Stevens, find it easier to write a first draft

and then let their law clerks have a go at it. Others, like Scalia, let the law clerks write the first draft, and then the justice rewrites, edits and refines." Everything necessary to sustain their varying interpretations of the amendment's meaning was contained in the body of their opinions. The footnotes gave them the opportunity to display something about styles of judging. Scalia's was personal—not only naming Stevens but insulting him. This is the style one sees in combative law reviews. Stevens's style was civil but heavy handed. Every point that Scalia made had to be confronted and refuted. This is the style required of appellate litigation, something that Stevens had done before he was appointed to the bench. Scalia never was a litigator. Instead, he was a government official and a law professor. Nothing could show the difference between these two career patterns than the footnotes in *Heller*.[45]

Even if, as some scholars have concluded, *Heller* firmly and finally established the legitimacy (even the ascendency) of originalist historical interpretation of constitutional texts, that achievement was a complicated one. For as an analysis of the footnotes shows, the history in the text and the history in the notes served different purposes. In the main, Scalia was focusing on primary sources—original documents, assuming that he (and the majority) were competent to understand what they meant in their context. He used secondary sources to buttress his interpretation, but he did not rely on them. In effect, he was the only historian who mattered. Although this was public meaning originalism, Scalia had substituted himself for the relevant past's "public." Stevens, by contrast, was relying on secondary sources of history, what commentators and scholars had to say about the terms and understandings of the amendment. His expertise piggybacked on theirs. If they were wrong, he had no rule to judge them wrong. He used primary sources as illustrations. Thus, the two kinds of historical analyses, primary source and secondary source, in works of history by historians, usually combined, were here set against one another. This explains in part the insight that law professor Cass Sunstein offered in his short essay on the case. His sense was that most legal scholars, including himself, thought that Scalia's reading of the history was entirely "plausible," even convincing. It

---

45 Nina Totenberg, "Skip the Legalese and Keep It Short, the Justices Say," NPR, June 13, 2011, www. npr.org. But they don't always practice what they preach, as the exchange in *Heller* demonstrated.

certainly convinced a broad spectrum of the public and politicians. At the same time, a good many historians, including specialists in the fields of early national American history and constitutional history, preferred Stevens's reading of the evidence. Thus, if the opinions represented some manner a triumph of legal history and the footnotes reflected that triumph, the type of history that triumphed remained uncertain.[46]

A final caveat. Why was it necessary for Scalia to carry his account into the pre–Civil War era and then into the twentieth century? Whether he was deploying old originalism (the framers' original intention) or new originalism (plain and public meaning of educated people at the time), both assumed that the meaning of the Constitution is and should be unchanged. That was the touchstone of all originalism—preserving the integrity of the document. Later writings on the amendment's meaning and impact were irrelevant unless they threw light on the amendment's original meaning. It was unimportant to originalism what later authorities themselves thought the amendment meant. This view of constitutional history, however, elided the court's own past thinking—precedent—particularly *Miller*. But even then, should *Miller* be interpreted in light of eighteenth-century meanings and intentions? Stevens had begun with the 1939 case. Throughout his dissent, he asked whether originalism, insofar as it privileged history, looked at only a narrow slice of that history from the time of the drafting and ratification of the amendment, or did history continue to dictate meanings to the present? That was the question that the later footnote war in *Dobbs* raised. For the majority opinion in that case ended its history (i.e., our "customs and traditions") in 1970 before *Roe*, actually before the movement that led to *Roe*, whereas the dissenters saw history coming up to the present.[47]

* * *

Although much of the legal scholarship on *Heller* assumed that Scalia's dogged originalism had led Stevens into a thicket of his own originalism,

---

46 Sunstein, "Second Amendment Minimalism," 251, 252, 253.

47 Eric Berger, "Originalism Pretenses," *University of Pennsylvania Journal of Constitutional Law* 16 (2013): 330 ("fixed, original meaning"). Scalia was caught in a version of Bishop Morton's fork, according to which, King Henry VII's archbishop of Canterbury was collecting a benevolence (tax) for the king by allegedly saying to the rich, "You can afford to pay," and to those who were living more modestly, "You must be concealing your wealth, and so you can pay." An anecdote probably invented by a later observer, however.

creating parallel tracks through a mire of ancient and modern history, an examination of the footnotes shows something quite different. The two justices were engaging in a conversation about history, albeit a charged conversation. They were fully aware of each other's evidence and interpretation, and each countered rather than ignored the other's arguments. This is similar to an exchange in a learned history journal or at a scholarly conference between two historians who have taken different views of an event or a figure. The "comments" on these occasions resemble the footnote exchange in *Heller*. On occasion, these exchanges among historians become quite heated. Seen in this light, the history they offered was not law office history but history office history.[48]

However parsed, the footnotes in *Heller* reflected a maturing of historical footnote use. The two opinions deployed footnotes in ways far more advanced, if that is the right word, than in *Carolene Products* and *Brown*. Some of the credit for this (if one believes that the evolution of the footnote is creditworthy) belongs to Scalia. Throughout his thirty-four years on the court, his footnotes were elegant, thoughtful, and pointed. They drew from his targets' equally able footnotes. Characteristically, the footnotes in *Heller* were not Post-its, additional citations, or mere opinion. They were integral to the reasoning of the two opinions, showing how Scalia and Stevens engaged in constitutional conversation on the highest level. The footnotes did not become law, however, for that very same reason. Set in relation to one another, they were an extrajudicial narrative on the firearms history of the country.

Scalia had the last word in *Heller*. His opinion is the law of the land. His footnotes, directed so sharply at Stevens, were in a way a tribute to Scalia's own passion for writing. He wrote, or at least he corrected, the footnotes in all his opinions, and he never pulled punches in them. But Stevens intended to have the last word on gun control. In his *Six Amendments: How and Why We Should Change the Constitution* (2014), he looked at the school shootings and warned, "Even as generously construed in *Heller*, the Second Amendment provides no obstacle to regulations prohibiting the ownership or use of the sorts of automatic

---

48 See, for example, Saul Cornell, "Originalism on Trial: The Use and Abuse of History in *District of Columbia v. Heller*," *Ohio State University Law Journal* 69 (2008): 625; Greene, "Heller High Water?," 325–26; Rory K. Little, "Heller and Constitutional Interpretation: Originalism's Last Gasp," *Hastings Law Journal* 60 (2008–09): 1418.

weapons" used in the school massacres. Congress should, he insisted, step into the gaps Scalia had left in his opinion and regulate possession of firearms by dangerous individuals and possession of firearms not used for personal defense. Add five words to the amendment, he offered, so it would read "keep and bear arms *when serving in the militia* shall not be infringed."[49]

---

49 William Jay, "Tribute: The Justice Who Said He Hated Writing," March 4, 2016, SCOTUS Blog, www.scotusblog.com; Kannon Shanmugam, "Most Memorable Footnote," *Law*, August 1, 2017, https://finance.yahoo.com; John Paul Stevens, *Six Amendments: How and Why We Should Change the Constitution* (Boston: Little, Brown, 2014), 128, 132.

PRECEDENT

Dobbs v. Jackson Women's Health Organization, 142 S.Ct. 2228 (2022)

After a fashion, the passage of arms in the *Heller* footnotes displayed the two justices' mutual respect. They neither asked for nor gave quarter. But to read the warring footnotes in the majority and dissenting opinions of *Dobbs v. Jackson Women's Health* (2022), it would seem that the rough comradery of the earlier court's senior members had vanished. True, no issue has so roiled American public life over the course of the past fifty years as reproductive rights, and no modern case so encompassed such a division as *Roe v. Wade* (1973). That case reflected an intense period of agitation for women's reproductive autonomy and choice. It ignited opposition, indeed created a party of opposition, calling itself pro-life. Nearly fifty years later, it was still being litigated. The footnotes in *Dobbs* traced that litigation, focusing on the doctrine of precedent. *Dobbs* overruled *Roe* and raised the question whether some precedents, particularly those rooted in "history and tradition," were more worthy of saving than other precedents of more recent vintage. Justice Samuel Alito wrote the majority opinion as he had wanted to write the opinion of the court in *Whole Woman's Health v. Hellerstedt* (2016) and *June Medical Services v. Russo* (2020). Now he had his chance, and he was taking no prisoners, as the footnotes, like Justice Scalia's in *Heller* but without the latter's brio, demonstrated. In effect, Alito had weaponized the Supreme Court footnote. Justice Elena Kagan's dissenting opinion itself revolutionized the footnotes, responding to Alito's vehemence in a different voice.[1]

---

1 Carol Gilligan, *In a Different Voice: Psychological Theory and Women's Development* (Cambridge, MA: Harvard University Press, 1982), suggested that women were raised more nurturing and men more competitive. Roe v. Wade, 410 U.S. 413 (1973); Whole Woman's Health v. Hellerstedt 579 U.S. 582 (2016); June Medical Services v. Russo, 591 U.S. 1101 (2020); Dobbs v. Jackson Women's Health Organization 142 S.Ct. 2228 (2022). The literature on *Roe* and the controversy surrounding it is vast. See, for example, the bibliographical essay in N. E. H. Hull and Peter Charles Hoffer, Roe v. Wade:

* * *

Precedent is the common-law doctrine of adherence to prior case law, as we saw in Justice Stevens's *Heller* opinion. In theory, stability in law has an intrinsic value. Lawyers and litigants can predict the outcomes of suits based on prior case outcomes, legal doctrines, and rules. Everyone can adjust their behavior to known law. That is why law reform movements in England and its colonies, as well as later in the United States, called for codification of laws. The result is a rule-of-law system, in which outcomes are not influenced by individual status or demographic characteristics. By contrast, when these doctrines and rules undergo rapid and unpredictable change, lawyers and litigants suffer uncertain expectations, as does everyone affected by law. Judges know this. As Justice Samuel Alito wrote in *Dobbs v. Jackson*, precedent "protects the interests of those who have taken action in reliance on a past decision. It 'reduces incentives for challenging settled precedents, saving parties and courts the expense of endless relitigation.' It fosters 'evenhanded' decision-making by requiring that like cases be decided in a like manner. It 'contributes to the actual and perceived integrity of the judicial process.' And it restrains judicial hubris and reminds us to respect the judgment of those who have grappled with important questions in the past" [citations omitted].[2]

Thus, doctrines like stare decisis (let the decision stand) and res judicata (the case has already been decided) are bedrock concepts in common-law systems like our own. They are "rooted in Article III" of the Constitution. But in constitutional adjudication, the controlling impact of precedent is weaker, and some judges argue that it is only a part of their reasoning. Precedent is a constraint, reining in activism; but with changing times precedent may hinder responsive judging. Indeed, upholding an old precedent in the face of an overwhelming national consensus to the contrary (think *Plessy v. Ferguson* and *Brown v. Board of Education*) would bring public scorn on the court. But what then hap-

---

The Abortion Rights Controversy in American History, 3rd ed. (Lawrence: University Press of Kansas, 2022), 391–403.

2 142 S.Ct. at 2261–2262 (2022) (Alito, J.); Richard A. Posner, *Sex and Reason* (Cambridge, MA: Harvard University Press, 1992), 328–29 (on consensual gay sex); Michael J. Gerhardt, *The Power of Precedent* (New York: Oxford University Press, 2008), 3–4, 5: the "golden rule" of precedent is that judges should treat other judges' precedents as they would treat their own.

pens to the law when precedent, particularly recent precedent, is overturned, and overturned for reasons not of obvious error or changing
social and economic conditions but for openly partisan shifts in the personnel of the courts?[3]

A second restraint on courts is prudential, that is, judge made. In the
words of Chief Justice William Rehnquist in *Washington v. Glucksburg*
(1997), "We have regularly observed that the Due Process Clause spe-
cially protects those fundamental rights and liberties which are, objectively, deeply rooted in this Nation's history and tradition." The modifier
objectively was there to prevent the allegation that the court was supply-
ing its own biased or partisan idea of history and tradition—importing
and abusing the doctrine of substantive due process. The problem with
this seemingly innocuous term was that the country's history and tradition included slavery and racial discrimination, dispossession of In-
digenous peoples, religious intolerance against minority churches, and
racialist immigration laws. Historians knew all about these. A second
qualifier may too easily escape notice. What does "deeply rooted in this
nation" mean? Are there traditions which are too shallow or too regional
(instead of national) that the court can ignore? For example, parts of
the country embraced chattel slavery and then Jim Crow segregation.
Are these part of our history and traditions? The invocation of a historical justification for a legal stance should worry justices, given the
poor reputation of history cited in judicial opinions. It certainly worries
historians.[4]

Still, could recitation of the umbrella phrase "history and tradition"
enable a new slate of justices on the Supreme Court sharing a particular set of political values to engage in wholesale nullification of well-
established precedent? The appointment process of federal judges from

---

3 142 S.Ct. at 2306 (Kavanaugh, J.).

4 Washington v. Glucksberg, 521 U.S. 702, 720–721 (1997) (Rehnquist, C. J.). Samples of leading
modern historians' concern about our oldest "history and traditions" include Alan Taylor, *American
Revolutions, A Continental History, 1750–1804* (New York: W. W. Norton, 2016) ("The American
Revolution validated rapid expansion but failed to settle what sort of society ultimately would take
shape," 480); Alan Waldstreicher, *Slavery's Constitution: from Revolution to Ratification* (New York:
Hill and Wang, 2014) ("We cannot have our creative founding fathers without their disturbingly
artful contributions to the politics of slavery," 14); and Claudio Saunt, *Unworthy Republic: The
Dispossession of Native Americans and the Road to Indian Territory* (New York: Norton, 2001) ("To
evoke the underlying violence of the act [of Indian removal] I also refer to the uprooting of Native
Americans as 'expulsion,' . . . and on certain occasions, [as] 'extermination,'" xiv).

different backgrounds and regions of the country is supposed to prevent such uniformity of opinion on the bench. But when presidents look for openly partisan judges and a majority of the Senate votes as a bloc to confirm the appointments, the bench may take on a distinctly partisan hue. Although Chief Justice John Roberts recently stated that there are no [President George W.] Bush judges and [Barack] Obama judges, over the course of second decade of the twenty-first century, the chief justice's claim of judicial neutrality underwent a severe test. Nowhere more than in abortion rights cases did the constitutional opinions of judges more closely align with the opinion of their congressional sponsors. Nowhere did the footnotes carry on the partisan combat more than in *Dobbs v. Jackson*.[5]

* * *

Roe v. Wade and the cases that followed it concerning abortion rights assured that some abortions were protected by law. Justice Blackmun's majority opinion had all but two of the members' signatures. The opinion also offered sixty-seven footnotes. Almost all were to medical or legal sources, although three concerned Texas's handling of similar cases. In other words, all except the comments on Texas could have been incorporated into the body of the decision. More to the point, none referred to the history and traditions of the nation. *Roe* was a reform decision, rooted not in long-standing history and tradition but in more recent shifts in medical, legal, and social opinion.

In *Roe*, Blackmun found, "The principal thrust of appellant's attack on the Texas statutes is that they improperly invade a right, said to be possessed by the pregnant woman, to choose to terminate her pregnancy. Appellant would discover this right in the concept of personal 'liberty' embodied in the Fourteenth Amendment's Due Process Clause; or in personal, marital, familial, and sexual privacy said to be protected by the Bill of Rights or its penumbras." In subsequent cases, the core holding of *Roe* resisted challenge, although the trimester formula for balancing the interests of pregnant women and the state Blackmun inserted into *Roe*

---

5 See, for example, Rachel Reed, "Politics, the Court, and the 'Dangerous Place We Find Ourselves in Right Now," *Harvard Law Today*, September 22, 2022, https://hls.harvard.edu/today; Simon Lazarus, "How to Rein in Partisan Supreme Court Justices," Brookings Institution, March 23, 2022, www.brookings.edu.

fell to the "undue burden" formula of *City of Akron v. Akron Center for Reproductive Health* (1983) affirmed in *Planned Parenthood of Southeast Pennsylvania v. Casey* (1992): "If the particular regulation does not 'unduly burden' the fundamental right, then our evaluation of that regulation is limited to our determination that the regulation rationally relates to a legitimate state purpose."[6]

Abortion rights in the post-*Roe* line of cases were not justified by history and tradition. The farthest back the due process right to reproductive autonomy could be traced was to *Griswold v. Connecticut* (1965). But in the years from 1973 to 2022, a history and tradition of third-generation feminism, reflected in the protection of women in the workplace as well as in reproductive rights, had emerged. It was this precedent, and its history and tradition, that the decision in *Dobbs v. Jackson* challenged. For in a short span of a single presidency, that very danger that Rehnquist warned against—an unchecked due process—turned a recent precedent and a longer-spanned history and tradition into opposing doctrines.[7]

If the history and tradition of abortion rights was comparably short, from 1973 to 2022, the end of abortion rights was even more abrupt. During President Donald J. Trump's administration from 2017 to 2021, *Roe* and its subsequent cases were under constant attack in the states. Despite over forty-three years of precedent protecting the core ruling, states from Alabama to Ohio passed restrictive legislation whose overt purpose, if one believed the stated intent of the sponsors, was the reversal of *Roe* rather than the protection of the health and welfare of the prospective mother. State political leaders whose antipathy to regulation of the economy, the environment, and other subjects was well documented were nevertheless eager to impose a wide variety of regulations on abortion practitioners and facilities. These included licensing of providers, limits by age of the fetus, exceptions limited to rape and incest, denial of insurance and state medical care coverage, opt-out provisions for health care providers, mandatory counseling of women seeking to end a pregnancy, and making the pregnant woman a party to the crime of abortion.[8]

---

6 Roe v. Wade, 410 U.S. 113, 129 (Blackmun, J.); Justice Harry Blackmun, oral history, June 1995, www.c-span.org. City of Akron v. Akron Center for Reproductive Health, 462 U.S. 416, 453 (1983) (O'Connor, J.); Planned Parenthood of Southeastern Pennsylvania v. Casey, 505 U.S. 833 (1992).
7 See, for example, Ruth Rosen, *The World Split Open: How the Modern Women's Movement Changed America* (New York: Penguin, 2000), 158f.
8 Roe v. Wade, 410 U.S. 113 (1973); text borrowed from Hull and Hoffer, *Roe v. Wade*, 334–35.

For example, in *June Medical Services v. Russo* (2020), a Louisiana law modeled on a Texas law that had been struck down three years previously in *Whole Woman's Health v. Hellerstedt* (2016), threatened the existence of abortion rights directly. Voting with the majority to strike down the Louisiana statute, Chief Justice Roberts, who did not favor *Roe*, explained his position: "I joined the dissent in *Whole Woman's Health* and continue to believe that the case was wrongly decided. The question today however is not whether *Whole Woman's Health* was right or wrong, but whether to adhere to it in deciding the present case." He had not changed his opinion on *Hellerstedt*, but the issue for him had changed. Was the court to abandon so recent a precedent? "The legal doctrine of stare decisis requires us, absent special circumstances, to treat like cases alike. The Louisiana law imposes a burden on access to abortion just as severe as that imposed by the Texas law, for the same reasons. Therefore Louisiana's law cannot stand under our precedents."[9]

The choice between his own view of abortion law and his desire to uphold the superordinate doctrine of stare decisis must have been a difficult one to make. Did it "save" the court in any sense? The chief justice had long wanted to take the court out of politics. To have abandoned *Hellerstedt* might have thrust the court into the very center of the 2020 national elections. There were jurisprudential reasons for restraint. Quoting an earlier case, Chief Justice Roberts added, "The doctrine also brings pragmatic benefits. Respect for precedent "promotes the even-handed, predictable, and consistent development of legal principles, fosters reliance on judicial decisions, and contributes to the actual and perceived integrity of the judicial process." Roberts's words were similar to those in Justice Alito's majority decision overturning *Roe* two years later, a similarity that should not be mistaken for Alito's adopting Roberts's logic. In fact, Alito's repetition of Roberts's language was nothing more than faint praise, or something even less conciliatory.[10]

* * *

When deployed in the court's opinions, most footnotes are indicators of precedent—giving the citations that tell which precedents apply to the

---

9 June Medical Services, LLC v. Russo, U.S. 591 U.S. 1101, 1148 (2020) (Roberts, C. J., concurring).
10 591 U.S. at 1162 (Roberts, C. J. concurring).

present case. Ironically, when the court overturns a long line of precedents, the footnote has even more work to do, because the opinion must
cut loose from an established line of precedent and create a new one.
As for example, in *Dobbs*, the dueling footnotes in the majority and dissenting opinions marked a corresponding contest in public opinion and
national politics. Justice Alito used 117 footnotes to ground his decision
in precedent of history and tradition. Dissenting Justice Elena Kagan's
thirty-one footnotes offered a different concept of precedent, or rather,
an attempt to reunite precedent with a different history and tradition.[11]

There are two narratives of reproductive rights in American history.
The first is a story of anti-abortion laws that sought to protect women
who were pregnant from the dangers of the abortion, a story played out
over two hundred years; the second is a far shorter story of the effort
to provide legal and safe abortions to women who wanted to end their
pregnancies. The footnotes in the opinions in *Dobbs* featured these alternative histories. But like the warring readings of historical texts in
the gun control cases, the historical scholarship was subject to opposing
readings in *Dobbs*. In other words, the justices looked at the history differently, some seeing the later history as part of the whole story, others,
under the doctrine of traditional values, seeing only one part of the history leading up to *Dobbs*. In the latter, recent precedent and older history warred with one another.

Justice Alito delivered the opinion of the court in *Dobbs*. His introductory passage was remarkably similar to that in *Roe*: "Abortion presents
a profound moral issue on which Americans hold sharply conflicting
views. Some believe fervently that a human person comes into being
at conception and that abortion ends an innocent life. Others feel just
as strongly that any regulation of abortion invades a woman's right to
control her own body and prevents women from achieving full equality.
Still others in a third group think that abortion should be allowed under
some but not all circumstances, and those within this group hold a variety of views about the particular restrictions that should be imposed."[12]

---

11 Justice Alito's clerks in the 2022–23 term were John C. Brinkerhoff Jr., Robert Flatow,
Christopher Pagliarella, and Laura Rupault. To date, none have spoken about the opinion or, more
controversially, about its early release.

12 *Dobbs v. Jackson Women's Health Organization*, 142 S.Ct. 2240, 2248 (Alito, J.). Compare with
"We forthwith acknowledge our awareness of the sensitive and emotional nature of the abortion
controversy, of the vigorous opposing views, even among physicians, and of the deep and seemingly

The opening passage seemed to view a balance of equities—legitimate but vying views of the abortion practice. But from the first moment he sat on the court, Justice Alito thought that *Roe* was badly reasoned and wrongly determined. He had no use for balance of equities doctrine. At his confirmation hearings, he said that he had an open mind on *Roe* and would be impartial, but his record on the Third Circuit and his general views on originalism suggested otherwise. He had been a conservative thinker from the time that he attended Princeton, then Yale Law School. He served on the Court of Appeals for the Third Circuit and was President George W. Bush's choice to replace the retired Sandra Day O'Connor on the court. Although there, he voted with Justice Scalia 75 percent of the time, he was never a Scalia clone. Unlike other conservatives, he looked to the legislative record (in the states) for statutory meaning but preferred judicial restraint to the court's acting as a super legislature. As he told the members of the Senate Judiciary Committee at his confirmation hearing in 2006, "Good judges develop certain habits of mind. One of those habits of mind is the habit of delaying reaching conclusions until everything has been considered. Good judges are always open to the possibility of changing their minds based on the next brief that they read or the next argument that is made by an attorney who is appearing before them or a comment that is made by a colleague during the conference on the case, when the judges privately discuss the case." Still, the confirmation vote was a highly partisan one, as Alito, predictably, would join with other conservative judges to form a bloc of six.[13]

As an originalist who believed in judicial restraint, it was not surprising that Justice Alito found no basis in the language of the Constitution for a right to an abortion. Instead, it was "the Court [that] held that [the Constitution] confers a broad right to obtain one. [*Roe*] did not claim that American law or the common law had ever recognized such a right, and its survey of history ranged from the constitutionally irrelevant (*e.g.*, its discussion of abortion in antiquity) to the plainly

---

absolute convictions that the subject inspires. One's philosophy, one's experiences, one's exposure to the raw edges of human existence, one's religious training, one's attitudes toward life and family and their values, and the moral standards one establishes and seeks to observe, are all likely to influence and to color one's thinking and conclusions about abortion" 410 U.S. at 416 (Blackmun, J.).

13 *Confirmation Hearing on the Nomination of Samuel A. Alito, Jr. to be an Associate Justice of the Supreme Court of the United States* (Washington, DC: US Government printing office, 2006), 56.

incorrect (*e.g.*, its assertion that abortion was probably never a crime under the common law)."[14]

Alito's statement of facts was incomplete. Historians are wary of bare facts, recitations of names and dates without broader context. A more nuanced and complex rendering of facts would include evidence that the first state laws were designed to protect the putative mother from the abortionist rather than to criminalize the mother's actions. They came at a time when white women were second-class citizens, without the right to vote, hold office, or own property if they were married. Black women and Native women faced even greater hardships. But to Alito, the history in the legal briefs raising these issues did not have a bearing on the constitutional status of abortion. The history that did matter was the history and tradition—the precedent—of criminalization.[15]

Alito was not interested in his judicial predecessors' struggle to define viability or the various formulas they assessed to weigh women's health versus the potential rights of the fetus or the unborn child. "The Court did not explain the basis for this line, and even abortion supporters have found it hard to defend *Roe*'s reasoning." For this, he quoted not a supporter of *Roe* but John Hart Ely of Yale Law School, an opponent: "One prominent constitutional scholar wrote that he 'would vote for a statute very much like the one the Court end[ed] up drafting' if he were 'a legislator,' but his assessment of *Roe* was memorable and brutal: *Roe* was 'not constitutional law' at all and gave 'almost no sense of an obligation to try to be.'" Later in the opinion, and then in the footnotes, Alito cited line and verse from academic commentators to demonstrate how inconsistent and incoherent Blackmun's opinion was. But he did not cite historians, in particular the historians in the various friends of the court briefs to the abortion cases. One supposes, perhaps naïvely, that an opin-

---

14 142 S.Ct. at 2248 (Alito, J.). *Roe v. Wade* did not offer much of a history of the crime. Its general conclusion was that "it perhaps is not generally appreciated that the restrictive criminal abortion laws in effect in a majority of States today are of relatively recent vintage. Those laws, generally proscribing abortion or its attempt at any time during pregnancy except when necessary to preserve the pregnant woman's life, are not of ancient or even of common law origin. Instead, they derive from statutory changes effected, for the most part, in the latter half of the 19th century" (410 U.S. at 128 [Blackmun, J.]).

15 See, for example, James Mohr, *Abortion in America* (New York: Oxford University Press, 1978), 247–48 (*Roe* at the "end of an era."); Hull and Hoffer, *Roe v. Wade*, 179 ("But now it was done").

ion resting on the doctrine of history and tradition would entail a wide and deep survey of historical writings. Not so here.[16]

Instead, like Scalia in *Heller*, Alito appointed himself the official court chronicler. Professional historians endure years of graduate training, and the results of Alito's spontaneous career change would not have impressed professional historians. His history was a bare recital of bits and pieces of statute without context or contemporary analysis. They came from different places at different times, but he lumped them together: "At the time of *Roe*, 30 States still prohibited abortion at all stages. In the years prior to that decision, about a third of the States had liberalized their laws, but *Roe* abruptly ended that political process." He gave evidence for this blanket statement in an appendix, then again at the end of the footnotes, but there again he simply recited the bare bones of the statutes, with their dates. There was no attempt to pierce the veil of the legislative debates or the surrounding events to reveal historical context. Legislative intent to bar the practice of abortion was assumed.[17]

By contrast with the variety of state laws, Alito found that *Roe* imposed a "highly restrictive regime on the entire Nation, and it effectively struck down the abortion laws of every single State." Footnote 3 and the appendix underlined the point. But it was wrong, for no sooner did the decision come down than protest against it led to various states' reimposition of restrictions. The opposition led to more litigation and ultimately to *Dobbs*. Although "Justice Byron White aptly put it in his dissent, the decision represented the 'exercise of raw judicial power,'" it was never an effective power, for as White continued, and Alito conceded, "it sparked a national controversy that has embittered our political culture for a half century."[18]

Alito's history of the abortion rights controversy after *Roe* demonstrated to him that the rationale for its holding was never really established. The court in *Webster v. Reproductive Health Services* (1989) and *Planned Parenthood of Southeastern Pennsylvania v. Casey* (1992) reconsidered *Roe* and split over the precedent. A switch of one vote would

---

16 142 U.S. S.Ct. at 2241 (Alito, J.) quoting John Hart Ely, "The Wages of Crying Wolf: A Comment on Roe v. Wade," *Yale Law Journal* 82 (1973): 920–49 (Court should not second guess legislative preferences), 923. Are poor pregnant women a discrete and insular minority? See chapter 4 herein.
17 142 S.Ct. at 2241 (Alito, J.).
18 142 S.Ct. at 2241 (Alito, J.).

have overturned *Roe*, but, although expected by many observers, that vote did not come. Instead, in fragmented opinions, members of the court defended, attacked, or revised *Roe*, supplanting the original trimester formula with an "undue burden" standard. In *Casey*, the idea that "*stare decisis*, which calls for prior decisions to be followed in most instances, required adherence to what it called *Roe*'s 'central holding'—that a State may not constitutionally protect fetal life before 'viability'—even if that holding was wrong." Actually, none of three justices in the latter "joint opinion" in *Casey*—Anthony Kennedy, Sandra Day O'Connor, and David Souter—said anything about a "wrong." But they did invoke the reliance that pregnant women had placed on *Roe* as one important reason to retain it.[19]

The persistence and political influence of the opponents of abortion rights proved to Alito that "as has become increasingly apparent in the intervening years, *Casey* did not achieve that goal. Americans continue to hold passionate and widely divergent views on abortion, and state legislatures have acted accordingly." What in fact some legislatures did was to ask the court to overturn *Roe*, while in the meantime undermining it. Alito continued: "And in this case, 26 States have expressly asked this Court to overrule *Roe* and *Casey* and allow the States to regulate or prohibit pre-viability abortions."[20]

In *Dobbs*, Mississippi wished "to uphold the constitutionality of [its] law that generally prohibits an abortion after the 15th week of pregnancy—several weeks before the point at which a fetus is now regarded as 'viable' outside the womb." Alito ignored that portion of the state's case and found that "the State's primary argument is that we should reconsider and overrule *Roe* and *Casey* and once again allow each State to regulate abortion as its citizens wish." In answer to the state's plea, Alito decided, "We hold that *Roe* and *Casey* must be overruled. The Constitution makes no reference to abortion, and no such right is implicitly protected by any constitutional provision, including the one on which the defenders of *Roe* and *Casey* now chiefly rely—the due process clause of the Fourteenth Amendment. That provision has been held to guarantee some rights that are not mentioned in the

---

19 142 S.Ct. at 2241 (Alito, J.).
20 142 S.Ct. at 2242 (Alito, J.).

Constitution, but any such right must be 'deeply rooted in this Nation's history and tradition' and 'implicit in the concept of ordered
liberty.'" So the end of *Roe* required rejection of substantive due process, the absence of deep rooting in the nation's history and tradition,
and a reading of the open-ended formula in *Palko* for the exceptions
(not the inclusions) of "ordered liberty" of the Bill of Rights in the
Fourteenth Amendment.[21]

It was the history and tradition portion of the majority-opinion decision that redefined precedent and required the display of historical
evidence. But among historians, one cannot simply offer historical text
without some explanation. In Alito's view, that enterprise did not require
a deep or broad historical account. The historians of abortion in the
friends of the court briefs had already provided some context, and Alito
discarded it. Instead, he offered the same kind of bare bones historical
recital that one found in *Heller*, as if history were simple and easily read,
like the language of the Second Amendment.

But unlike *Heller*, which was something of a novel case, *Roe* had lots
of baggage that had to be thrown overboard. "*Roe*'s defenders character-
ize the abortion right as similar to the rights recognized in past decisions involving matters such as intimate sexual relations, contraception,
and marriage, but abortion is fundamentally different, as both *Roe* and
Casey acknowledged, because it destroys what those decisions called
'fetal life' and what the law now before us describes as an 'unborn human
being.'" Quoting from the decision that he was discarding was clever,
but the definition of *unborn* was itself subject to a long history, which
was not even alluded to in Alito's opinion. It was simply implied. That is,
Alito assumed that the embryo was a human being waiting to be born.
The fetus was an intermediate stage. The dissenters feared that the next
step would be the undoing of privacy rights like birth control, but Alito
insisted that *Griswold v. Connecticut* was not in danger.[22]

The other difference from *Heller* was that *Roe* was not long-established
precedent. Alito pit recent precedent against precedent rooted in history and tradition. The latter won. "*Stare decisis*, the doctrine on which

---

21 142 S.Ct. at 2242 (Alito, J.).

22 142 S.Ct. at 2243 (Alito, J.). There was a parallel argument in the opinions whether the end of *Roe*
sounded the death knell for privacy rights, hence for birth control, same sex marriage, and so forth.
On Heller as new case, see Phillips and Blackmun, "Corpus Linguistics," 612.

Casey's controlling opinion was based, does not compel unending adherence to *Roe*'s abuse of judicial authority. *Roe* was egregiously wrong from the start. Its reasoning was exceptionally weak, and the decision has had damaging consequences. And far from bringing about a national settlement of the abortion issue, *Roe* and *Casey* have enflamed debate and deepened division." That was certainly so—abortion rights had become, for many Americans, more important than the wars in the Middle East at the time.[23]

The decision seemed to end here. "It is time to heed the Constitution and return the issue of abortion to the people's elected representatives. The permissibility of abortion, and the limitations, upon it, are to be resolved like most important questions in our democracy: by citizens trying to persuade one another and then voting." But the opinion was only just beginning; more than 80 percent of the opinion was yet to come. One senses that the opinion was something like the historian who has more note cards and wants to put all of them into their essay. So the opinion, like Scalia's in *Heller*, piled detail on detail when all the surprise was gone. But Alito wanted to rehearse another history that went back to his and Justice Breyer's opinions in *Hellerstedt* and *Russo*. Then, Breyer's majority opinion had rehearsed at great length the details of the lower courts' findings. Alito, now able to write for the court, had been storing up his note cards for five years. He was not going to omit any of them. He relished the account of the Mississippi legislature's factual findings. He relitigated *Casey*, this time coming up with the right answer. He reimposed original intent, quoting Joseph Story's *Commentaries on the Constitution of the United States*. By contrast, *Roe* was "loose" in its interpretation (ignoring the fact that during his lifetime, Story was routinely accused of loose construction of the Constitution.)[24]

Alito dismissed an equal protection clause defense of *Roe* because "neither *Roe* nor *Casey* saw fit to invoke this theory, and it is squarely foreclosed by our precedents, which establish that a State's regulation of abortion is not a sex-based classification and is thus not subject to the 'heightened scrutiny' that applies to such classifications." (Here, one

---

23 142 S.Ct. at 2243 (Alito. J.). Pew Research Center, Public Opinion on Abortion, "Views on Abortion, 1995–2022," May 17, 2022, www.pewresearch.org.
24 142 S.Ct. at 2243 (Alito, J.).

notes, stare decisis was fully operational, when for *Roe*, it was not.) The constitutional theory lesson continued with concern for the misuse of substantive due process. He conceded that the first eight amendments were indeed incorporated in the Fourteenth Amendment. Where did the Fourteenth Amendment say this? It did not. It was the court, over the long course of the first half of the twentieth century, that adopted, piece by piece, the doctrine of incorporation. But if this process stopped with *Palko v. Connecticut* (1937), and were Alito's logic followed to its natural conclusion, *Brown v. Board of Education* would have to go, and separate but equal would have to be reinstated.[25]

A second category of permissible incorporation was those fundamental rights that were part of a scheme of ordered liberty. Presumably, this included *Brown*. But Alito had to connect this to his mantra of "deeply rooted in our history and tradition." The problem was that Jim Crow segregation of schools was more deeply rooted in American history than the far more recent desegregation, and even more so than integration of schools. "We have engaged in a careful analysis of the history of the right at issue," Alito promised, excluding other rights equally contested at the time, contested over time, and still not accepted in many quarters—like integration. "History and tradition" was simply no more definitive than any other constitutional doctrine for deciding which precedent to retain and which to discard.[26]

The majority opinion concluded that "historical inquiries of this nature are essential whenever we are asked to recognize a new component of the 'liberty' protected by the Due Process Clause because the term 'liberty' alone provides little guidance." The history that Alito provided was unilluminated by any professional historical commentary. The only citations to historians were not to historians at all but to philosophers of history whom Alito mistook for experts in legal history. Thus, "In a well-known essay, Isaiah Berlin reported that 'historians of ideas' had cataloged more than 200 different senses in which the term had been used." Isaiah Berlin was a philosopher. His work in the history of ideas in early modern Europe was of a philosophical nature—he did not work in archives, libraries, or the field, he did not

---

25 142 S.Ct. at 2245 (Alito, J.).
26 142 S.Ct. at 2235 (Alito, J.).

write histories, and he had no expertise in American law or history. He simply sat in his library and dictated his thoughts into a recorder, and the transcriptions were published.[27]

Alito warned that when the court had departed from the "teachings of history," "it has fallen into the freewheeling judicial policymaking that characterized discredited decisions such as *Lochner v. New York, 198 U.S. 45* (1905)." Actually, there is almost no history in the *Lochner* majority opinion. There was the accusation, by Oliver Wendell Holmes Jr. in dissent, that the majority was captured by Herbert Spencer's social statistics, but that was a work of sociological theory, not a history, and the majority did not actually rely on it. Alito ignored the glaring errors of his historical aside and continued, "The Court must not fall prey to such an unprincipled approach. Instead, [it must be] guided by the history and tradition that map the essential components of our Nation's concept of ordered liberty."[28]

Put in different terms, Alito's extensive account of pre-*Roe* legal sources does not offer any of what historians routinely call (and produce) secondary sources—the work of trained academic historians working in the archives and old records. Not a one. There is a cottage industry out there of modern scholarly articles and books on abortion and infanticide. To be sure, the authors of these, read in objective fashion, would not support Alito's position, so why include them in the opinion or the notes?[29]

Instead, there is in Alito's recital of old treatises and commentaries—combined with the absence of modern scholarship—something like satirist Jonathan Swift's "Battle of the Books" (1704), in which ancient and modern books leap off the shelves to contest their authority:

> Respondents and their *amici* have no persuasive answer to this historical evidence. . . . A few of respondents' *amici* muster historical arguments,

---

27 142 S.Ct. at 2247 (Alito, J.).

28 142 S.Ct. at 2248 (Alito, J.).

29 In assessing the weaknesses of historical theory and fact in the majority, am I perhaps too protective of my own, historical, discipline? In full disclosure, I am coauthor, with legal scholar N. E. H. Hull, of *Murdering Mothers: Infanticide in England and New England, 1558–1803* (New York: New York University Press, 1983); and *Roe v. Wade: The Abortion Rights Controversy in American History*, 3rd ed. (Lawrence: University Press of Kansas, 2023), and coeditor of *The Abortion Rights Controversy in America, A Legal Reader* (Chapel Hill: University of North Carolina Press, 2004).

but they are very weak. . . . Instead of following these [eighteenth century] authorities, *Roe* relied largely on two articles by a pro-abortion advocate who claimed that Coke had intentionally misstated the common law because of his strong anti-abortion views. These articles have been discredited, and it has come to light that even members of Jane Roe's legal team did not regard them as serious scholarship.

In fact, the author of these was not a historian. He was a lawyer. He had no historical training and no history credentials. But why, although the shooting range was the wrong one, would such facts matter when an easy target presented itself?[30]

A harder target for criticism was the joint Organization of American Historians (OAH)/American Historical Association (AHA) brief. The OAH and the AHA are the leading professional organizations of historians in America. Why it sponsored a friend of the court brief may be questioned, but its scholarly qualifications were unquestioned. Shortly after the opinion was announced, a joint statement responded to the treatment accorded the brief in the majority opinion: "We are dismayed that the Court declined to take seriously the historical claims of our brief. . . . The OAH and AHA consider it imperative that historical evidence and argument be presented according to high standards of historical scholarship. The Court's majority opinion in Dobbs v. Jackson does not meet those standards, and has therefore established a flawed and troubling precedent." In aid of their claim to historical accuracy, the two organizations appended a list of other historical associations subscribing to their position. Among the thirty was the American Society for Legal History, an elite group of law professors, political scientists, and historians.[31]

The brief argued that "the new and stricter statutes enacted in the 1840s to 1850s were often a response to alarming newspaper stories about women's deaths from abortion" and "yet despite these new laws on the books, abortion convictions remained rare." Even after the campaign to criminalize abortion, "abortions continued taking place, and many ordinary citizens continued to believe that abortion prior to quickening

---

30 142 S.Ct. at 2254 (Alito, J.).
31 Joint OAH-AHA Statement on the *Dobbs v. Jackson* decision July 2022, https://www.oah.org.

was not a crime." That is, the practice of abortion and the legal effort to suppress abortion did not coincide. This was because those women, and their helpers, were not part of the legal regime itself. The nineteenth-century legislators were all white males, almost all propertied Protestants. That was hardly a cross section or a representative group of Americans. One did not have to be a professional historian to surmise that such a limited demographic segment of American society might share values at odds with other Americans or that their view of the world might be strikingly different from our own. In effect, the authors of the brief urged the court to consider the motives of the legislators. Recall that these were the days when sending birth control information through the federal mails was also a crime.[32]

To its detriment, the AHA brief bore a remarkable similarity to the nineteenth-century history section of the far more voluminous and authoritative "historians' brief" in *Webster*, submitted thirty-three years earlier. The historians' brief in *Webster* was far more comprehensive, carried the story up to *Webster*, and included a twelve-page appendix of leading scholars in law and history. Although the two organizations agreed to sign on to the brief in September, 2021, the OAH/AHA amicus had not one historian, legal or otherwise, putting their name to it. It was an institutional submission that seemed tired and halfhearted, perhaps because the councils of the two organizations thought that their advocacy was sufficient in itself.[33]

Alito responded that the evidence for the 2021 brief was "based almost entirely on statements made by one prominent proponent [Dr. Horatio Storer] of the statutes." Whether or not this evidence was a smoking gun, "This Court has long disfavored arguments based on alleged legislative motives . . . [citations omitted]. The Court has recognized that inquiries into legislative motives 'are a hazardous matter.'" One notes the irony

---

32 Brief for amici curiae American Historical Association and Organization of American Historians in support of respondents, available at https://www.historians.org/news-and-advocacy/aha-advocacy/aha-amicus-curiae-brief-in-dobbs-v-jackson-womens-health-organization-(september-2021), on pages 1, 3, 4, and 21 of the associated PDF.

33 "AHA Signs Amicus Curiae Brief in Dobbs v. Jackson Women's Health Organization," American Historical Association, www.historians.org; Clyde Spillenger, Jane E. Larson, and Sylvia A. Law, "Brief of 281 American Historians As Amici Curiae Supporting Appellees," *Public Historian* 12, no. 3 (Summer 1990): 57–75; Webster v. Reproductive Health Services, 88–406; Roy M. Mersky and Gary R. Hoffman, comps., *Documentary History of the Legal Aspects of Abortion in the United States: Webster v. Reproductive Health Services* (Littleton, CO: F. B. Rothman: 1990), 109–70.

that indifferent to their motives, the court readily assigns abortion rights to state legislatures. Mississippi's legislature is hardly a good example for this argument, given its past embrace of chattel slavery and its creation of citizens' councils to ferret out integrationists in the Jim Crow era. To be fair, Alito did score one solid point based not on modern scholarship but on modern source criticism: "Here, the argument about legislative motive is not even based on statements by legislators, but on statements made by a few supporters of the new 19th-century abortion laws, and it is quite a leap to attribute these motives to all the legislators whose votes were responsible for the enactment of those laws."[34]

Like Scalia in *Heller*, Alito devoted the rest of the opinion to refuting the dissent. "Instead of seriously pressing the argument that the abortion right itself has deep roots, supporters of *Roe* and *Casey* contend that the abortion right is an integral part of a broader entrenched right." That was an opening to a discussion of precedent. For "nor does the right to obtain an abortion have a sound basis in precedent." The key words were *sound* and *basis*. "Attempts to justify abortion through appeals to a broader right to autonomy and to define one's 'concept of existence' prove too much. . . . Those criteria, at a high level of generality, could license fundamental rights to illicit drug use, prostitution, and the like." The key word here was *illicit*. But the long curve of history has shown (to historians at least) that drug criminalization is relatively recent (opiates were not illegal in the nineteenth century; nor was prostitution). Regulation of substances and sex does not make them illicit. Again, the argument was circular—allowing abortion on demand would be like allowing the use of marijuana on demand. But what if the latter had become permitted? Would that be part of the history and traditions of the nation?[35]

Again, a good place to stop, but Alito did not stop. He repeated that "the dissent does not identify *any* pre-*Roe* authority that supports such a right—no state constitutional provision or statute, no federal or state judicial precedent, not even a scholarly treatise." The dissent has no historical evidence, historical evidence now being the key to any successful defense of the abortion right. By saying this, Alito moved the history

---

34 142 S.Ct at 2255 (Alito, J.).
35 142 S.Ct at 2257 (Alito, J.).

and tradition definition of precedent of the majority opinion from the periphery to the center. "The dissent's failure to engage with this long tradition is devastating to its position." Why? Because "we have held that the "established method of substantive-due-process analysis" requires that an unenumerated right be 'deeply rooted in this Nation's history and tradition' before it can be recognized as a component of the 'liberty' protected in the Due Process Clause."[36]

All of which makes the historical references in the footnotes not only vital to the majority's rationale but part of that rationale. "So without support in history or relevant precedent, *Roe*'s reasoning cannot be defended even under the dissent's proposed test, and the dissent is forced to rely solely on the fact that a constitutional right to abortion was recognized in *Roe* and later decisions that accepted *Roe*'s interpretation." In short, the dissent's logic was circular.[37]

With history and tradition sitting at the head of the table of precedent, the majority opinion returned to the doctrine of stare decisis. A precedent based on history and tradition was not an absolute command, for "there are occasions when past decisions should be overruled, and as we will explain, this is one of them." The proof would be a footnote even longer than Scalia's best effort in *Heller*. It would document in how many cases the court had overturned its own precedents. It would be a historical coup de grace to *Roe*. It would demolish the "reliance" argument that precedent based on usage need not rest also on history and tradition.[38]

* * *

Before the promised omnibus note came an appendix, in which the majority opinion listed the anti-abortion laws of thirty-seven states to 1868 and thirteen territories thereafter that "contain statutes criminalizing abortion at all stages of pregnancy in the States." It could have been abbreviated to say that thirty-seven states and thirteen territories criminalized abortion practice before *Roe*. The appendix did not have notes, and it did not mention that all the statutes criminalized the acts of the abortion providers rather than the women seeking abortions. In any case, there was no particular reason to turn the opinion into a miniature

---

36 142 S.Ct at 2259 (Alito, J.).
37 142 S.Ct at 2261 (Alito, J.).
38 142 S.Ct at 2261 (Alito, J.).

encyclopedia, and one may surmise that without the aid of the four clerks in his office, Alito would not have bothered. No one was expected to read it, because everyone who supported *Roe* would argue that those laws came at a time when women could not vote, or get into college, or practice law—hence they were irrelevant. And those who favored voiding *Roe* would argue that there was no constitutional basis for the abortion right, and it did not matter that some states allowed it (i.e., the ones not in the list, like California, New York, Hawai'i, and Connecticut) before *Roe*. Why then append it?

The way to explain the presence of the appendix is to view it as the introduction to the footnotes. There were 117 of them, more than triple the number in Scalia's *Heller* opinion, and they, too, were pieces of history and tradition—not proof, but history and tradition itself. For they marked the long campaign to overturn *Roe*. They went back to Justice Byron White's and William Rehnquist's original opposition to the decision, then further back to the beginning of the United States, then carried the story up to the present. They were an answer to the claim that the shift in political alignment on the court was the only reason for the end of the *Roe* era. They were yet another kind of history and tradition, this one internal.

The first, the citation to *Roe*, is immediately followed by the most robust and academically respected criticism of *Roe*, Yale Law professor John Hart Ely's "The Wages of Crying Wolf: A Comment on *Roe* v. *Wade*." It was published soon after the decision came down in the *Yale Law Journal* and repeated in Ely's later *Democracy and Distrust* (1980).[39] Alito was fair to Ely's views, then followed with a clever (mis)use of the views of Ely's counterpart, Laurence Tribe of Harvard Law School. Tribe was a defender of *Roe* who had little use for Blackmun's opinion. His piece in the *Harvard Law Review*, "Toward a Model of Roles in the Due Process of Life and Law," lamented that "in *Roe v. Wade* and *Doe v. Bolton*, when the Court had its most dramatic opportunity to express its supposed aversion to substantive due process, it carried that doctrine to lengths few observers had expected." Worse, Tribe opined, "The Court says even less to justify its crucial conclusion that the state's interest in

---

39 Ely, "The Wages of Crying Wolf." John Hart Ely, *Democracy and Distrust* (Cambridge, MA: Harvard University Press, 1980), 73–77.

potential life does not become 'compelling' until viability.'" Later in the article, however, Tribe supplied a very different, much fuller reading of abortion rights. In effect, it supplanted Blackmun's muddled prose with Tribe's version of what Roe really said:

> The Court was not, after all, choosing simply between the alternatives of abortion and continued pregnancy. It was instead choosing among alternative allocations of decision-making authority, for the issue it faced was whether the woman and her doctor, rather than an agency of government, should have the authority to make the abortion decision at various stages of pregnancy. The appellant's argument in Roe was not that the Court should decide "for abortion," but rather that the Court should transfer the role of decisionmaker from the government to the woman herself. Despite what the Court's opinion seemed to say, the result it reached was not the simple "substitution of one non-rational judgment for another concerning the relative importance of a mother's opportunity to live the life she has planned and a fetus's opportunity to live at all," but was instead a decision about who should make judgments of that sort."[40]

Historians have a term for what Alito had done in the footnote. It is called quoting out of context. One chooses words or a group of words from the target source and quotes them, although they are the opposite of what the author of that source, and the rest of that source, meant to say. It is a first-year graduate school historical methods mistake (that reappears in movie advertisements). And Alito enlarged it by bundling *Roe* supporters into the same footnote as *Roe* opponents, then by selectively quoting from the former to make them appear to belong in the latter category. Few jurists (except Blackmun) liked the way he explained his decision, but the bulk of the legal academic community supported the underlying policy.

In a more general sense, this footnote was an example of law office history, the historical sources being the writings of legal academics, twisted, chopped, and reassembled to support positions which they did

---

40 Laurence Tribe, "Toward a Model of Roles in the Due Process of Life and Law," *Harvard Law Review* 87 (1973): 2, 11.

not actually hold. This will hardly be persuasive to the legal historian who comes along later and compares the snippets in the footnote with the complete version of articles. What use has the collection of snippets? One must conclude that the audience for the footnote is not the legal historian or indeed any expert in historical methods. The audience was not the general public, and its members did not read footnotes. The audience was the dissenters, just as the audience for Justice Scalia's many footnotes in *Heller* was Justice Stevens. Alito had no intent to make the footnote part of the law, unlike Stone in *Carolene Products* or Warren in *Brown*. They served a different purpose.

That purpose was evident in subsequent notes, where cases regarding different subjects and quotations from cases from widely separated periods in our history were linked together, as if they had been written by the same hand at the same time to the same purpose. It was patchwork or mosaic reasoning, or, as termed in historical methodology, "source mining." It is another of the many fallacies that young historians are taught to shun. Worse still, sometimes the patchwork did not even mesh. So in footnote 19, "See also, *e.g.*, *Duncan v. Louisiana, 391 U.S. 145*, 148 (1968) (asking whether 'a right is among those "fundamental principles of liberty and Justice which lie at the base of our civil and political institutions"'); *Palko v. Connecticut, 302 U.S. 319*, 325 (1937) (requiring 'a "principle of Justice so rooted in the traditions and conscience of our people as to be ranked as fundamental"' (quoting *Snyder v. Massachusetts, 291 U.S. 97*, 105 (1934)." Alito had joined a quote from *Duncan*, in which the court ruled that a jury trial was a fundamental part of the county's criminal Justice, to *Palko*, in which a court, some thirty years earlier, had ruled that a jury trial (along other parts of the Bill of Rights) was not part of our ordered liberty. At that time, according to Justice Cardozo, writing for the court in *Palko*, "The right to trial by jury and the immunity from prosecution except as the result of an indictment may have value and importance. Even so, they are not of the very essence of a scheme of ordered liberty." A history that did this ill-fitting source mining would be marked "F". A Supreme Court footnote that did this leaves one shaking one's head.[41]

---

41 Duncan v. Louisiana, 391 U.S. 145, 148 (1968); Palko v. Connecticut 302 U.S. 319, 325 (Cardozo, J.). See Galloway v. United States, 319 U.S. 372, 397 (1943) (Black, J.): "The founders of our government thought that trial of fact by juries rather than by judges was an essential bulwark of civil

Then there is nitpicking. This goes on all the time in historical scholarship, but here the death by a thousand papercuts has a different purpose. Undermine your opponents' accuracy in some small thing, and you can accuse them of inaccuracy throughout. "If they got this wrong, how can they be trusted?" So in footnote 34, "The *amicus* brief for the American Historical Association asserts that only 26 States prohibited abortion at all stages, but that brief incorrectly excludes West Virginia and Nebraska from its count. Compare Brief for American Historical Association 27–28 (citing Quay), with Appendix A, *infra*."[42]

Next, turn to motive. "Other *amicus* briefs present arguments about the motives of proponents of liberal access to abortion. They note that some such supporters have been motivated by a desire to suppress the size of the African-American population. See Brief for African-American Organization et al. as *Amici Curiae* 14–21; see also *Box v. Planned Parenthood of Ind. and Ky., Inc.*, 587 U. S. ___, ___–___ (2019) (Thomas, J., concurring) (slip op., at 1–4). And it is beyond dispute that *Roe* has had that demographic effect." This was an accusation that was widely made against *Roe* by a special-interest group. They were not experts of any kind, but they had the support of Justice Clarence Thomas. Thomas was the most vocal, open, and consistent opponent of *Roe*, and in effect, the amici were quoting Thomas back to Thomas. He honored them with citation in his concurring opinion. This back and forth did not make the argument any stronger, although it seemed to multiply the voices clamoring for the end of *Roe*. A little demography shows that declining Black birth rate is related to the choice of Black women to have smaller families. In any case, even if the total number of abortions were of Black women, it would not have changed Black birth rates very much. Then, having made an inflammatory and unfounded claim of racial suicide through voluntary

---

liberty. For this reason, among others, they adopted Article III, § 2 of the Constitution, and the Sixth and Seventh Amendments." Trial by jury in founding era: James Oldham, *Trial by Jury* (New York: New York University Press, 2006), 5.

42 Nitpicking works both ways, of course; see Aaron Tang, "After Dobbs: History, Tradition, and the Uncertain Future of a Nationwide Abortion Ban," *Stanford Law Review* 75 (2023), 31–46, available at the Social Science Research Network; finding evidence that the footnote was factually incorrect; twenty-one of the thirty-seven states continued the common-law pre-quickening exemption, not nine.

birth control options, the majority backed away: "For our part, we do not question the motives of either those who have supported or those who have opposed laws restricting abortions."[43]

Footnote 48 was the crowning glory of the majority opinion citations. There is no doubt that the court has overturned its own decisions. The "big three" of *Brown, West Coast v. Parrish*, and *Barnett v. West Virginia* in the text make the point. Why, then, the exhaustive list in the footnote? It is not because Justice Alito wanted to prove he could do basic historical research. Indeed, one cannot see Justice Alito poring through the *U.S. Reports* to find all the cases in which the court overruled an earlier precedent. One or more of his clerks did the spade work. I can only find one missing case, *Skinner v. Texas* (1942), rather pointedly overruling *Buck v. Bell* (1927) (Justice William O. Douglas wrote with a sharp pen).

This footnote is gaining a reputation of its own, not always glowing. As law professor Eric Segall wrote in one of the many law blogs, "The more contestable point is how much, if at all, the Court cares about its own prior case law. This factor leads us to the very lengthy footnote 48 . . . and what Justice Angry Alito called a "partial list" of the times when the Court reversed itself. I strongly suggest you read it. I predict it will leave you breathless." In any case, the footnote is here reproduced as appendix C.[44]

The court does indeed overrule earlier precedent. The "string cite" in footnote 48 seeks to add what might be called inverse precedent, the history and tradition of overturning decisions, to the history and tradition of the court. What had the cases to do with the issues in *Roe*? Was it not much easier for the court to overturn any one of the cases cited than to overturn *Roe*? Who can tell from the list? (In some cases, it probably was; in others the question was a technical one. Most of the cases were irrelevant to the majority opinion however.)

The penultimate section of the notes reminded the reader that the majority had always been right on the abortion issue, even when (actually, especially when) writing in dissent. The notes then closed with a

---

43 142 S.Ct (Alito, J.). According to the Centers for Disease Control and Prevention, fertility rates for all races are declining. The Black fertility rate, historically higher than the white rate, is simply moving closer to the national average. As the marital rate declines for all races, the fertility rate has declined. Again, the rates for whites and Blacks are simply closing.

44 Eric Segall, "Dobbs Footnote 48, Precedent, and Why the Supreme Court Is Not a Court" Dorf on Law, August 19, 2022, www.dorfonlaw.org.

coda—a return to citations for the various state bans on abortion, for the third time. The state histories framed the beginning, middle, and end of the notes, reiterating that states had always criminalized abortions. In effect, the notes served as the chorus of the opinion. The notes did not show an "angry" Alito, however, so much as a frustrated one, in so far as he believed that the end of *Roe* was long past due. History had shown him and his fellow justices that the decision should never have been handed down.

* * *

Justice Kagan's dissent, for herself and Justices Sonia Sotomayor and Stephen Breyer, told a different historical story, which her footnotes reflected. It was as if she and Justice Alito occupied different constitutional planets. The only history that mattered was that between *Roe* and 2022. "For half a century, *Roe* v. *Wade, 410 U.S. 113* (1973), and *Planned Parenthood of Southeastern Pa.* v. *Casey, 505 U.S. 833* (1992), have protected the liberty and equality of women." The liberty and equality of women were not part of the deep history and tradition of the nation but a precedent of more recent provenance. "*Roe* held, and *Casey* reaffirmed, that the Constitution safeguards a woman's right to decide for herself whether to bear a child. *Roe* held, and *Casey* reaffirmed, that in the first stages of pregnancy, the government could not make that choice for women." The two decisions protected women from an intrusive, male-dominated government. The government was the enemy, something so foreign from Alito's thinking that Kagan might have been writing about a criminal justice case rather than a women's rights case. "The government could not control a woman's body or the course of a woman's life: It could not determine what the woman's future would be."[45]

The justices' different understanding of precedent rested on a different way of reading history. Kagan's idea of precedent, like her idea of history, was holistic; Alito's idea of precedent, like his history, was staccato. The justices were standing on the two sides of a deep and wide crevasse across which Kagan summarized while Alito particularized.

---

45 142 S.Ct at 2317 (Kagan, J. dissenting). Kagan's clerks in the 2022–23 term were Gavin W. Duffy Gideon, Danial J. B. Kane, Hilary R. Ledwell, and Kyle Schneider.

Kagan: "Respecting a woman as an autonomous being, and granting her full equality, meant giving her substantial choice over this most personal and most consequential of all life decisions." She conceded what Alito had labored to prove, that "*Roe* and *Casey* well understood the difficulty and divisiveness of the abortion issue. The Court knew that Americans hold profoundly different views about the 'moral[ity]' of 'terminating a pregnancy, even in its earliest stage.'" And the court recognized that "the State has legitimate interests from the outset of the pregnancy in protecting" the "life of the fetus that may become a child."[46]

Kagan's presentation of history, hence her view of precedent, was softer, compassionate, where Alito's was tough minded. Kagan read history in terms of its emanations rather than its bare details. Such a history allowed for a nuanced weighing of values and needs:

> So the Court struck a balance, as it often does when values and goals compete. It held that the State could prohibit abortions after fetal viability, so long as the ban contained exceptions to safeguard a woman's life or health. It held that even before viability, the State could regulate the abortion procedure in multiple and meaningful ways. But until the viability line was crossed, the Court held, a State could not impose a "substantial obstacle" on a woman's "right to elect the procedure" as she (not the government) thought proper, in light of all the circumstances and complexities of her own life.[47]

This was the kind of lived experience that Alito's precedents excluded from both his history of the abortion issue in the courts and his history of the abortion issue in the women's world. The conflicting use of history in the notes, mirroring the different views of precedent, was a difference that historians recognize. The doctrine of "separate spheres" of American social and cultural history, introduced in Nancy Cott's 1977 book *The Bonds of Womanhood: "Women's Sphere" in New England, 1780–1835*, and carried to perfection in Laurel Thatcher Ulrich's *A Midwife's Tale: The Life of Martha Ballard, Based on Her Diary, 1785–1812* (1990) rests on the simple notion that women's work and women's attitudes are different from men's.

---

46 142 S.Ct at 2317 (Kagan, J. dissenting).
47 142 S.Ct at 2317 (Kagan, J. dissenting).

Women work in the home; men work in the field; women adopt caring approaches to life; men are competitive and combative. While more accurate in describing pre-twenty-first-century life and not without critics among today's historians, the theme rests on an even broader foundation: that men and women see history in different ways. The balancing of interests, rather than an absolute view of rights, fits one side in this divide.[48]

Thus, Kagan:

> Today, the Court discards that balance. It says that from the very moment of fertilization, a woman has no rights to speak of. A State can force her to bring a pregnancy to term, even at the steepest personal and familial costs. An abortion restriction, the majority holds, is permissible whenever rational, the lowest level of scrutiny known to the law. And because, as the Court has often stated, protecting fetal life is rational, States will feel free to enact all manner of restrictions.

What evidence from precedent could Kagan summon to support holistic reading of the law's proper treatment of women? How would it reflect the difference ways that historians prove their case? Bear in mind that in past time pregnancy and child bearing, along with birthing, was an intensely female, domestic, and private event. Women gathered with the pregnant, midwives presided at the birth, and women continued care after the birth for both the mother and the child. Doctors were called when there was a complication. With the introduction of hospital birth and the obstetrics and gynecology medical practice, bearing and birthing crossed over into a gendered world that now included men, typically in positions of authority. Should law have followed this direction? "Whatever the exact scope of the coming laws, one result of today's decision is certain: the curtailment of women's rights, and of their status as free and equal citizens. Yesterday, the Constitution guaranteed that a woman confronted with an unplanned pregnancy could (within reasonable limits) make her own decision about whether to bear a child, with all the life-transforming consequences that act involves."[49]

---

48 Nancy Cott, *The Bonds of Womanhood: "Women's Sphere" in New England, 1780–1835* (New Haven, CT: Yale University Press, 1977); Laurel Thatcher Ulrich, *A Midwife's Tale: The Life of Martha Ballard, Based on Her Diary* (New York: Alfred A. Knopf, 1990); and Gilligan, *In a Different Voice.*
49 142 S.Ct 2317 (Kagan, J. dissenting).

Justice Kagan early committed herself to public life. She crossed the boundary from the private to the public spheres. Born and raised in New York City, educated at Princeton University, Worcester College, Oxford, and Harvard Law School, she clerked for Supreme Court Justice Thurgood Marshall. Choosing a legal teaching career over work in a law firm, she began at the University of Chicago Law School, which she left to serve in President Bill Clinton's White House. Clinton nominated her to the United States Court of Appeals for the DC Circuit, but the Senate Republican majority did not proceed with the hearings, and she joined the faculty at Harvard Law School, later becoming its dean. In 2009, Kagan became the first female solicitor general of the United States. The capstone of her public career came on May 10, 2010, when President Barack Obama appointed her to the court. The United States Senate confirmed her nomination by a vote of 63–37. She has served since August 7, 2010. On the court, she is not confrontational, and her writing style is similarly accommodating, except in *Dobbs*.[50]

In *Dobbs*, Kagan saw change over time not in discrete and isolated moments but as part of larger movements: "The majority has no good reason for the upheaval in law and society it sets off. *Roe* and *Casey* have been the law of the land for decades, shaping women's expectations of their choices when an unplanned pregnancy occurs." The general rule for overturning precedent was a change in the society. "No recent developments, in either law or fact, have eroded or cast doubt on those precedents. Nothing, in short, has changed. Indeed, the Court in *Casey* already found all of that to be true." Now the unpleasant truth that Alito completely avoided: "The Court reverses course today for one reason and one reason only: because the composition of this Court has changed. . . . Today, the proclivities of individuals rule. The Court departs from its obligation to faithfully and impartially apply the law."[51]

We are not politicians, Chief Justice Roberts insisted on another occasion. But you are, Justice Kagan replied in *Dobbs*. And if Kagan's assertion was valid, was the intervention of *Roe* not also the product of the politics of the court? Was all the precedent on divisive national issues subject to partisanship on the court? Kagan had opened a door that historians and

50 Elena Kagan biography, "Supreme Court of the United States." Accessed March 17, 2023. See, www.supremecourt.gov.
51 142 S.Ct 2319, 2320 (Kagan, J. dissenting).

political scientists had long peered around. After all, "Some half-century ago, *Roe* struck down a state law making it a crime to perform an abortion unless its purpose was to save a woman's life. The *Roe* Court knew it was treading on difficult and disputed ground." The immediate aftermath of *Roe* (indeed the years preceding it as well) promised that it would be controversial outside the court. The "balance" that the court struck was actually a compromise rather than a jurisprudential move, "turning on the stage of the pregnancy at which the abortion would occur." Women's choices were balanced against legislative majorities that wanted to protect fetal life from the point of conception. The years after *Roe* saw additional compromises, partial retreats, and reaffirmations of the core of *Roe*, "of a woman's right to choose." *Roe* sailed through the years escorted by an armada of decisions protecting liberty interests in privacy. None of these rested on explicit constitutional text. None were explicitly guaranteed in the Constitution. The right to marry a person of one's choice, to have or not have children, to engage in sex with another adult, were all part of the *Roe* regime, sometimes preceding it, sometimes flowing from it, sometimes merely sailing alongside it. These rights were not old, not part of a long history and tradition. They were modern, and they were rooted in the evolution of modern society. In this, too, Kagan's was a vision and version of history, hence of precedent, entirely different from Alito's.[52]

Of course, the dissent had to answer the majority opinion. But the majority opinion's strict chronology of abortion law before *Roe* and *Casey* was not central to that reply. It was the larger pattern of events that mattered. "*Roe* and *Casey* invoked powerful state interests in that protection, operative at every stage of the pregnancy and overriding the woman's liberty after viability." The history and tradition in the majority opinion was irrelevant. While "the majority makes this change based on a single question: Did the reproductive right recognized in *Roe* and *Casey* exist in 1868, the year when the Fourteenth Amendment was ratified? The majority says (and with this much we agree) that the answer to this question is no: In 1868, there was no nationwide right to end a pregnancy, and no thought that the Fourteenth Amendment provided one."[53]

---

52 142 S.Ct at 2320 (Kagan, J. dissenting); Confirmation Hearing on the Nomination of John G. Roberts . . . September 15, 2005, 109 Cong. 1st Sess., www.govinfo.gov/content/pkg/GPO-CHRG-ROBERTS/pdf/GPO-CHRG-ROBERTS.pdf, 56.
53 142 S.Ct at 2323 (Kagan, J. dissenting).

But so what? That was then, this is now. "First, it is not clear what relevance such early history should have, even to the majority." It was a field full of straw men. "If the early history obviously supported abortion rights, the majority would no doubt say that only the views of the Fourteenth Amendment's ratifiers are germane." Then: "On the other side of 1868, the majority occasionally notes that many States barred abortion up to the time of *Roe*. That is convenient for the majority, but it is window dressing." For what the majority is saying is, "We in the 21st century must read the Fourteenth Amendment just as its ratifiers did." Fair point. The majority decision did rest on original meaning. It had no room for a living constitution in which liberty interests had shifted from property to personal dignity. And no pricking of the majority's toes was going to change that attitude. But Kagan could not resist. "Of course, 'people' did not ratify the Fourteenth Amendment." States did. Men did. "So it is perhaps not so surprising that the ratifiers were not perfectly attuned to the importance of reproductive rights for women's liberty, or for their capacity to participate as equal members of our Nation."[54]

For whom was Kagan writing? Whom did she see as her audience? The six members of the majority were not wavering in their views. Even Roberts, who had switched sides again, and Kavanaugh, who wanted to be the new swing vote, were not likely to be swayed. Sotomayor and Breyer agreed with the dissent, but even Breyer wanted, in his dissent, a different tone. Was Kagan writing for later generations of justices, as many dissenters did, going back to Justice William Johnson on the Marshall court and later Justice John Marshall Harlan on the Fuller and White courts? Or perhaps she was writing because she was freed to write what she really believed, no more politics, no more pulling punches. "Indeed, the ratifiers—both in 1868 and when the original Constitution was approved in 1788—did not understand women as full members of the community embraced by the phrase 'We the People.' In 1868, the first wave of American feminists were explicitly told—of course by men— that it was not their time to seek constitutional protections." This is history, but it does not resemble the history that Alito offered. Historians recognize it as women's history.[55]

---

54 142 S.Ct at 2323 (Kagan, J. dissenting).
55 142 S.Ct at 2324, 2325 (Kagan, J. dissenting).

Kagan continued, reframing the subject of abortion from the perspective of those who did not take part in the formal legal process. "To be sure, most women in 1868 also had a foreshortened view of their rights: If most men could not then imagine giving women control over their bodies, most women could not imagine having that kind of autonomy." The core point was this: "When the majority says that we must read our foundational charter as viewed at the time of ratification (except that we may also check it against the Dark Ages), it consigns women to second-class citizenship." But times and attitudes and women's part in society and public life had changed. "*Casey* itself understood this point." And that was the point of Kagan's history: history is ongoing. It is not like Zeno's paradox—a collection of finite moments. And the history of modern America was the history that was relevant to the *Roe* precedents: "Times had changed. A woman's place in society had changed, and constitutional law had changed along with it." *Casey* said, "Our Constitution, read now, grants rights to women." *Casey* "rejected the majority's pinched view of how to read our Constitution. . . . And over the course of our history, this Court has taken up the Framers' invitation. It has kept true to the Framers' principles by applying them in new ways, responsive to new societal understandings and conditions." The answer to my question of Kagan's intended audience was now clear: she was writing for her law students, for this generation and the next generation of lawmakers and law interpreters. She was the law professor, this was her classroom, and the dissent was a lecture.[56]

From the standpoint of history—women's history—"nowhere has that approach been more prevalent than in construing the majestic but open-ended words of the Fourteenth Amendment—the guarantees of 'liberty' and 'equality' for all. And nowhere has that approach produced prouder moments, for this country and the Court." For those moments, the court discarded the circumscribed, mincing history, chopping precedent into

---

56 142 S.Ct at 2325 (Kagan, J, dissenting). See, for example, Linda K. Kerber, Jane Sherron DeHart, Cornelia Hughes Dayton, and Judy Tzu-Chu Wu, "Introduction," *Women's America: Refocusing the Past*, 8th ed. (New York: Oxford University Press, 2016), 5: "Historians also argue that gendered differences exemplify broader power hierarchies. These social differences and hierarchies have been *systemically created* over time. Economics, politics, law and religion—each has been permeated by assumptions, practices, and expectations that are deeply gendered. . . . These are so widely shared and so much a part of the ordinary, everyday average experience that they acquire an aura of naturalness, rightness, and even inevitability."

pieces, of "today's majority." Instead, the court followed the larger arc of our history, leading to an inclusive and affective version of precedent. She cited *Obergefell v. Hodges* as an example, in which "the Constitution does not freeze for all time the original view of what those rights guarantee, or how they apply." Take *Loving v. Virginia*. Take *Griswold*. Or take *Casey*: "*Casey* explicitly rejected the present majority's method. '[T]he specific practices of States at the time of the adoption of the Fourteenth Amendment,' *Casey* stated, do not 'mark['] the outer limits of the substantive sphere of liberty which the Fourteenth Amendment protects.'"[57]

One of those liberty interests especially important to modern women was "bodily integrity":

> Or to put it more simply: Everyone, including women, owns their own bodies. So the Court has restricted the power of government to interfere with a person's medical decisions or compel her to undergo medical procedures or treatments. . . . There are few greater incursions on a body than forcing a woman to complete a pregnancy and give birth. For every woman, those experiences involve all manner of physical changes, medical treatments (including the possibility of a cesarean section), and medical risk. Just as one example, an American woman is 14 times more likely to die by carrying a pregnancy to term than by having an abortion."

This was history, in the form of medical facts. They had been gathered over a course of years and here were summarized.[58]

The medical facts were part of a history of the courts' own making (primarily the district courts' making), and they should be read, Kagan argued, as a whole rather than in pieces. "*Roe* and *Casey* fit neatly into a long line of decisions protecting from government intrusion a wealth of private choices about family matters, child rearing, intimate relationships, and procreation." Casey rested on them, as did *Hellerstedt* and *Russo*. "Those cases safeguard particular choices about whom to marry; whom to have sex with; what family members to live with; how to raise children—and crucially, whether and when to have children. In varied cases, the Court explained that those choices—'the most intimate and

---

57 142 S.Ct at 2326 (Kagan, J. dissenting).
58 142 S.Ct at 2328 (Kagan, J. dissenting).

personal' a person can make—reflect fundamental aspects of personal identity; they define the very 'attributes of personhood.'"[59]

Kagan thus rejected the punctuated history, and the piecemeal precedent, that Alito preferred. "And liberty may require it, this Court has repeatedly said, even when those living in 1868 would not have recognized the claim—because they would not have seen the person making it as a full-fledged member of the community." Kagan returned to her larger point, in case anyone had missed it: "Throughout our history, the sphere of protected liberty has expanded, bringing in individuals formerly excluded. In that way, the constitutional values of liberty and equality go hand in hand; they do not inhabit the hermetically sealed containers the majority portrays." Values, embedded in the history of women and the precedent that equality established, trumped a sterile reading of precedent.[60]

Kagan looked to the future. With concern, she read the possible impact of *Dobbs* forward. "The majority tells everyone not to worry. It can (so it says) neatly extract the right to choose from the constitutional edifice without affecting any associated rights. (Think of someone telling you that the Jenga tower simply will not collapse.) Today's decision, the majority first says, 'does not undermine' the decisions cited by *Roe* and *Casey*—the ones involving 'marriage, procreation, contraception, [and] family relationships'—'in any way.' Should the audience for these too-much-repeated protestations be duly satisfied? We think not."[61]

Kagan had decided to abandon the pose of collegiality. Her purpose was getting on the record her belief that *Dobbs* was the first of a series of decisions striking at the privacy doctrine. "The first problem with the majority's account comes from Justice Thomas's concurrence—which makes clear he is not with the program." She saw intent where Thomas denied it. "In saying that nothing in today's opinion casts doubt on non-abortion precedents, Justice Thomas explains, he means only that they are not at issue in this very case. But he lets us know what he wants to do when they are. '[I]n future cases,' he says, 'we should reconsider all of this Court's substantive due process precedents, including *Griswold*, *Lawrence*, and *Obergefell/*.'" Alito had said that the majority decision in

---

59 142 S.Ct at 2329 (Kagan, J. dissenting).
60 142 S.Ct at 2329 (Kagan, J. dissenting).
61 142 S.Ct at 2330 (Kagan, J. dissenting).

Dobbs was a one-way ticket. For Kagan, the chilling prospect was that "at least one Justice is planning to use the ticket of today's decision again and again and again."[62]

Accusing a fellow justice of duplicity was not unheard of—Justice Robert H. Jackson accused Justice Hugo Black of undermining his chance to become chief justice, Justice Curtis was so angry at Chief Justice Taney that he resigned, Justice McReynolds would read newspapers when Justice Brandeis spoke during oral argument, and Justice Douglas would leave the room when Justice Frankfurter began one of his miniature lectures in the judicial conference. But putting an accusation into an opinion was something else. "Nor does it even help just to take the majority at its word. Assume the majority is sincere in saying, for whatever reason, that it will go so far and no further. Scout's honor. Still, the future significance of today's opinion will be decided in the future. And law often has a way of evolving without regard to original intentions." The unraveling of more precedent by the new majority was not just an idle fear. "Rights can contract . . . because whatever today's majority might say, one thing really does lead to another. We fervently hope that does not happen because of today's decision."[63]

One final historical foray completed the dissent. "The majority today lists some 30 of our cases as overruling precedent, and argues that they support overruling *Roe* and *Casey*. But none does, as further described below and in the Appendix." Alito had offered squibs of the cases to show how they overturned predecessors. Kagan's clerks went back to the pairs of cases and claimed, "In some, the Court only partially modified or clarified a precedent. And in the rest, the Court relied on one or more of the traditional *stare decisis* factors in reaching its conclusion. The Court found, for example, (1) a change in legal doctrine that undermined or made obsolete the earlier decision; (2) a factual change that had the same effect; or (3) an absence of reliance because the earlier decision was less than a decade old." None of them was as galvanic as *Dobbs*. In playing Alito's game, Kagan departed from her own holistic view of constitutional history. Whether or not the Court had overturned the precedent in any particular case required the kind of precise, detailed, narrow analysis

---

62 142 S.Ct at 2331 (Kagan, J. dissenting).
63 142 S.Ct at 2332 (Kagan, J. dissenting).

that Alito preferred. Some of the examples were every bit as profound as *Dobbs*. Had the world changed so much between 1918 and 1937? 1927 and 1943? 1940 and 1944? 1937 and 1961? Constitutional law had changed, but only because the composition of the courts had changed. But change was the center of Kagan's historical method, and conceding that precedent had been overturned did not undermine that method.[64]

The benchmark for overturning precedent remained *Brown*'s overturning of *Plessy*, however, not *Casey*. Could Kagan get around that? "*Brown* . . . protected individual rights with a strong basis in the Constitution's most fundamental commitments; [it] did not, as the majority does here, take away a right that individuals have held, and relied on, for 50 years." Analogies in law are common. So are analogies in history. Kagan did not find the connection between *Brown* and *Dobbs* persuasive, because a vital element was missing. "Society's understanding of the facts" in 1954 was "fundamentally different" from its understanding of the facts in 1896. So the court needed to reverse course. And because such dramatic change had occurred, the public could understand why the court was acting. "[T]he Nation could accept each decision" as a "response to the Court's constitutional duty." But that would not be true of a reversal of *Roe*—"[b]ecause neither the factual underpinnings of *Roe*'s central holding nor our understanding of it has changed." (In fact, Warren's opinion in *Brown* did not explicitly overrule *Plessy*.)[65]

Roe was not *Plessy*. It was *Brown*. "Only a dozen years before *Roe*, the Court described women as 'the center of home and family life,' with 'special responsibilities' that precluded their full legal status under the Constitution. By 1973, when the Court decided *Roe*, fundamental social change was underway regarding the place of women—and the law had begun to follow." By 1992, when the court decided *Casey*, "the traditional view of a woman's role as only a wife and mother was 'no longer consistent with our understanding of the family, the individual, or the Constitution.' Under that charter, *Casey* understood, women must take their place as full and equal citizens. And for that to happen, women must have control over their reproductive decisions. Nothing since *Casey*—no changed law, no changed fact—has undermined that promise."[66]

---

64 142 S.Ct at 2334 (Kagan, J. dissenting).
65 142 S.Ct at 2342 (Kagan, J. dissenting).
66 142 S.Ct at 2343 (Kagan, J. dissenting).

* * *

Kagan, a former law professor and law school dean, assayed a double-layered assault on the majority—an appendix refuting its reading of precedent, and then a series of notes to support the appendix. I suspect that a clerk did the scut work, matching Alito's clerk's footnote 48 case for case. "This Appendix analyzes in full each of the 28 cases the majority says support today's decision to overrule *Roe v. Wade*, 410 *U.S.* 113 (1973), and *Planned Parenthood of Southeastern Pa. v. Casey*, 505 *U.S.* 833 (1992). As explained herein, the Court in each case relied on traditional *stare decisis* factors in overruling." Actually, the squibs accompanying each of the cases hardly amounted to "in full," but the point of the appendix was clear enough. The justice appended a note to the appendix: "A great many of the overrulings the majority cites involve a prior precedent that had been rendered out of step with or effectively abrogated by contemporary case law in light of intervening developments in the broader doctrine." This was not true, she had already argued, in the case of *Roe* and *Dobbs*. Nothing had changed. Appendix D at the end of this essay contains Kagan's appendix.[67]

Kagan's opinion rehearsed the argument for precedent, the reliance that women had on the right to a safe and obtainable abortion, and a rearguard action against the anticipated attack on contraception. All that was in the dissent, although dissents have a way of becoming majority opinions in time. (Look at the appendix to her dissent.) But if *Roe* failed because the right to an abortion was nowhere stated in the Constitution, and if abortion was not a traditional right, then contraception, based on the right to privacy, was similarly vulnerable. For the right to privacy was itself a relatively recent one, based in *Griswold v. Connecticut* on inferred rather than stated protections in the "penumbras" of the Bill of Rights.

Looking at the footnotes to the dissent, one sees how Kagan had made Alito's insistence on history and tradition irrelevant. Precedent was once again more important. This was not unusual for Kagan. With Scalia, with Kavanaugh, and here with Alito, she used the footnotes to dismantle opposing arguments. It kept the adversarial cut

---

67 142 S.Ct at 2350 (Kagan, J. dissenting).

and thrust out of the body of her opinions, and presumably, out of any part of the law. These footnotes are closer to those in law reviews than in opinions.

Take the first note's focus: "We do not understand the majority's view that our analogy between the right to an abortion and the rights to contraception and same-sex marriage shows that we think '[t]he Constitution does not permit the States to regard the destruction of a 'potential life' as a matter of any significance.'" This is entirely different from the standard footnote content. Scalia waited a bit before he tore into Stevens. Kagan did not delay:

> To the contrary. The liberty interests underlying those rights are, as we will describe, quite similar. But only in the sphere of abortion is the state interest in protecting potential life involved. So only in that sphere, as both *Roe* and *Casey* recognized, may a State impinge so far on the liberty interest (barring abortion after viability and discouraging it before). The majority's failure to understand *this fairly obvious point* stems from its rejection of the idea of balancing interests in this (or maybe in any) constitutional context. . . . The majority thinks that a woman has *no* liberty or equality interest in the decision to bear a child, so a State's interest in protecting fetal life necessarily prevails" (Italics added).

"Fairly obvious point" strongly suggests that the majority did not understand the case at all.

Or footnote 5:

> In a perplexing paragraph in its opinion, the majority declares that it need not say whether that statement from *Casey* is true. But how could that be? Has not the majority insisted for the prior 30 or so pages that the "specific practice[ ]" respecting abortion at the time of the Fourteenth Amendment precludes its recognition as a constitutional right? It has. And indeed, it has given no other reason for overruling *Roe* and *Casey*. *We are not mindreaders*, but here is our best guess as to what the majority means. It says next that "[a]bortion is nothing new." So apparently, the Fourteenth Amendment might provide protection for things wholly unknown in the 19th century; maybe one day there could be constitutional

protection for, oh, time travel. But as to anything that was known back then (such as abortion or contraception), no such luck (Italics added).

Or footnote 7:

Indulge a few more words about this point. The majority had a choice of two different ways to overrule *Roe* and *Casey*. It could claim that those cases underrated the State's interest in fetal life. Or it could claim that they overrated a woman's constitutional liberty interest in choosing an abortion. (Or both.) The majority here rejects the first path, and we can see why. Taking that route would have prevented the majority from claiming that it means only to leave this issue to the democratic process—that it does not have a dog in the fight. And indeed, doing so might have suggested a revolutionary proposition: that the fetus is itself a constitutionally protected "person," such that an abortion ban is constitutionally *mandated.* The majority therefore chooses the second path, arguing that the Fourteenth Amendment does not conceive of the abortion decision as implicating liberty, because the law in the 19th century gave that choice no protection. The trouble is that the chosen path—which is, again, the solitary rationale for the Court's decision—provides no way to distinguish between the right to choose an abortion and a range of other rights, including contraception.

Footnote 8 carries on in the same vein: "The majority briefly (very briefly) gestures at the idea that some *stare decisis* factors might play out differently with respect to these other constitutional rights. But the majority gives no hint as to why. And the majority's (mis)treatment of *stare decisis* in this case provides little reason to think that the doctrine would stand as a barrier to the majority's redoing any other decision it considered egregiously wrong."

The primary purpose of these footnotes was to tear apart the logic of the majority case. A few notes contained supporting citations from various amicus briefs, but overall, the first batch of notes focused on the majority opinion's mistakes, as if the majority opinion were a third-year law student paper and the dissent were the extended comments of the professor/grader.

Then came something quite remarkable, a transformation of footnotes into a law review article–like account of medical practice. Consider footnote 11 on state abortion regulation variations:

> The rest of the majority's supposed splits are, shall we say, unimpressive. The majority says that lower courts have split over how to apply the undue burden standard to parental notification laws. See *ante*, at 60, and n. 54. But that is not so. The state law upheld had an exemption for minors demonstrating adequate maturity, whereas the ones struck down did not. The majority says there is a split about bans on certain types of abortion procedures. But the one court to have separated itself on that issue did so based on a set of factual findings significantly different from those in other cases. Finally, the majority says there is a split about whether an increase in travel time to reach a clinic is an undue burden. But the cases to which the majority refers predate this Court's decision in *Whole Woman's Health v. Hellerstedt*, (2016), which clarified how to apply the undue burden standard to that context.

The remaining notes provided medical information, made analogies among medical procedures, and in general lectured the majority on actual abortion practice as opposed to abstract legal notions of abortion. They showed how the *Roe* decision would or would be likely to affect decisions in related medical matters like miscarriages (footnote 12), mortality rates (footnote 13), medical insurance (footnotes 14, 15), "safe haven laws" (footnote 16), adoption (footnote 17), fetal life (footnote 18), unintended pregnancy (footnote 19), infant mortality (footnotes 20, 21), public funding for adoption (footnote 21), contraceptives (footnote 24), interstate travel to abortion providers (footnote 25), costs of abortions (footnotes 26, 27), and abortion rates (footnote 29). The information came from various amicus briefs and was accepted as accurate.

Kagan's footnotes had diverged from her dissent in unique fashion. They were of two parts. The first part, including notes 1–8, summarized her refutation of the majority opinion. The most common quotation and cite in them is to the text of the majority opinion, not to her own dissent. (I have removed all of these references, for clarity.) The remaining notes were a summary, with detailed source citations, of current medical practice. In effect, they brought together material from amicus briefs to constitute a scholarly article on the subject. Kagan had repurposed the footnote, finding a new use for them. She demonstrated how versatile the footnote was and would remain—and how central it had become to judicial writing.

* * *

The controversy over women's reproductive rights will no doubt continue, and the court's decision in *Dobbs v. Jackson Women's Health Organization* will join the parade of precedent rather than ending it. In legislative chambers antipathetic to women's rights, attempts to ban distribution of birth control pills are already replacing restrictions on abortion providers. These will find their way to the high court. Perhaps a new era of Comstockery is upon us. As Justice Kagan feared, *Griswold v. Connecticut* (1965) and the right of privacy may be next. After all, the Constitution does not mention privacy. Certainly, same-sex marriage and protection of gay and lesbian rights are already at risk. If no precedent is safe, where is the rule of law?

One conclusion is obvious. The fierceness of these struggles over constitutional rights and wrongs in the justices' opinions now routinely find their way into the footnotes of the justices' opinions. Whether they belong there is no longer the question. Perhaps because the notes are largely the work of the justices' clerks, something no one disputes (or apologizes for), they now resemble the extensive notes in law review articles. After all, the clerks were the editors of those law reviews before they were the justices' clerks, and one of the duties of law review editors is to "cite check" the references in submissions. The articles in the law review are the work, largely, of law professors. They know but are not bound by the same rules of collegiality as the justices on the court. They use the articles to do battle over constitutional issues with other law professors, a proxy of the combat in the justices' chambers. Thus, the notes, and the opinions, resemble the mentality of the law professor rather than the judge.

CONCLUSION

Wither the Footnote?

At the start of his *The Footnote*, Anthony Grafton celebrated the footnote for offering "empirical support for stories told and arguments
presented." That is certainly true of footnotes to US Supreme Court
cases. He also warned that "full of unexpected human and intellectual
interest . . . the footnote is not so uniform and reliable as some historians believe." But no one can doubt that in increasingly scholarly and
acerbic footnote exchanges, the lowly footnote has been elevated to a
higher plane. It has become part of an argument about how law should
be made or unmade. The notes in *Heller* and *Dobbs* were directed by the
justices at one another, continuing the dialogue begun in oral argument,
expanded in the conference, and then developed in the exchange of
drafts. The notes allowed the lay public to peek into the justices' chambers and hear their thinking. Most important, the modern note not only
became part of the law; it became a meta-law, a running commentary on
the law as it was made.[1]

By continually reinventing the footnote and putting it to new uses,
James Wilson, the justices of the Taney court, Horace Gray, David
Brewer, Harlan Fiske Stone, Earl Warren, Antonin Scalia, John Paul
Stevens, Samuel Alito, and Elena Kagan had found ways to expand the
limits of the traditional appellate opinion. Over time, the notes changed
from mere reference citations to miniature arguments. The contemporary footnote revealed how judicial opinions had become more academic, more tied to legal scholarship, and more responsive to the world
outside of courtrooms and law libraries. The footnotes themselves began
to resemble those in law reviews, not surprising given that the authors
of the footnotes had almost certainly been editors of major law reviews

---

1 Grafton, *Footnote*, vii, viii.

at their law schools before they became the justices' clerks. In this sense, the footnotes show the triumph of an academic version of legal realism (reflecting the reality of the law school—law clerk connections). Where the opinions may still discourse on doctrine and claim that the law has not changed—that is, that the justice adopted an originalist stance—the footnotes prove that claim misleading. They track changes in the law over time in a context of novel ideas and interests.

Footnotes are clearly here to stay, although in the future, they may disappear into hyperlinks, another addition to the cloud. As the court becomes more of a manager of the sprawling federal court system, the notes also serve as directions (some hints, others more persuasive) to lower court judges and magistrates. Scholars and laypeople will pore over the footnotes, looking for clues to the justices' thinking, a game of guessing where the court will go in the future.

To be sure, a footnote to the Supreme Court opinion is still a footnote, an appendage to the opinion, no matter how extensive it is, how scholarly, how argumentative, how relevant to today or to tomorrow, until it is incorporated in the body of later opinions. Some notes will never attain this high station. But others will. Studying them will help us understand the logic and appreciate the contribution of the opinion itself. For the footnote, more than the body to which it is attached, opens the door to a conversation with the justice. For the footnote, more than the opinion, is addressed to the community of legal scholars, inviting them to share and to comment.

ACKNOWLEDGMENTS

I am grateful to Mark Graber, N. E. H. Hull, Mark Tushnet, and John Fabian Witt for reading and commenting on the manuscript. Their insights and contributions were immensely helpful. Theodora Light did the spadework on appendices A and B. Clara Platter and the acquisitions team at NYU Press were exemplary in their handling of the manuscript. Richard Feit copyedited with skill. All errors are, of course, my own.

APPENDIX A

Selection of William Cranch's Annotations to U.S. Reports

7 United States Reports (Cranch 3), HUIDEKOPER'S LESSEE v. DOUG-
LASS. (a), Feb 1805, 1, 29–49, (a) This question has been agitated in a variety of forms in the state of Pennsylvania, and a great degree of sensibility
is said to have been excited upon the subject. In the year 1800, a rule was
obtained in the supreme court of Pennsylvania, by the Holland Company,
upon the secretary of the land-office, to show cause why a mandamus
should not be awarded, commanding him to prepare and deliver patents
for various tracts of land, for which they had obtained warrants under the
act of April 3d, 1792. The judges delivered their opinions in the following
terms:

SHIPPEN, Ch. J. The legislature, by the act of 3d April, 1792, meant to
sell the remaining lands of the state, particularly those lying on the
north and west of the rivers Ohio and Alleghany. The consideration
money was to be paid on issuing the warrants. They had, likewise,
another object, namely, that, if possible, the lands should be settled
by improvers. The latter terms, however, were not to be exacted from
the grantees at all events. The act passed at a time when hostilities
existed on the part of the Indian tribes. It was uncertain when they
would cease; the legislature, therefore, contemplated that warrants
might be taken out during the existence of these hostilities, which
might continue so long as to make it impossible for the warrantees
to make the settlements required, for a length of time; not, perhaps,
until these hostilities should entirely cease. Yet, they make no provisions that the settlements should be made within a reasonable time
after the peace; but expressly within two years after the dates of the
warrants. As, however, they wished to sell the lands, and were to
receive the consideration money immediately, it would have been
unreasonable, and, probably, have defeated their views in selling, to

require settlements to be made on each tract of four hundred acres, houses to be built, and lands to be cleared, in case such acts should be rendered impossible by the continuance of the Indian war. They, therefore, make the proviso, which is the subject of the present dispute, in the following words: "*Provided always, nevertheless,* That if any such actual settler, or any grantee, in any such original or succeeding warrant, shall, by force of arms of the enemies of the United States, be prevented from making such actual settlement, or be driven therefrom, and shall persist in his endeavours to make such actual settlement as aforesaid, then, in either case, he and his heirs shall be entitled to have and to hold the said lands, in the same manner as if the actual settlement had been made and continued."

When were such actual settlements to be made? The same section of the act which contains the above proviso, gives a direct and unequivocal answer to this question: "within the space of two years next after the date of the warrant." If the settlements were not made within that time, owing to the force or reasonable dread of the enemies of the United States, and it was evident that the parties had used their best endeavours to effect the settlement, then, by the express words of the law, the residence of the improvers for five years afterwards, was expressly dispensed with, and their title to the lands was complete, and patents might issue accordingly. It is contended, that the words "persist in their endeavours," in the proviso, should be extended to mean, that fi within the two years they should be prevented by the Indian hostilities from making the settlement, yet, when they should be no longer prevented by those hostilities, as by a treaty of peace, it was incumbent on them then to persist to make such settlement. The legislature might, if they had so please, have exacted those terms, (and they would not, perhaps, have been unreasonable,) but they have not done so: they have expressly confined the time of making such settlements to the term of two years from the date of the warrant. Their meaning and intention can alone be sought for, from the words they have used, in which there seems to me, in this part of the act, to be no great ambiguity. If the contrary had been their meaning, they would not have made use of the word "endeavours," which supposes a possibility, at least, if not a probability, as things then stood, of those endeavours failing on account of the hostilities, and would, therefore, have expressly exacted actual settlements to be made, when the purchasers should no longer run any risk in making them.

(31) The state having received the consideration money, and required a settlement within two years, if not prevented by enemies; and in that case dispensing with the condition of settlement and residence, and declaring that their title shall be then good and as effectual as if the settlement had been made and continued, I cannot conceive they could mean to exact that settlement at any future indefinite time. And although it is said they mean that condition to be indispensable, and that it must be complied with in a reasonable time, we have not left to us that latitude of construction, as the legislature have expressly limited the time themselves.

It is urged, that the main view of the legislature was to get the country settled, and a barrier formed; this was, undoubtedly, one of their views, and for that purpose, they have given extraordinary encouragement to individual settlers; but they had, likewise, evidently another view, that of increasing the revenue of the state, by the sale of the lands. The very title of the act is "for the sale of the vacant land within this commonwealth;" this latter object they have really effected, but not by the means of the voluntary settlers; it could alone be effected by the purses or rich men, or large companies of men, who would not have been prevailed upon to lay out such sums of money as they have done, if they had thought their purchases were clogged with such impracticable conditions. I have hitherto argued upon the presumption that the words "persist in their endeavours," relate to the grantees as well as the settlers; but, in considering the words of the proviso, it may be well doubted whether they relate to any other grantee or settler than those who have been driven from their settlements; the word "persist" applies very properly to such: the words of the proviso are, "If such actual settler, or any grantee, shall, by force of arms of the enemies of the United States, be prevented from making such settlement, or be driven therefrom, and shall persist in his endeavours to make such an actual settlement; then, in either case, he and his heirs shall be entitled," &c. Here, besides that the grammatical construction of referring to the word "persist" to the last antecedent is best answered, but the sense of it is only applicable to settlements begun, and not to the condition of the grantees. There are two members of the sentence; one relates to the grantees, who, it is supposed, may be prevented from making their settlements; the other to the settlers, who are supposed to be driven away from their settlements. The latter words, as to them, are proper; as to the grantees, who never began a settlement, improper. The act says, in either case, that is, if the grantees are prevented from making their settlements, or if the settlers are driven away, and persist in their endeavours to complete their settlements, in either case they shall be entitled to the land.

I will not say this construction is entirely free from doubt; if it was, there would be an end of the question.

But taking it for granted, as it has been done at the bar, that the (32) words relate to the grantees, as well as the settlers; yet, although inaccurate with regard to the former, it seems to me, the legislature could only mean to exact from the grantees their best endeavours to make the settlements, within the space of two years from the date of their warrants; at the end of which time, if they have been prevented from complying with the terms of the law, by the actual force of the enemy, as they had actually paid for the land, they are then entitled to their patents. If the legislature really mean differently, all I can say is, that they have very unfortunately expressed their meaning.

The propriety of awarding a *mandamus* is another question, which I mean not to discuss, as I presume a decision of a majority of the court will make it unnecessary.

8   United States Reports (Cranch 3), LAMBERT'S LESSEE v. PAINE., February 1805, 96, 118, (a) JOHNSON, J. Does not the last clause of the will of 1780 show that the testator meant, by that will, to dispose of his *whole* estate?

> *Mason.* That clause relates only to personal estate. The word *property* is coupled with negroes and horses, which shows in what sense he meant to use it. But if it comprehends the reversion of the real estate, yet, as he appointed no person to make the sale, the reversion would descend to the heir at law, until some person should be appointed by proper authority, to carry that clause of the will into effect.
>
> *(b)* WASHINGTON, J. Is the will of 1782 so executed and recorded as to pass lands?
>
> *Key.* The jury have found that he executed it, and it is not necessary that a *will* of *lands* should be recorded under the laws of England, and the law is considered the same in Maryland. I do not object to the will on that account.

APPENDIX B

The First State High Court Footnotes

Alabama: WARD v. LEWIS, 1 Ala 8–9, (Jan 1827) p. 9 "NOTE. See acts of 1825, p.6, by which sheriffs are authorized to serve process in cases of forcible entry and detainer."

Arkansas: McKEE *against* MURPHY.—HESTER *against* MURPHY. ERROR *to Conway Circuit Court.* 1 Ark. 55 (1838), p. 57 "*Atterm, A.D. 1838."

California: THE PEOPLE v. SMITH, *et al.* 1 Cal. 9 (1850), p. 9; "Cited as authority in *Brumagim v. Bradshaw*, 39 Cal. 40; *Ex parte Cottrell*, 59 Cal. 422."

Connecticut: Tyler v. Marsh., 1 Conn. 1 (1802) (Supreme Court of Errors), p. 2 "(*a*) The Superior and County Courts are authorized, by Statute, to try issues in fact, when joined to the Court, by agreement of parties. *Stat. 27.*"

Delaware: 1 Del (Delaware Cases 1792–1830, Doorstin), ANONYMOUS. *Wilson's Red Book*, 1 (July and Aug 1792), p. 5" note 1 In the manuscript this page number appears as '637', but there is no such page, and 137 is plainly intended."

Florida: HOLTEN v. THE STATE, 2 Fla. 476 (1849), p. 507 "* NOTE.—The Reporter understands that Justice HAWKINS did not assent to all the views taken by the court in the foregoing opinion. No expression of dissent was heard from him, however, and it is believed he concurred in the judgment pronounced by the court."

Georgia: State v. Roberts, 1 Ga (Ga Decisions) 13 (Chatham Cty, 1805), p. 13, "*See State v. Monaquas and Segar, T.U.P. Charlton 16." [Ga had no supreme court until 1846.]

Illinois: Taylor v. Sprinkle, 1, Ill. 1 (1819), "* Justice BROWNE having decided this cause in the court below, gave no opinion."

Indiana: M'Dowell v. Davis, 1 Ind., 2 (1818), p. 2 fn (1) "Similar orders were made in several other causes, during the term."

Iowa: In the matter of RALPH (a colored man), on HABEUS CORPUS 1
Iowa 1 (1839), page 1: "(a.) the questions involved in this case are no longer
of any great practical importance. The distinction between *free* and *slave
states* within the Union no longer exists; for within its bounds all are now
free. No *slave* can tread the soil or breathe the air of free America."

Kansas: Kansas *ex rel.* Adams v. Hillyer, 2 Kan. 17 (1863) at 17: "This case and
'THE STATE OF KANSAS ex rel. DANIEL W. ADAMS V. JOHN W. ROB-
INSON,' were submitted on the same agreed statement of facts, and the two
cases submitted and determined at the same time."

Kentucky: McConnell v. Kenton, 1 Ken. 257 (1799) fn 1 at 316, "In the case of
Smith v. May and Curd an interlocutory judgement was given in the court
of appeals, and then removed to the district court held in Bardstown, and
from thence to the general court, The judgement being opened and a new
trial granted the plaintiff dismissed this caveat."

Louisiana: Patton v. The Cities of Philadelphia & New Orleans, 1 La. 98 (1846),
page 100: "EUSTIS, C.J., having been of council in this case, did not sit on
the trial."

Maine: Peterson v. Loring, 1 Me 64 (1820), p. 67: The Reporter has since
ascertained that the first report, in the case cited, was in favour of Short;
and that the second, by two of the referees, was in favour of Pratt & al.
The observations of Parsons C.J., are therefore applicable to a new report,
different from the former, and made by two of the referees, the third not
having been present at the hearing;— and the case, thus explained, is not
contradicted by the case of *May v. Haven.*"

Maryland: State of Maryland v. Jarrett and Harwood, 17 Md, 309 (1861) p. 330:
"*Note by the Reporter*:- It will be observed that in this case no motion was
made to dismiss the appeal, and no question raised or argued on either side
as to the *right of appeal* in such a case, under *Art. 5, sec. 25* of the Code, as
was done in the case of *Steigerwald vs. Winans, et al., ante.*"

Massachusetts: Gold v. Eddy, 1–2 Mass. 1 (1804), p. 2: "(a) In the case of
Dwight vs. Wilcox, the note had been negotiated to *Dwight* several months
before it fell due—that case, therefore, could not be considered as governing the present."

Michigan: May v. Rumney, 1 Mich. 7 (1847), pp. 7–8 "NOTE.—Widow of
a nonresident of the state has dower in those lands only of which her
husband died seized. Comp. L. 1871, § 4269; Pratt v. Tefft, 14 Mich.
91; entitled to dower in wild lands, Campbell, 2 Doug. 141; if she is a

nonresident at the time he makes an absolute conveyance of all seizin and estate, she has no right of dower. Ligare v. Semple, 32 Mich. 438; see, also, 4 Mich. 230; 19 Mich. 224; 12 Barb. 537; 11 Wend. 392; 1 Paige 634. For general statutes of limitation, see code of 1820, pp. 243, 384; rev. of 1827, pp. 223, 258; laws of 1829, p. 95; rev. of 1833, pp. 408, 569; R. S. of 1838, pp. 573, 576; laws of 1843, p. 43; laws of 1863, p. 388; laws of 1869, pp. 11, 218; Comp. L. 1871, §§ 7137 to 7147. For statutes of limitation as to dower, in other states, see Washburne on Real Property, 3d ed. Pp. 249–251, and notes.

—Possession, under sheriff's deed, of the husband's title, is not adverse to the previously acquired inchoate dower right of the widow so as to bar her right of action after ten years. Cowan v. Lindsay, 30 Wis. 586.

—Under limitation act of 1839, in Illinois, widow must pursue her remedy within the seven years prescribed by the statute against party in possession under color of title, and paying taxes, or she will be barred. Owen v. Peacock, 38 Ill. 33. But statute does no[t] commence to run until right of action has accrued by the death of the husband. Steele v. Gallatly, 41 Ill. 39; Whiting v. Nichol, 46 id. 481. Widow has dower in equitable estate, but only in such as would, at death of husband, descend as real estate, not in such as would pass to personal representatives as a chose in action. Misoll v. Todd, 70 Ill. 295. As to dower in riparian accretions, Lombard v. Kinzie, 73 id. 446; dower in mines opened, worked and abandoned, and in mineral lands, Leufers v. Heuke, 73 id. 405.

By statute of 1874, in Illinois, estate of curtesy was abolished, and the surviving husband or wife is endowed in one-third part of all lands whereof deceased wife of husband was seized at any time during the coverture, unless relinquished in due form, including equitable estates wherein the title may be completed after decease. R. R. 1877, Hurd, 416; 75 Ill. 223; 78 id. 600; 79 id. 465; 80 id. 132."

Minnesota: Holcombe v. McKusick, 1 Minn. 334 (1856) p. 339: "The pleadings in this cause would of themselves make a respectable book in size, but as there is no Opinion on file, and the record very imperfect, I have stated the issues in as few words as possible.-REPORTER."

Mississippi: FLETCHER v. WILSON et al., 1 Miss. 146 (1843), p. 152: "The counsel for Fletcher fell into an error, as to Conn's not being a party to Wilson's case-bill, and have thereby misled the Court. An examination of the record shows that he was a party defendant."

Missouri: COLLIER *v.* WHELDON AND WIFE., 1 Mo 5–7, (1820) p. 5, "*
When it is not shown what Judge delivered the opinion of the Court, it
commences thus: *"Per Curiam."*

Nebraska: Franklin v. Kelley, 2 Ne, 79–118 (1873), p. 111 "* The question determined in this judgment has, since its delivery, been finally decided by
the Supreme Court of the United States. The opinion of that court will be
found in the Appendix of this volume."

Nevada: 1–2 Nev (Republication Hawley 1865–1866), T.W. STEEL, RESPON-
DENT, *v.* JOHN STEEL, APPELANT. (1 Nev. 27–30, 27), (Jan 1865), "(1) 1
Nev. 82."

New Hampshire: TOMSON *versus* WARD, 1 NH, 9–11, (Sept 1816), p. 11
"*RICHARDSON, C.J. having been of counsel, did not sit in the cause."

New Jersey: BEAKE'S EXECUTORS v. BIRDSALL., 1 NJ, 15–19 (1790), p. 16
"(a) See 1 *Bac. Abr.* 584, *Letter B,* Judge Wilson's edition, where the cases are
collected; *Peake's Evid.* 133, and the case of *De Lisle v. Priestman,* 1 *Browne*
182, how far this principle extends."

New York: 1 NY (Caine's New York Term Reports), BOGERT AND LEWIS,
EXECUTORS OF BOGERT, *against* HILDRETH, SHERIFF OF MONT-
GOMERY, 1–4, 1, (May 1803), "(a) See *Mellor v. Barber,* 3 D.&E. 387.
Pinkney v. Collins, 1 D.&E. 571. *Clissold v. Clissold, ibid.* 647."

North Carolina: 1 NC (Martin v. 1), ANDERSON'S ADM'RS vs. ANDERSON
(Page 19), 3, 3, "*1786, 14, 15, 585."

Ohio: 1–2 OH (Hammond), SMITH v. GODDARD, 189–232, 232, (Dec 1823)
"NOTE BY THE REPORTER—See the case of Hunt v. Rousmanier's
Adm'r, Wheat. 174. In this case, the Supreme Court of the United States
decided that where a party through *mistake* and *ignorance of law,* executes
a writing which does not carry into effect the contract and the intention
of the parties, parol evidence may be received to establish the fact, and the
true contract and real intention of the parties enforced in equity; and this
where no fraud is alleged, nor no mistake in a matter of fact, but a mistake
in point of law only, the legal effect and operation of the writing not being
such as the parties intended."

Oregon: 2 OR (Wilson), ELIHU LINDLEY, Appellant, *v.* M. and E. WALLIS,
Respondents, 203–204, 204, (Sept 1867), "NOTE.—The court affirmed
certain rulings and constructions of law heretofore made, in addition to the
4th, applicable peculiarly to this case.—REP."

Pennsylvania: 1 Penn (Dallas Reports), The Lessee of HYAM and Others v. EDWARDS, 2–3, 2, (Sept 1754),"* 11 Mod. 2. C. 2."

Rhode Island: 1 RI, NEWELL MOWRY ET UX. V. THOMAS N. STAPLES, 10–16, 16, (Sept 1835), "'The same question decided in this case, was decided in *Amy Weatherhead v. Nathaniel Newell*, at the same term of the court; a short opinion of the court on file, referring to the above case of *Mowry et ux.*"

South Carolina: 1 SC (New Series, Richardson), HENRY A. MEETZE vs. W. PADGETT AND ANOTHER., 127–128, 127, (April 1869), 9 "(a) The law now provides that sales of real estate shall be made in the county where it lies by the Sheriff of the County, or by a referee. See Code, § 310, p. 490."

Tennessee: 1 Tenn (Overton), MURFREE v. LEEPER, 1–2, 1, (Nov 1791), "*2 Term Rep., 735; 5 Term Rep., 251, 626; 6 Term Rep., 194."

Texas: 1 Tex, THOMAS G. WESTERN VS. ZADOC WOODS—APPEAL FROM HARRIS COUNTY., 1–8, 3, (Dec 1846), "* The Reporters have not been furnished with Mr. Buckley's brief."

Vermont: 1 Vt, HIECOCK vs. HIECOCK, 133–135. 133, (Jully adj'd term 1797), "* By a subsequent statute, one Judge is authorised [sic] to take such recognizance."

Virginia: 3 Va, PETER KAMPER VS. MARY HAWKINS, 21–98, 22, (Dec 1792) "* Passed in 1792."

West Virginia: 1 WV, HOBBS, TAYLOR & CO. *vs.* THE STEAMBOAT IN-TERCHANGE, 57–68, 57, (Jan 1865), "* The 5th section provides that, when any person has instituted suit against the commander of any steamboat or other vessel, &c., or against the owner of any such vessel, of any raft or river craft navigating the Ohio river, &c., for materials, supplies or labor furnished or bestowed in the building, repairing, equipping, navigating or attending upon the same, &c., he may forthwith sue out of the clerk's office an attachment against the defendant's estate, or against the vessel, raft or river craft, of which he is the owner or commander with all her tackel [sic], apparel and furniture."

Wisconsin: 1 Wis (Wisconsin Pinney's Reports), MURDOCK VS. ARNDT., 70–72, 71–72, (July 1839), "* The indorsement of a negotiable note, after dishonor, is itself negotiable without writing the words "or order." The note does not lose its negotiable character by being dishonored, and an indorse-ment, although made after dishonor, follows the nature of the original contract, and is negotiable, unless it contains express words of restriction. *Leavitt v. Putnam*, 3Comst. 494. Such an indorser [sic] will be held liable to the indorsee [sic] or subsequent holder, if the requirements respecting demand and notice, proper to notes on demand, are all complied with. 2 Parsons on Notes and Bills, 13.

The following authorities will be found to hold that a parol [sic] agreement between an indorser and his immediate indorsee, that the former shall not be charged on his indorsement, is a valid defense to an action on such indorsement as between the immediate parties, but it will be of no avail as against a subsequent *bona fide* holder or indorsee without notice of such agreement. 2 Parsons on Notes and Bills, 24; 1 Chitty on Bills (7th ed.), 139; *Pike v. Street*, 1 Mood. & Malk 226; *Wright v. Latham*, 3 Murph. 298; *Hill v. Ely*, 5 Serg. & R. 363; *McDonough v. Goale*, 8 La. 472.—REP."

APPENDIX C

Footnote 48 to Majority Opinion in Dobbs v. Jackson

"See, *e.g.*, *Obergefell* v. *Hodges*, 576 U.S. 644 (2015) (right to same-sex marriage), overruling *Baker* v. *Nelson*, 409 U.S. 810 (1972); *Citizens United* v. *Federal Election Comm'n*, 558 U.S. 310 (2010) (right to engage in campaign-related speech), overruling *Austin* v. *Michigan Chamber of Commerce*, 494 U.S. 652 (1990), and partially overruling *McConnell* v. *Federal Election Comm'n*, 540 U.S. 93 (2003); *Montejo* v. *Louisiana*, 556 U.S. 778 (2009) (Sixth Amendment right to counsel), overruling *Michigan* v. *Jackson*, 475 U.S. 625 (1986); *Crawford* v. *Washington*, 541 U.S. 36 (2004) (Sixth Amendment right to confront witnesses), overruling *Ohio* v. *Roberts*, 448 U.S. 56 (1980); *Lawrence* v. *Texas*, 539 U.S. 558 (2003) (right to engage in consensual, same-sex intimacy in one's home), overruling *Bowers* v. *Hardwick*, 478 U.S. 186 (1986); *Ring* v. *Arizona*, 536 U.S. 584 (2002) (Sixth Amendment right to a jury trial in capital prosecutions), overruling *Walton* v. *Arizona*, 497 U.S. 639 (1990); *Agostini* v. *Felton*, 521 U.S. 203 (1997) (evaluating whether government aid violates the Establishment Clause), overruling *Aguilar* v. *Felton*, 473 U.S. 402 (1985), and *School Dist. of Grand Rapids* v. *Ball*, 473 U.S. 373 (1985); *Seminole Tribe of Fla.* v. *Florida*, 517 U.S. 44 (1996) (lack of congressional power under the Indian Commerce Clause to abrogate States' Eleventh Amendment immunity), overruling *Pennsylvania* v. *Union Gas Co.*, 491 U.S. 1 (1989); *Payne* v. *Tennessee*, 501 U.S. 808 (1991) (the Eighth Amendment does not erect a *per se* bar to the admission of victim impact evidence during the penalty phase of a capital trial), overruling *Booth* v. *Maryland*, 482 U.S. 496 (1987), and *South Carolina* v. *Gathers*, 490 U.S. 805 (1989); *Batson* v. *Kentucky*, 476 U.S. 79 (1986) (the equal protection clause guarantees the defendant that the State will not exclude members of his race from the jury venire on account of race), overruling *Swain* v. *Alabama*, 380 U.S. 202 (1965); *Garcia* v. *San Antonio Metropolitan Transit Author-*

ity, 469 U.S. 528, 530 (1985) (rejecting the principle that the Commerce Clause does not empower Congress to enforce requirements, such as minimum wage laws, against the States "'in areas of traditional governmental functions'"), overruling *National League of Cities v. Usery, 426 U.S. 833* (1976); *Illinois v. Gates, 462 U.S. 213* (1983) (the Fourth Amendment requires a totality of the circumstances approach for determining whether an informant's tip establishes probable cause), overruling *Aguilar v. Texas, 378 U.S. 108* (1964), and *Spinelli v. United States, 393 U.S. 410* (1969); *United States v. Scott, 437 U.S. 82* (1978) (the Double Jeopardy Clause does not apply to Government appeals from orders granting defense motions to terminate a trial before verdict), overruling *United States v. Jenkins, 420 U.S. 358* (1975); *Craig v. Boren, 429 U.S. 190* (1976) (gender-based classifications are subject to intermediate scrutiny under the Equal Protection Clause), overruling *Goesaert v. Cleary, 335 U.S. 464* (1948); *Taylor v. Louisiana, 419 U.S. 522* (1975) (jury system which operates to exclude women from jury service violates the defendant's Sixth and Fourteenth Amendment right to an impartial jury), overruling *Hoyt v. Florida, 368 U.S. 57* (1961); *Brandenburg v. Ohio, 395 U.S. 444* (1969) (*per curiam*) (the mere advocacy of violence is protected under the First Amendment unless it is directed to incite or produce imminent lawless action), overruling *Whitney v. California, 274 U.S. 357* (1927); *Katz v. United States, 389 U.S. 347*, 351 (1967) (Fourth Amendment "protects people, not places," and extends to what a person "seeks to preserve as private"), overruling *Olmstead v. United States, 277 U.S. 438* (1928), and *Goldman v. United States, 316 U.S. 129* (1942); *Miranda v. Arizona, 384 U.S. 436* (1966) (procedural safeguards to protect the Fifth Amendment privilege against self-incrimination), overruling *Crooker v. California, 357 U.S. 433* (1958), and *Cicenia v. Lagay, 357 U.S. 504* (1958); *Malloy v. Hogan, 378 U.S. 1* (1964) (the Fifth Amendment privilege against self-incrimination is also protected by the Fourteenth Amendment against abridgment by the States), overruling *Twining v. New Jersey, 211 U.S. 78* (1908), and *Adamson v. California, 332 U.S. 46* (1947); *Wesberry v. Sanders, 376 U.S. 1*, 7–8 (1964) (congressional districts should be apportioned so that "as nearly as is practicable one man's vote in a congressional election is to be worth as much as another's"), overruling in effect *Colegrove v. Green, 328 U.S. 549* (1946); *Gideon v. Wainwright, 372 U.S. 335* (1963) (right to counsel for indigent defendant in a criminal prosecution in state court under the Sixth and Fourteenth Amendments), overruling *Betts v. Brady*, 316 *U.S.* 455 (1942); *Baker v. Carr*, 369 *U.S.* 186 (1962) (federal courts have jurisdiction to consider constitutional challenges to state redistricting plans), effectively overruling in part *Colegrove*, 328 *U.S.* 549; *Mapp v. Ohio*, 367 *U.S.* 643 (1961) (the exclusionary rule regarding the inadmissibility of evidence obtained in violation of the Fourth Amendment applies to the States), overruling *Wolf v. Colorado*, 338 *U.S.* 25 (1949); *Smith v. Allwright*, 321 *U.S.* 649 (1944) (racial restrictions on the right to vote in primary elections violates the equal protection clause of the Fourteenth Amendment), overruling *Grovey v. Townsend*, 295 *U.S.* 45 (1935); *United States v. Darby*, 312 *U.S.* 100 (1941) (congressional power to regulate employment conditions under the Commerce Clause), overruling *Hammer v. Dagenhart*, 247 *U.S.* 251 (1918); *Erie R. Co. v. Tompkins*, 304 *U.S.* 64 (1938) (Congress does not have the power to declare substantive rules of common law; a federal court sitting in diversity jurisdiction must apply the substantive state law), overruling *Swift v. Tyson*, 16 Pet. 1 (1842).

APPENDIX D

Comment on Cases Overturned, from Dissent in Dobbs

There is an Amendment [that] requires a unanimous jury verdict in state prosecutions for serious offenses, and overruling *Apodaca* v. *Oregon, 406 U.S. 404* (1972), because "in the years since *Apodaca*, this Court ha[d] spoken inconsistently about its meaning" and had undercut its validity "on at least eight occasions"); *Ring* v. *Arizona, 536 U.S. 584,* 608–609 (2002) (recognizing a Sixth Amendment right to have a jury find the aggravating factors necessary to impose a death sentence and, in so doing, rejecting *Walton* v. *Arizona, 497 U.S. 639* (1990), as overtaken by and irreconcilable with *Apprendi* v. *New Jersey, 530 U.S. 466* (2000)); *Agostini* v. *Felton, 521 U.S. 203,* 235–236 (1997) (considering the Establishment Clause's constraint on government aid to religious instruction, and overruling *Aguilar* v. *Felton, 473 U.S. 402* (1985), in light of several related doctrinal developments that had so undermined *Aguilar* and the assumption on which it rested as to render it no longer good law); *Batson* v. *Kentucky, 476 U.S. 79,* 93–96 (1986) (recognizing that a defendant may make a prima facie showing of purposeful racial discrimination in selection of a jury venire by relying solely on the facts in his case, and, based on subsequent developments in equal protection law, rejecting part of *Swain* v. *Alabama, 380 U.S. 202* (1965), which had imposed a more demanding evidentiary burden); *Brandenburg* v. *Ohio, 395 U.S. 444,* 447–448 (1969) *(per curiam)* (holding that mere advocacy of violence is protected by the First Amendment, unless intended to incite it or produce imminent lawlessness, and rejecting the contrary rule in *Whitney* v. *California, 274 U.S. 357* (1927), as having been "thoroughly discredited by later decisions"); *Katz* v. *United States, 389 U.S. 347,* 351, 353 (1967) (recognizing that the Fourth Amendment extends to material and communications that a person "seeks to preserve as private," and rejecting the more limited construction articulated in *Olmstead* v. *United States, 277 U.S. 438* (1928), because "we have since departed from the narrow view on which that decision rested," and "the underpinnings of *Olmstead* . . . have been so eroded by our subsequent decisions that the 'trespass' doctrine there enunciated can no longer be regarded as controlling"); *Miranda* v. *Arizona*, 384 U.S. 436, 463–467, 479, n. 48 (1966) (recognizing that the Fifth Amendment requires certain procedural safeguards for custodial interrogation, and rejecting *Crooker* v. *California*, 357 U.S. 433 (1958), and *Cicenia* v. *Lagay*, 357 U.S. 504 (1958), which had already been undermined by *Escobedo* v. *Illinois*, 378 U.S. 478 (1964)); *Malloy* v. *Hogan*, 378 U.S. 1, 6–9 (1964) (explaining that the Fifth Amendment privilege against "self-incrimination is also protected by the Fourteenth Amendment against abridgment by the States," and rejecting *Twining* v. *New Jersey*, 211 U.S. 78 (1908), in light of a "marked shift" in Fifth Amendment precedents that had "necessarily repudiated" the prior decision); *Gideon* v. *Wainwright*, 372 U.S. 335, 343–345 (1963) (acknowledging a right to counsel for indigent criminal defendants in state court under the Sixth and Fourteenth Amendments, and overruling the earlier precedent failing to recognize such a right, *Betts* v. *Brady*, 316 U.S. 455 (1942));[31] *Smith* v. *Allwright*, 321 U.S. 649, 659–662 (1944) (recognizing all-white primaries are unconstitutional after reconsidering in light of "the unitary character of the electoral process" recognized in *United States* v. *Classic*, 313 U.S. 299 (1941), and overruling *Grovey* v. *Townsend*, 295 U.S. 45 (1935)); *United States* v. *Darby*, 312 U.S. 100, 115–117 (1941) (recognizing Congress's Commerce Clause power to regulate employment conditions and explaining as "inescapable" the "conclusion . . . that *Hammer* v. *Dagenhart*, [247 U.S. 251 (1918)]," and its contrary rule had "long since been" overtaken by precedent construing the Commerce Clause power more broadly); *Erie R. Co.* v. *Tompkins*, 304 U.S. 64, 78–80 (1938) (applying state substantive law in diversity actions in federal courts and overruling *Swift* v. *Tyson*, 16 Pet. 1 (1842), because an intervening decision had "made clear" the "fallacy underlying the rule").

Additional cases the majority cites involved fundamental factual changes that had undermined the basic premise of the prior precedent. See *Citizens United* v. *Federal Election Comm'n*, 558 U.S. 310, 364 (2010) (expanding First Amendment protections for campaign-related speech and citing technological changes that undermined the distinctions of the earlier regime and made workarounds easy, and overruling *Austin* v. *Michigan Chamber of Commerce*, 494 U.S. 652 (1990), and partially overruling *McConnell v. Federal Election Comm'n, 540 U.S. 93* (2003)); *Crawford v. Washington, 541 U.S. 36,* 62–65 (2004) (expounding on the Sixth Amendment right to confront witnesses and rejecting the prior framework, based on its practical failing to keep out core testimonial evidence, and overruling *Ohio v. Roberts, 448 U.S. 56* (1980)); *Mapp v. Ohio, 367 U.S. 643,* 651–652 (1961) (holding that the exclusionary rule under the Fourth Amendment applies to the States, and overruling the contrary rule of *Wolf v. Colorado, 338 U.S. 25* (1949), after considering and rejecting "the current validity of the factual grounds upon which *Wolf* was based").

Some cited overrulings involved *both* significant doctrinal developments *and* changed facts or understandings that had together undermined a basic premise of the prior decision. See *Janus v. State, County, and Municipal Employees,* 585 U. S. ___, ___, ___–___ (2018) (slip op., at 42, 47–49) (holding that requiring public-sector union dues from nonmembers violates the First Amendment, and overruling *Abood v. Detroit Bd. of Ed., 431 U.S. 209* (1977), based on "both factual and legal" developments that had "eroded the decision's underpinnings and left it an outlier among our First Amendment cases" (internal quotation marks omitted)); *Obergefell v. Hodges, 576 U.S. 644,* 659–663 (2015) (holding that the Fourteenth Amendment protects the right of same-sex couples to marry in light of doctrinal developments, as well as fundamentally changed social understanding); *Lawrence v. Texas, 539 U.S. 558,* 572–578 (2003) (overruling *Bowers v. Hardwick, 478 U.S. 186* (1986), after finding anti-sodomy laws to be inconsistent with the Fourteenth Amendment in light of developments in the legal doctrine, as well as changed social understanding of sexuality); *United States v. Scott, 437 U.S. 82,* 101 (1978) (overruling *United States v. Jenkins, 420 U.S. 358* (1975), three years after it was decided, because of developments in the Court's double jeopardy case law, and because intervening practice had shown that government appeals from midtrial dismissals requested by the defendant were practicable, desirable, and consistent with double jeopardy values); *Craig v. Boren, 429 U.S. 190,* 197–199, 210, n. 23 (1976) (holding that sex-based classifications are subject to intermediate scrutiny under the Fourteenth Amendment's Equal Protection Clause, including because *Reed v. Reed, 404 U.S. 71* (1971), and other equal protection cases and social changes had overtaken any "inconsistent" suggestion in *Goesaert v. Cleary, 335 U.S. 464* (1948)); *Taylor v. Louisiana, 419 U.S. 522,* 535–537 (1975) (recognizing as "a foregone conclusion from the pattern of some of the Court's cases over the past 30 years, as well as from legislative developments at both federal and state levels," that women could not be excluded from jury service, and explaining that the prior decision approving such practice, *Hoyt v. Florida, 368 U.S. 57* (1961), had been rendered inconsistent with equal protection jurisprudence).

Other overrulings occurred very close in time to the original decision so did not engender substantial reliance and could not be described as having been "embedded" as "part of our national culture." *Dickerson v. United States, 530 U.S. 428,* 443 (2000); see *Payne v. Tennessee, 501 U.S. 808* (1991) (revising procedural rules of evidence that had barred admission of certain victim-impact evidence during the penalty phase of capital cases, and overruling *South Carolina v. Gathers, 490 U.S. 805* (1989), and *Booth v. Maryland, 482 U.S. 496* (1987), which had been decided two and four years prior, respectively); *Seminole Tribe of Fla. v. Florida, 517 U.S. 44* (1996) (holding that Congress cannot abrogate state-sovereign immunity under its Article I commerce power, and rejecting the result in *Pennsylvania v. Union Gas Co., 491 U.S. 1* (1989), seven years later; the decision in *Union Gas* never garnered a majority); *Garcia v. San Antonio Metropolitan Transit Authority, 469 U.S. 528,* 531 (1985) (holding that local governments are not constitutionally immune from federal employment laws, and overruling *National League of Cities v. Usery, 426 U.S. 833* (1976), after "eight years" of experience under that regime showed *Usery's* standard was unworkable and, in practice, undermined the federalism principles the decision sought to protect).

The rest of the cited cases were relatively minor in their effect, modifying part or an application of a prior precedent's test or analysis. See *Montejo v. Louisiana, 556 U.S. 778* (2009) (citing workability and practical concerns with additional layers of prophylactic procedural safeguards for defendants' right to counsel, as had been enshrined in *Michigan v. Jackson, 475 U.S. 625* (1986)); *Illinois v. Gates, 462 U.S. 213,* 227–228 (1983) (replacing a two-pronged test under *Aguilar v. Texas, 378 U.S. 108* (1964), and *Spinelli v. United States, 393 U.S. 410* (1969), in favor of a traditional totality-of-the-circumstances approach to evaluate probable cause for issuance of a warrant); *Wesberry v. Sanders, 376 U.S. 1,* 4 (1964), and *Baker v. Carr, 369 U.S. 186,* 202 (1962) (clarifying that the "political question" passage of the minority opinion in *Colegrove v. Green, 328 U.S. 549* (1946), was not controlling law).

INDEX

ABOUT THE AUTHOR

PETER CHARLES HOFFER is Distinguished Research Professor at the University of Georgia. He earned his PhD at Harvard in 1970, after which he taught at the Ohio State University and the University of Notre Dame. He held a visiting fellowship at Harvard Law School 1986–1987. He has authored or coauthored books on the Supreme Court, the federal court system, impeachment, abortion rights, and slavery.